TO GET UKRAINE
A REPORT FROM INSIDE THE COUNTRY,
FOR THOSE LOOKING ON FROM THE OUTSIDE

GLAGOSLAV PUBLICATIONS

TO GET UKRAINE
A REPORT FROM INSIDE THE COUNTRY,
FOR THOSE LOOKING ON FROM THE OUTSIDE

by Oleksandr Shyshko

Translated by Huw Davies
Book created by Max Mendor

© 2014, Oleksandr Shyshko

© 2015, Glagoslav Publications, United Kingdom

Glagoslav Publications Ltd
88-90 Hatton Garden
EC1N 8PN London
United Kingdom

www.glagoslav.com

ISBN: 978-1-78384-025-0

A catalogue record for this book is available
from the British Library.

Glagoslav Publications neither shares nor assumes responsibility for author's political and other views and opinions as expressed in or interpreted from this book.

This book is in copyright. No part of this publication may be reproduced, stored in a retrieval system or transmitted in any form or by any means without the prior permission in writing of the publisher, nor be otherwise circulated in any form of binding or cover other than that in which it is published without a similar condition, including this condition, being imposed on the subsequent purchaser.

CONTENTS

FOREWORD BY THE AUTHOR 7

WHY ARE WE REQUIRED
TO PROVIDE PROOF THAT WE EXIST? 10

WHO ARE THE UKRAINIAN PEOPLE? 14

THE ORIGINS OF THE NAME UKRAINE 19

RUS, MUSCOVY AND UKRAINE 21

WHO STOPPED US FROM FORMING AN ALLIANCE WITH POLAND? 25

THE COSSACKS 27

UKRAINE'S FIRST ATTEMPT TO GAIN INDEPENDENCE 30

UKRAINE'S SECOND ATTEMPT TO GAIN INDEPENDENCE 32

THE LEFT BANK OF UKRAINE UNDER RUSSIAN RULE 34

THE RIGHT BANK OF UKRAINE UNDER THE RZECZPOSPOLITA 36

AN ASSOCIATION OF UKRAINIAN
LANDS INSIDE THE BORDERS OF THE RUSSIAN EMPIRE 39

THE FIRST RENAISSANCE OF UKRAINIAN SELF-CONSCIOUSNESS 45

THE UKRAINIANS UNDER THE RULE OF AUSTRIA-HUNGARY 50

THE EVENTS OF THE FIRST WORLD WAR
IN THE TERRITORY OF UKRAINE 52

THE THIRD ATTEMPT TO OBTAIN INDEPENDENCE –
AND THE MOST LIKELY TO SUCCEED? 54

THE OCCUPATION OF UKRAINE BY AUSTRO-GERMAN FORCES 60

ANOTHER ATTEMPT TO CREATE A UKRAINIAN STATE 62

THE UKRAINIAN PEASANTRY TAKES UP ARMS 63

FRENCH TROOPS IN UKRAINE 65

THE ACT ZLUKY (THE ACT OF UNIFICATION) 66

THE RED ARMY IN UKRAINE	67
THE WHITE ARMY IS IN UKRAINE – YET THE RED ARMY TRIUMPHS. UKRAINE IS CARVED UP ONCE AGAIN	68
RELATIONS BETWEEN THE COMMUNIST POWERS AND THE UKRAINIAN PEOPLE	71
THE MANOEUVRINGS OF THE BOLSHEVIKS TO QUELL UKRAINE'S RESISTANCE	73
THE BOLSHEVIKS SHOW HOW THEY REALLY FEEL ABOUT UKRAINE	76
WHY DID THE BOLSHEVIKS IN MOSCOW HARBOUR SUCH HATRED FOR UKRAINE? A FEW THOUGHTS ON THE MATTER	79
WHAT EXACTLY IS A "COLLECTIVE FARM"?	81
THE CONSEQUENCES OF FORCING THE PEASANTS TO JOIN COLLECTIVE FARMS	84
PARANOID STALINIST TERROR IN UKRAINE	87
UKRAINE BEFORE THE SECOND WORLD WAR	90
THE SECOND WORLD WAR AND UKRAINE	93
THE UKRAINIAN REBEL ARMY	94
THE POST-WAR PERIOD. WHAT CHANGED FOR UKRAINE?	100
THE PERIOD WHICH BECAME KNOWN AS THE 'THAW'	104
A MOUTHFUL OF ETHNIC FREEDOM?	106
UKRAINE'S 'MEN OF THE SIXTIES'	108
THE 'PERIOD OF STAGNATION'	112
THE DISASTER AT CHERNOBYL	116
THE ATTEMPT TO MODERNIZE THE USSR	118
A NEW ERA APPROACHES	120
THE POPULATION OF UKRAINE TODAY	123
UKRAINIANS LIVING OUTSIDE THEIR NATIVE LAND	125
RELIGIONS IN UKRAINE	128

LANGUAGES IN UKRAINE	130
THE NATIONAL CHARACTER OF THE UKRAINIAN PEOPLE	135
RELATIONS BETWEEN THE SEXES	139
FINANCIAL RELATIONS IN THE FAMILY	143
PROSTITUTION	146
UKRAINIAN MAIL-ORDER BRIDES	148
A TOUCH OF THE EXOTIC: AGE-OLD TRADITIONS AND CUSTOMS	152
EMBROIDERY	157
THE NATIONAL CHARACTER OF THE UKRAINIAN PEOPLE	157
LET'S TALK ABOUT FOOD	161
WHAT DO UKRAINIANS REALLY EAT, THEN?	164
PORK "SALO"	167
PUBLIC HOLIDAYS AND FESTIVALS IN UKRAINE	169
THE ECONOMIC AND SOCIAL ENVIRONMENT IN MODERN-DAY UKRAINE	179
THE CAPTAINS OF UKRAINE'S MARKET ECONOMY	191
THE HETMANS OF MODERN-DAY UKRAINE	197
STATISTICS AND REAL LIFE	207
SLAYING THE DRAGON	210
A FEW CONCLUSIONS THAT CAN BE DRAWN AT THIS STAGE	216
THE THINGS WE DISLIKE	224
A FEW THINGS THAT WE LIKE	228
IN PLACE OF AN EPILOGUE	230
SOME TRADITIONAL UKRAINIAN RECIPES WHICH YOU SHOULD TRY IN ORDER TO GET A FULLER UNDERSTANDING OF THE IDEAS SET OUT IN THIS BOOK	231

FOREWORD BY THE AUTHOR

I would like to stress that all the views set out in this book are my own personal opinions. Plenty of my compatriots would disagree with some of them. Yet I also know that many of them share my assessments of the events and processes taking place.

There will no doubt be some who will feel entitled to express stronger opinions, giving vent to more radical and aggressive views, evaluating facts from the past and the present day and passing judgment, in an uncompromising way, on aspects of society, saying who is in the right and who is in the wrong, and 'judging' the public figures of the past and the present.

One thing is certain: I am not going to foist my opinion on readers, nor am I willing to get dragged into arguments. I am going to set out my own personal opinion about my country, its past and its present, and it is for you to decide for yourself to what extent it coincides with your own personal impressions of Ukraine.

I have taken the step of offering my vision to readers from other countries for a number of reasons.

Firstly, I am getting on a bit now, and I have spent most of my life in this country; I love it, and genuinely think of myself as a Ukrainian. My narrative is thus a report by a Ukrainian, for people from other countries.

Secondly, unlike many of my fellow citizens, I have driven all over the country in my time, and have even covered quite a bit of it on foot. I have been to all of Ukraine's big cities, as well as dozens of small towns, villages and hamlets. In the past I used to make these trips on business, but nowadays I tend mostly to travel as a tourist. So I am fairly knowledgeable not only about my home and my hometown, but also about the country as a whole.

Thirdly, I have had occasion to spend time in other countries. In my time I have visited New York, Miami, Vienna, London, Istanbul, Amsterdam, Bremen, Belgrade, Budapest, the Canary Islands, Hawaii, the Seychelles…the list goes on. This was simply the way my life panned out: my business affairs and a natural sense of curiosity led me to visit various parts of the world and gave me an insight into the way various peoples live. I am therefore aware of the things my country has in common with these other countries, and the ways in which it differs from them.

Fourthly, when I was younger I used to attend lectures alongside Arabs, Vietnamese, Nigerians, Ethiopians, Bulgarians, Czechs and Cubans. In later years I had occasion to work with people from America, the United Kingdom, Australia, Hungary, France, Switzerland, India, Pakistan and Japan.

I would like to think that I have managed, to a certain extent, to grasp the differences in mentality between these various nations, and to form an awareness of specific aspects of the way in which the Ukrainian people interpret the world around them.

The fifth reason is that I spent the first part of my life in Soviet Ukraine, when my country was one of the many nations incorporated into the Soviet Union, and the second part in the independent Ukraine which came into being in 1991, when the state of 'Ukraine', like a phoenix from the flames, was reborn once again. I say 'once again' because for many centuries, attempts to assert Ukrainian statehood had met with failure, in spite of the efforts and sacrifices made by Ukrainian patriots.

I therefore decided to reflect upon what happened in the past and what is happening now, and to have a think about where the country known as 'Ukraine' is headed. People aged under 30 find it hard to do this: their worldview was formed in a new era.

People approaching the age of eighty are unable to talk about such issues calmly. Just think about it: a little over 20 years ago, when a fundamental shift in the socio-economic order in the country occurred, their careers were already coming to an end, and they were looking forward to a quiet retirement surrounded by the beaming faces of their grandchildren.

And suddenly all that was turned upside down...

The mighty Soviet empire came crashing down, and Ukraine became an independent state. But was this something to be welcomed by the elderly, who in an instant lost everything they had saved up over the course of decades of life and work? They felt oppressed, as though the ancient Chinese curse, "May you live in a time of change!" had been put on them.

And here I am, right in between these two generations. I am glad that I lived to see the day when information is available that has not been put through ideological filters. After all, the younger generation – and this is quite natural – is not in a position to be able to comprehend just how drastically things have changed, and how deep the impact of these changes has been. But I can recall a great deal, I find it easy to reflect on it, and I do not seek to thrust my opinion on readers, it is for you to form your own conclusions...

I am going to attempt to draw a small ethnographic, historical, economic and cultural portrait of my native land. I have heard many times what people from other countries think of us. Can I now tell you how we see ourselves, and give you 'an insider's view'?

It may be that some readers will begin to think more highly of us after reading my book. After all, we are all neighbours, when it comes down to it. You can fly right round the world these days in a day or even an hour, depending on your chosen method of transport. It's nice to be able to see for yourself that your neighbours are a good lot.

If there are readers who end up feeling disillusioned, so be it. This book is in no way intended as a brochure, nor is it a tourist guidebook which wants to say: "Come and visit us and give us some of your money." Those who wish to do business with us must be given an opportunity to achieve greater success in their business affairs by gaining a better understanding of their Ukrainian partners. And those who, after reading this book, refuse to have anything to do with Ukraine whatsoever, ought to thank me for saving them a good deal of unpleasantness.

In my narrative I sometimes refer to people whose names will mean nothing to you. Some of them are long-forgotten here, too. The collective memory of every nation holds onto images of great leaders, generals and heroes whose names mean nothing to the rest of the world, but who are extremely significant to that particular people. To relate the country's history without mentioning these names would result in a dry and formal narrative, which would lack authenticity. It is beside the point that all the historical figures of note have long since been rated and ranked in order by their descendants. The descendants always seem incredibly sure about which historical figures were in the right and which were in the wrong.

Let us not protest that the history of human civilization has been one continuous battle, in which everyone is pitted against everyone else. At any given moment there will be someone who is the victor and someone who is on the losing side. History is always written by the victors. But the victor is different every time, and therefore history is rewritten once again – is this not the way it works in your countries too?

I have therefore tried to steer clear of long-held clichés when forming judgments about our Ukrainian heroes. You won't find any reference to the opinions of established authors on this subject in my book, either: I decided for myself which names to mention, which ones to omit, and how to evaluate them. Any similarities between my judgments and those commonly held are therefore purely coincidental.

WHY ARE WE REQUIRED TO PROVIDE PROOF THAT WE EXIST?

I must say it feels strange to be starting to tell the story of the Ukrainian people with an explanation of the fact that we are, indeed, a nation.

The Ukrainian people have an ancient history, a culture dating back to primordial times, an authentic language and, as many would assert, a distinct national character. Over the course of many centuries, however, the territory of present-day Ukraine, either in full or in part, has been incorporated into several empires, and on each occasion those running the empire have attempted to integrate the local population into their system of values, and destroy Ukrainians' sense of their own national identity.

Their efforts led to a situation in which a nation of many millions, living on a vast area of land, became almost invisible. It is enough to make one wonder how we managed to preserve our authenticity and our collective historical memory.

To this day many people in Europe and North America describe anyone who lives beyond the eastern border of the EU as Russian. The term 'Ukrainians' is not one with which the average man in the street, as opposed to politicians or historians, is overly familiar.

I have even grown accustomed to the fact that a large number of the foreigners I know do not think of Ukrainians as a separate nation, and were unaware of the existence of the Ukrainian language. It is hardly surprising: over the course of the last three centuries, when the territory of Ukraine formed part of the Russian empire, and throughout seventy years of Soviet rule (with Moscow the centre of power, again), a colossal ideological, financial, propaganda-spreading and penal machine was in operation, the objective of which was to crush the Ukrainians' awareness of their own national identity.

I am minded of a good friend of mine from Moscow. Thirty years ago he tried to convince me, in all seriousness, that the Ukrainian language was dying out, and disappearing, and that before long everyone would be speaking Russian. There would be no distinct nationalities, either, just a single, unified people.

This, as it happens, was the official policy in the USSR: to establish a new historical community, the 'unified Soviet people', whose members would all converse in the same language – and Russian had been chosen as this language. I was brought up in the Soviet ideological environment, and this policy appealed to me greatly. It made the state in which I lived at the time seem limitless, from Brest in the West to Khabarovsk in the East, from the Baltic Sea to the Tian Shan mountain range. It was comforting to think that you were a tiny part of such a mighty phenomenon.

Be that as it may, the Ukrainian roots deep within my soul forced me, committed Komsomol member as I was, to object to what my friend back then in Moscow said: "What do you mean, the Ukrainian language will disappear? We teach children in our schools in Ukrainian, we have huge areas where Ukrainian is not just the only language people speak: they think in it, too, we have our own Ukrainian literature, both classic and modern. I enjoy reading books written in Ukrainian myself, given that I'm bilingual, and take pleasure in hearing the language, with its luscious sounds, precision and melodic tone."

What one must understand is that the official Soviet ideology sought to water down the Ukrainian people's self-recognition by citing the shared past of these two peoples – the Russians and the Ukrainians. The idea was put about that Russians and Ukrainians share the same roots, that they are brother-peoples who were torn asunder by a whim of history, but then reunited once again. The Russians were of course portrayed as the more senior, and the Ukrainians as the younger of the two peoples.

I'm afraid my Russian friend may not have too many positive things to say about Ukraine today. It is always hurtful when events unfold in completely the opposite way to the one you forecasted.

In the last 20 years a different historical narrative has become accessible to Ukrainians, one that has not been dissected by the official imperial historians, but is founded on evidence and documents which were previously subject to a ban on being freely studied. It has suddenly emerged that Ukrainians and Russians are not the same, and are far from being brothers: there is reason to believe that they are not even particularly closely related, but are simply neighbours, who have had very different attitudes towards one another throughout history.[1]

---

1   It is worth reading the book by the second President of independent Ukraine, Leonid Kuchma, *Ukraine is not Russia*. The book's title alone is telling.

OLEKSANDR SHYSHKO

In 1991 it became clear that the Communists had failed to form a single people. When the USSR collapsed, the economic disparities and political ambitions of the regional leaders caused a whole series of conflicts and wars between countries whose citizens had until recently referred to one another as 'brother-peoples'. Nationalist tensions began to ferment, and bones of contention going back a hundred years were recalled. One must not forget, either, the 'assistance' provided by foreign states, which had an interest in stepping up their influence in the former Soviet republics.

Interestingly, the formal liquidation of the Soviet Union took place by a mutual decision by the leaders of Russia, Ukraine and Belarus. As for whether they were driven, at that moment, by an awareness of the historical inevitability that the Communist empire would disintegrate, or by personal ambition, and the desire to become a head of state – head of a small state, admittedly, but one that would be their own – is for history to decide. The die was cast, and the process of political delimitation had begun. Above all, however, the process of the dividing up of the single economic complex of a vast country had begun, and this was to have devastating consequences for the people.

I can well understand where the Russians – or rather, the Russian citizens of the Russian Federation – are coming from. It is one thing for us Ukrainians to feel that we have found independence from an empire; it is quite another

---

This is a man who held one of the most influential positions of all in the Soviet Union: he was the director of the flagship Soviet rocket-building plant, Yuzhmash, a member of the Central Committee of the Ukrainian Communist Party (i.e. he was part of the apparatus of power in Soviet times) – and then suddenly, when he was President of Ukraine, came up with this explosive work. He did not write anything with a title such as Ukrainians and Russians are brother-peoples. On the contrary, his book emphasizes in sundry ways the difference differences between the two ethnicities, not only in their culture and traditions, but also in their mentality and psychology.

To be honest, I am genuinely of the belief that any comparison of the peoples based on anthrometric or psychological criteria is a perverse exercise; and any comparison of their natures and psychological traits - even more so. The genes of the modern Ukrainian nation (like the Russian one) now contain a mixture of so many ethnicities that any attempt to distinguish 'true' Ukrainians based on anthropometric characteristics would seem stupid.

A recent trend among people in the mass media, who love to invent all kinds of sensations, is to look for traces of some sort of 'special' line of descent among the Ukrainian people, in their DNA. 'Studies' such as this are of course nothing more than juggling with quasi-scientific concepts, using comments made by academics and taken out of context, and other forms of verbal sleight of hand. Yet these shows are often watched by people who would describe themselves as intellectuals, and I can understand this: they are an instinctive reaction to the attempts made over many centuries by the Russians, who held sway over the empire of peoples, to oppress the consciousness of the Ukrainians as an independent nation. It is not hard to understand the train of thought of the average person: "How about that, we've been told for so long that we don't even exist as a separate people, and now it turns out that we're special in some way!"

Today, as I see it, anyone who identifies himself as a Ukrainian and sees benefit for the country in its independence and territorial integrity should be thought of as a Ukrainian. As for what's in our DNA, I don't believe this is relevant at all in the 21st century. Noah's Ark contained just two of every bird and beast, and yet they arrived safely in Ararat. We shall do likewise.

for the central nation in that empire to come to terms with the fact that it has lost its spheres of influence, and that its former vassals want to negotiate with it on an equal footing. This is quite distressing for people who have always seen themselves as the more senior, more important partner, and looked on the others as younger and in need of wise guidance.

And I know that such feelings can be attributed not only to the effect of the official Russian propaganda machine, which inflates them out of all proportion, creating the notion of the 'ungrateful' Ukrainians. This reaction is as natural as the reaction of people living in a metropolis to declarations of independence by its colonies. It is not as if European nations need to be told about this. There have been ample occasions in the history of the European countries when they have experienced precisely this feeling.

We, on the other hand – the Ukrainian people – are obliged to begin our story by identifying ourselves, and by explaining we ought not to be lumped together with other nations. What are we to do? To a large extent, Ukrainians themselves are to blame for the fact that their national identity has become so blurred.

The Ukrainian people have had so many opportunities throughout history to assert and strengthen their statehood. They have another such opportunity now.

In the past, the failures of the national project were rooted not only in the aggression of the country's neighbours, but in the lack of outstanding and lasting national leaders, and in the people's inability to put to one side local, regional, narrow interests, to forget insults, both real and imagined, suffered by their ancestors, and to advance, on the basis of the common idea of national independence and territorial integrity.

We shall see how things work out on this occasion.

WHO ARE THE UKRAINIAN PEOPLE?

I do not intend to begin an academic debate about the origins of the Ukrainian people, the sources of Ukrainian statehood or the process of forming a Ukrainian national and literary language. I shall merely set out my understanding of these phenomena, which is founded on a study of many official and less official sources. It may be that some readers will seek to put their own interpretation on the facts I am going to set out – and they are entitled to do so.

Today's political leaders love to cite incidents from history in order to back up their theories. Often, though, their wilful interpretation of historical facts has a pragmatic, utilitarian objective.

I would not feel the need to venture into historical episodes, were it not for the attempts by the leaders of neighbouring states to justify their present-day political ambitions by citing history, and coming up with statements such as: "this territory belongs to us by rights," or "these regions were historically part of our state". It is easy to understand the desires they have: the land is incredibly good land, fertile and offering very thick soil; it is in a favourable geographical location, and deep rivers run across the country from north to south; it has a moderate, temperate climate, with no tornadoes or earthquakes to worry about, and it has both low mountains and useful minerals. And in the modern world, the fact that it has infrastructure, industry, a well-qualified workforce and a high level of education among the population, it makes perfect sense to try to convince Ukraine to join all manner of unions and associations – preferably to such an extent that it loses its sovereignty altogether.

Before we once again get lost in a tangle of political and historical intrigues, let us first establish what we mean when we refer to the Ukrainian people.

There can be no doubting the fact that we are Europeans. In any event, of the five points in four different countries which lay claim to the title of 'The geographical centre of Europe', two are located on Ukrainian soil. Our history was bound up in the history of the other European countries, this land and this people have been part of empire after empire, have enjoyed independence and statehood for a short period (in the historical sense) and then fallen once again into the clutches of its more powerful neighbours.

Since ancient times, Ukrainians have lived in the central and eastern part of European territory, adjoining two seas – the Black Sea and the Azov. The kernel of the ethnic territory of the Ukrainian people has always been situated inside the territory of Ukraine itself.

Let us not join in with the various Ukrainian historians and enthusiasts who have estimated that there have been 80 different states on the territory of Ukraine in…12,000 years. It begins to look a little bit made up.

All the same, which civilizations can we find traces of on this land?

There are some signs that the Cimmerians (remember Conan the Barbarian? He was a Cimmerian) may have lived on this land 2500 years ago. They were followed by the Skiffs, the Goths, the Huns and the Sarmates…

And then at last these lands were settled by the Veneti, the Antes and the Sclavines – these were the names given by Byzantine authors to people from the tribes which were later given the name of 'Slavs'. This supposedly took place in the 5th century AD, i.e. some 1600 years ago. The Slavic race is considered to have originated in the north-western areas of present-day Ukraine. The Slavs were of course divided into tribes, each with its own name. One of them, for example, is known in Russian as the *polyane*, and this name no doubt came from the word for field, *polye*.

The Polyane tribes were founded at the site of the capital of Ukraine – the city of Kiev. According to various experts, the city was founded at some point in the 5th to 7th centuries AD. It was a very good site from a strategic point of view, being at higher altitude than the surrounding area, on the banks of a broad river, the Dnieper, with its abundant waters. According to legends written down many centuries later, the city was founded by three brothers, the leaders Kiy, Shchek and Khoriv, with the city getting its name from the eldest of these three. This is the story told to tourists visiting the city, and several hills and streets in the city are to this day named after the middle brother and the youngest brother; there is also a stream in the city named after their sister, 'Lybid' (meaning Swan), which was once abundant with water but has now run dry and is hidden away inside a sewer.

Alternative accounts, which do not have quite the same legendary status, but which are cited in the written sources, indicate that Kiev was ruled by the commanders of Varangian brigades. As many of my readers will be aware, the Varangians were bandits from Scandinavia, who seized power over the Slavic peoples and laid the foundations for statehood on their land.[2]

---

2   The theory that the Varangians were Vikings from the Swedish fjords was drawn up, strange to say, by order of the Russian Empress in the 18th century. It had come about that for the last three

The 'Scandinavian' hypothesis is not particularly convincing, however.

The Slavs had in fact *invited* the Varangian leaders to govern them, so they were probably very similar to the Slavs in terms of their language, culture and outer appearance. It is very doubtful that Rurik, who was invited by the northern Slavs and the Finno-Ugric peoples to govern them and to defend their land from attacks by their neighbours, was descended from the Scandinavians – a people with a completely different language and culture and different gods.

The most likely theory is that the Varangians were descended from the Slavic peoples of the Obotrites, who lived on the banks of the Baltic Sea (which was then known as the Varangian Sea), who were skilled and warrior-like, and were adept at seafaring. They lived more by war than by peaceful labours, and were therefore better warriors and had better weapons than their enemies. They plundered enemy territory and protected their own kind. The people working the land, who had founded a settlement at the site of present-day Kiev, were certainly in need of such protection.

Among the rulers of Kiev who are often evoked are the Varangian Askold and the warrior Rurik. Prince Oleg, a relative of Rurik's who killed Askold, and Rurik's son Igor, who ruled Kiev after Oleg, were also Varangians – of that there is no doubt.

And what of their descendants? Often we find among their number some outstanding leaders, and occasionally some who were not particularly successful or capable. Under their guidance the city grew larger and stronger, then collapsed and grew weak; by turns it was a capital city then a province. They invaded neighbouring states, established diplomatic relations with them and married the daughters of Byzantine emperors, Scandinavian kings and Huns from nomadic tribes (Cumans). In a word, the DNA of the local aristocracy consisted of an extremely diverse range of material.

Take Prince Yaroslav, for example, who ruled Kiev between 1016 and 1054. Yaroslav himself was married to the daughter of a Swedish king; one of his daughters, Anna, married the Henry I, King of France, and the other married Andrei I, King of Hungary; his sister Maria married the Polish king Casimir I; and his son married a Byzantine princess. Kiev's rulers were eager

---

centuries the monarchs ruling over the Russian state had been people of Germanic stock. Attempts to demonstrate that the Slavic peoples were incapable of any form of state-building were an important component of the ideological battle. From this stemmed the belief that it was the Germanic peoples' mission to act as a civilizing force. Incidentally, in order to destroy any possible counter-arguments at the time this theory was devised, a thorough check was made of the monasteries where historical chronicles were kept, accompanied by the confiscation and destruction of manuscripts. As Bismarck once said, "Nations are ruled by Kings, Kings are ruled by bankers, but above all of these are the chroniclers – for they hold sway over history."

to intermarry with powerful ruling dynasties from neighbouring states, and the latter were no less eager, for their part, to establish ties with the powerful state on the banks of the Dnieper.

These lands were known as Rus, and chroniclers from other areas referred to the people who lived on them variously as Rusins, Rutens or Roksolans. It is very unlikely they thought of themselves as a fully-formed ethnic group, or that they identified themselves as belonging to a particular tribe, region or principality. The area was surrounded by Lithuania to the north, Poland to the west, Muscovy to the east and, to the south, the Wild steppes and some nomadic tribes.

Since Kiev was seen as the most important city in Rus, and its ruler – the prince – was known as the 'Grand Prince', the city was at the centre of intense conflicts between the Rurikoviches themselves. As a result, the city was burned to the ground several times and its people were massacred, and the competing grandsons and great-grandsons of the great Kievan princes departed for the north-west and founded new cities, new fortresses and new duchies. It was in this manner, for example, that the Grand Duchy of Moscow came into being – a duchy which was at loggerheads with the duchy of Kiev practically from the very outset. The people of the Duchy of Moscow bore no relation to the Slavs from an ethnic point of view – most of them were descended from Urgo-Finnish tribes – but their conflicts with the Duchy of Kiev were not inter-ethnic ones. All of the princes fought each other for power and for territory which they would be able to tax. This was known as 'feudal fragmentation', and is something you will have read about in your history books.

Eventually, the princes and the population of Rus, who would one day become the Ukrainian people, preoccupied as they were with internecine warfare, proved unable to resist an invasion by nomadic tribes from the East, led by the grandson of Ghengis Khan, Batu Khan. Their invasion in 1240 found Kiev without a prince and without an army. By then, the former capital of the Great Dukedom was already ruled by Danila Galitsky, whose court was six hundred kilometres west of Kiev. The people of Kiev tried to defend the city against the Mongols but were defeated, and Kiev was razed to the ground once again.

In a manuscript housed at the Gustinsky monastery (in the Chernigov Region, 160 km from Kiev), a historian refers to the warlike nature of the 'rusian' people, which had led to infighting, and to the fact that great troubles were brought to the 'Russian land' from Poland, Lithuania and Moscow: "Since it first came into being, our Rusian people has always had to do battle, and began by mastering the art of weaponry, and then, at the time of the duchies, this warlike people waged war unceasingly, either with the peoples surrounding it – the Greeks, the Polovtians or the Pechenegs – or, failing that, with one another.

And this continued until the Tatar Tsar Baty (that was the name given to Batu Khan in Rus) laid waste to our land, and great damage was done by the Liakhs, Lithuania and Moscow, and by the infighting."

THE ORIGINS OF
THE NAME UKRAINE

In ancient times, a substantial part of the territory we now know as the Ukrainian state was called 'Rus', or the 'Rusian land'. One often sees the names 'White Rus', 'Black Rus' and 'Red Rus' on maps from those times. So where did the word 'Ukraine' come from?

The similarity between Ukraine and the Russian word *okraina*, meaning a place removed from the centre, has prompted a handful of jingoistic Russian historians to come up with the theory that the name 'Ukraine' stands for a place which is on the outskirts by comparison with the central, Muscovite land.

This is pure fantasy, of course. When the word 'Ukraine' was first used, there were not yet any traces of even a small Duchy of Moscow, and Russia's future capital, Moscow, was a border outpost for Kievan princes at the edge of Ukraine. These lands were known as Rus right up until the mid-16th century, as countless documents and manuscripts testify. The word 'Ukraine' dates back to the 12th century, however, and simply meant 'country'. The oldest of all the documents containing the word 'Ukraine' is the so-called Hypatian Codex (a copy of an ancient manuscript found at the Ipatiev Monastery outside Kostroma). The manuscript tells of the heroic death of the Prince of Pereyaslavl[3], Vladimir Glebovich, in 1187, reporting: "Ukraine grieved for him very much."

The term 'Ukraine' was well-known in European countries, too. Levassaire de Beauplan, who served in the Polish-Lithuanian Commonwealth from 1630 to 1647, refers, in his work 'A description of Ukraine', to a Ukrainian territory, "which lies between the borders of Muscovy and Transylvania." The traditional names Rus and Rusian lands continued to be used to describe the Ukrainian lands which were part of the Polish-Lithuanian Commonwealth.

Russian Imperial historians later coined the term *velikoross* (i.e. *veliky russky*, meaning 'great Russian') to describe the people of the state of Moscow, and

---

3   *Pereyaslavl is an ancient town not far from Kiev*

maloross (i.e. Russian as well, but 'little', 'junior') – to describe the people of Ukraine.

It was for this reason that our people began to go by the name of Ukrainians – so as to avoid being 'little Russians': after all, the epithet 'Russians' had already been appropriated by a different people.

RUS, MUSCOVY AND UKRAINE

Disputes over the origins of 800-year-old words still give rise to fresh offence and accusations today. When jingoistic nationalists in modern-day Russia start spouting ideas about Ukraine being the *okraina* – the area on the fringes, the part which was broken off and which is home to the lost younger brothers of the great Russian people, the swift response they get are snide and well-directed remarks to the effect that the ethnonym 'Russian' is a 'stolen' name, and that the core component of the people who lived in the muscovite lands were of Urgo-Finnish descent, rather than being Slavs. As for the population of the territory which eventually came to be known as Moscow, Muscovy, the manuscripts tell us that they were not Slavs and that this was not Rus, but that other peoples lived here, who had to pay a levy to Rus: the Chud, Merya, Ves, Muroma and Cheremis peoples; and that the lands of Suzdal, Vladimir and Rostov, which eventually came to be known as Muscovite land, were never referred to as Rus and were not considered to be Rus.[4]

Russia has roughly the same attitude in respect of the historic and cultural legacy of Kievan Rus as the one adopted in relation to the legacy of the Roman Empire by its former colony, Romania.

We are living in the 21st century, though.

To focus the debate on the issue of which people inherited the legacy of the south-western part of the Eastern European flatlands in the time of the Duchies of Kiev, Chernigov and Pereslavl a thousand years ago is tantamount to arguing about whether the French are descended from the Franks, or the people of Germany from the Germanic tribes.

The author is well aware that the multi-ethnic Russian Federation is currently one of the biggest states in the world, that it has a huge say on the fate of the world, and that the world is obliged, whether it likes it or not, to listen to what it says. We are linked to the population of our northern

---

[4] According to the Lavrentievskaya chronicles, they rebelled in 1176 against the prince and demanded that he not bring any 'Rusians' their lands or give them any positions in high office

neighbour by a huge number of financial ties and blood-ties. Had the Russian leaders exhibited a little less imperial ambition, Ukraine would be more than happy to work with Russia, in true neighbourly fashion. The constant attempts to put Ukraine back inside the womb of the Russian Empire have led to a situation today when Ukrainians say to themselves: "The Russians aren't our brothers."

Ukraine, it must be acknowledged, has not yet identified once and for all the route it must follow, is experiencing serious economic hardship and is not coping all that well with the challenges of the modern world. But we are not Russia and Moscow is not our capital. What's more, we have accumulated plenty of grudges against the Kremlin's power over the course of history, and the more Russia strives to bring the Ukrainians back under their guardianship, the more we call these grudges to mind.

Let us return, though, to the 13th century. The cavalry of Batu-Khan, after reaching the Andriatic Sea during a seven-year military campaign, returned to its native steppes. The north-western duchies, which were ruled by the descendants of Rurik, were not included within the nomads' state, which was known as Ulus Dzhuchi, but served as a base for the acquisition of material wealth in the form of a levy collected on a regular basis. In some cases, moreover, their princes chose instead to become allies of the nomads.

The famous 13th century warrior Alexander Nevsky, who fought the Swedes, the Livonians and the Teuton knights, put in a great deal of diplomatic effort to strengthen ties with the rulers of Ulus Dzhuchi, and called on their military support on several occasions in order to restore order over his subjects, including his own sons, who were trying to organize the resistance against the Golden Horde. As a result he was canonized by the Russian Orthodox Church.[5]

Paradoxically, the invasion by the hordes from the east brought an end to the infighting which had sapped the strength from the north-western duchies of Suzdal, Vladimir, Tver, Kostroma, among others. The unifying centre of these lands was the duchy of Moscow, whose rulers proved to be more talented, far-sighted and cunning than the others.

Ultimately, the fall of the Mongol Empire, and the defeat of the army of Tokhtamysh the Hun, the ruler of the Golden Horde, by Timur, the conqueror

---

5   In early 2013 the Russian financial analyst Alexander Razuvaev, who was interested in history but was not bound by the official dogma and the 'generally accepted' version of events, wrote an interesting article in which he talked about the "historic, imperial choice made by Alexander Nevsky and Batu-Khan," which had determined Russia's "national, Eurasian and orthodox identity." He added that this choice went against the "over-atrching Slavic Catholic project". As he sees it, Russia is associated with Asia, the Mongols and orthodoxy, and Ukraine is associated with Europe, the Slavs and Catholicism. It is a stretch to associate the Orthodox Church with the Mongols, admittedly, because in Ulus Dzhuchi, which ruled over the future Russian lands, Islam was adopted as the state religion in 1312.

from Central Asia, and the resistance put up by the defeated peoples, including the people of the Great Duchy of Moscow, meant the beginning of the end for the Golden Horde, and its eventual disappearance.

And in the 16th century it was not the dukes of Moscow and Vladimir who were requesting the reins of power from the Huns of the Golden Horde; rather, a direct descendant of Ghenghis Khan, Sain-Bulat, agreed to serve the Russian Tsar, converted to the Christian faith, married a Russian countess and, for an 11-month period in 1575-1576, bore the title Grand Duke of Moscow named Simeon Bekbulatovich.

The Golden Horde's State was destroyed, but the Turkic peoples residing on its territory (Bulgarians, Mari, Tatars and so on from the Volga region) were still very much there. The Europeans described all the peoples living to the east of the duchy of Moscow as Tatars, and it was towards the east that the duchy of Moscow, whilst it was growing stronger and flourishing, directed most of its efforts as regards conquering new land. The 'Tatars' therefore became no more than component parts of the population of an ever-expanding kingdom with Moscow at its centre, which, over time, started to become known as Russia.

The territory which was later to become Ukraine was laid waste to by Batu Khan's invasions. The Horde controlled land to the south of Kiev and to the east and west, as far as the Dunai. Its core population consisted of the Kipchak (also known as the Cumans). It is beyond doubt that over the following centuries, in the post-Horde period, this population was involved in the formation of the Ukrainian genotype. The duchy of Kiev probably existed in name only. Prince Alexander Nevsky, who was referred to above, bore the title of Grand Duke of Kiev from 1249 to 1263, but who was much bothered about a city that had been destroyed and burnt to the ground?

The only duchy which was still going in the Ukrainian territory at the time was the Galitsko-Volyn duchy, under the leadership of the most wise ruler Danila I Galitsky. An ancestor of Rurik, who had become a fully-fledged duke at just 10 years of age, this outstanding politician and military leader built up, developed and defended his state. He received permission from the Roman Catholic Pope to be known as the King of Rus. At one time his territory stretched along the Dnieper and Dunai rivers and across the Carpathians, which made it the biggest state in Europe at the time. Danilo resisted Mongol expansion with varying degrees of success, but managed to save his kingdom from destruction.

His son, Lev, ruled for another 32 years, although to do so he had to form an alliance with the Golden Horde and do battle against Lithuania, Poland and Hungary. For 30 years, Lev Danilovich was, among other things, the

Grand Duke of Kiev, though this was of course with the blessing of the Huns from the Horde.

Their ancestors, however, were unable to preserve the achievements of their forefathers.

In the 14th – 16th centuries, most of the Ukrainian lands were annexed by the duchy of Lithuania, and after the signing in 1569 of the so-called Lyublinsk Union, the Polish eagle, spreading its wings, formed an alliance with the Lithuanian State called the Rzeczpospolita (the Polish-Lithuanian Commonwealth), which incorporated modern-day Ukraine within its borders, and got caught up in a lengthy confrontation with the state of Moscow. This confrontation ultimately ended with the victory of the Russian empire, and to Ukraine being annexed to the victors' territory. There were still two hundred years to go before that happened, however.

In the meantime, the Ukrainian and Polish peoples began to co-exist within a single state. These centuries of co-existence were characterised by common battles against the Ottomans, the Tatars and Moscow. It must be said, however, that the history of these two co-existing peoples – the Ukrainians and the Poles – over several centuries included not only examples of cooperation, but also periods of irreconcilable national and religious enmity, which led to there being countless victims on both sides.

WHO STOPPED US FROM FORMING AN ALLIANCE WITH POLAND?

A fateful role on the historical fate of the Ukrainian and Polish peoples was played by the political ambitions of rulers acting from the outside. Poland was one hundred percent a catholic country. The Vatican had set the Polish crown the task of ensuring that Catholicism flourished in the east. In the Ukrainian territories this mission was put into effect by all possible means. People who were not members of the Catholic Church were considered inferior to Catholics, and suffered all kinds of persecution – not only the lower classes and peasantry but also the wealthy and military classes.

The Ukrainian people (who at that time called themselves 'rusins', from the word Rus), were adherents of the Greco-Byzantine, orthodox faith, unlike the population of the Rzeczpospolita.

Among the leaders of the Rzeczpospolita there were a fair few cold-blooded, clear-headed sorts individuals who suggested that Catholics and those of the Orthodox faith should be put on an equal footing, and that the Rzeczpospolita of two peoples (to give it its full title) be turned into a Rzeczpospolita of three peoples[6].

The arrogance of the so-called Polish military and aristocratic class (the so-called 'gentry') and a stubborn desire not to recognize the Rusin (Ukrainian) gentry as an equal, coupled with the strong differences as regards religion (the attempts to enforce Catholicism on the Orthodox population of the Ukrainian lands) led, ultimately, to a civil war in the mid-17th century, and to the breaking off of a sizeable part of the land populated by the Ukrainians from the Rzeczpospolita.

The state of Muscovy had become attractive in the eyes of both ordinary Ukrainian peasants and Cossacks, and the Cossack officers, due to the orthodox religion which held sway there. And when the Cossack state, which

---

6   In 1658 an agreement was signed on the creation of a three-way Rzeczpospolita (the so-called Gadyachskaya Uniya). The Polish Sejm, however – not without pressure from the Vatican – rejected the idea that the Rusins and the Poles could be considered equals.

had come into being during the insurrection in 1648-1654 in Ukraine's Left-bank area, became a protectorate of Moscow, the Ukrainians acquired not only allies who shared the same faith as them, but also equal rights. The senior Cossack leaders were given the same rights as the nobility. This came to embody its eternal desire to be given confirmation of its achievements, of its standing; to achieve what the Polish crown had refused to give it. It is not surprising, therefore, that the Ukrainians evinced plenty of signs of loyalty to the Russian empire.

THE COSSACKS

It should be noted that the Rzeczpospolita recognized the special nature of the Ukrainian lands, and that a specific state was formed on this territory: the so-called Hetmanshchina, ruled over by the most senior military commander, the Hetman. The fact that its special status was recognized was due in large part to an attempt by the Polish crown to turn the Ukrainian lands into a buffer zone, to protect Polish territories from incursions by the Ottoman Empire.

The first Hetman was of course a Pole – Predslav Lyantskoronsky.

And it was this Pole who enabled a class of people to be established in Ukrainian land that became, and remains to this day, a symbol of our people, our freedom and our sense of identity: the Cossacks.

One of the chroniclers writes: "King Sigismund I the Old despatched Lyantskoronsky to Ukraine to gather some men, and along with these men he made a very successful attack against the Tatars and the Turks. And then this warlike people began to call itself 'Cossacks' and began venturing into the Tatar lands on its own.

The Cossacks selected a military leader from among their own number, "in accordance with their ancient custom", spent their summers in Zaporozhye[7] and catch fish, which they leave to dry in the sun, "and then in winter they disperse and go back to their own cities," i.e. in winter they return home to Ukraine, and "in summer they meet up again" in Zaporozhye.

This manuscript pertained to the year 1516.

The term 'Cossack' had existed long before this date, of course. Cossacks were men, of course; they were free, naturally; and they were always armed. What options were open to a free, armed man at that time? He could either become a mercenary, a security guard or a highwayman. The Cossacks were all three of these things.

The Cossack brigades were very much a mixed bag: they might include both Slavs-Rusins, and Turkic nomads. If one's looking for a group that paid

---

7   An area downstream of the Dnieper River.

no heed to ethnic origins, the Cossacks certainly tick that box! The only condition for joining the Cossack brotherhood was to adopt the Orthodox faith.

When it came to transforming them into a powerful and well-organized military force, however, equipped with guns which were very advanced by the standards of the day, key roles were played by both the Polish Hetman, Lyantskoronsky, and the Lithuanian prince and Kosh chieftain Dashkevich, who had enlisted to serve the Polish king.

In 1550 the Polish king appointed the *rusin* Dmitry Vishnevetsky – the son of a nobleman from Volinsky – as praepostor (i.e. ruler) in the Cherkassian and Kanevsky territories (a huge expanse in the centre of Ukraine). Vishnevetsky assembled a large force of Cossacks and in 1552, after leaving the area, they boarded ships and set off for the island of Khortytsia.[8] There, using his own money, Vishnevetsky built a wood-and-earth castle, which historians consider to be the prototype for the Zaporozhian Sich – an autonomous Cossack settlement, a military order of a kind, which served as both sword and shield for the Rzeczpospolita along its south-eastern borders.[9]

Soon the "father of Ukrainian Cossackhood" began to construct an entire city on the island, surrounding it with moats and erecting ramparts around it. When the Sech was built, the Cossacks built columns made of oak for the walls and towers along the tops of the ramparts.

Vishnevetsky was elected Hetman by the Cossacks and sent letters to the King of Poland, Sigismund, and to Tsar Ivan the Terrible in Moscow, requesting their help in his great invasion of the Crimea. The Crimea was at that time inhabited by Tatars. The Crimean Khanate was a subject of the Ottoman rulers, and warriors from the Crimea had for centuries committed incursions into lands settled by the Ukrainians, in order to plunder them

---

8   Khortytsia is an island in the lower part of the Dnieper. Before the dams of a hydroelectric power plant were built in the 20th century, lifting the water level in various sections, this island was behind a barrier of rocky outcrops coming up from the bottom of the river, which rendered attacks by large vessels from upstream impossible. And from downstream – who would be capable of rowing against the tide of such a powerful river? The rocky outcrops in the river were known as POROGI (RAPIDS). Everything that was located lower down in the river was known as the ZAPOROZHYE, i.e. the area on the other side of the RAPIDS.

9   The Zaporozhian Sich existed for over 200 years and was destroyed by order of the Russian Empress Catherine II, because, on the one hand, it had lost its significance as a defensive outpost against Russia's southern neighbours, and on the other hand, the Cossacks had supported insurrections against the monarchy by the peasants on numerous occasions, so a pocket of resistance such as this simply could not continue to exist within an absolute monarchy.
Some time later the Zaporozhskoe force was restored by Catherine herself, and renamed the Chernomorskoe (Black Sea) force, and the Cossack troops were resettled in Kuban, where there was a lot of free land, where the borders of the empire needed protecting, and generally so that Ukraine would cause fewer problems for the Muscovite monarchs.

and capture people for use as slaves. Neither the Polish ruler nor the ruler of Moscow came to the aid of the Ukrainian hetman, however. Nevertheless, in 1556 the Hetman made his attack on Ochakov and, by laying waste to the surrounding area, managed to rescue a considerable number of prisoners. This feat was followed by many other victories. Under Vishnevetsky's leadership, the Cossacks captured all of the steppes, from the Bug right up as far as the Don.

UKRAINE'S FIRST ATTEMPT TO GAIN INDEPENDENCE

By a twist of fate, Dmitry Vishnevetsky's grandson, Ieremiah, was the main opponent to the much-celebrated leader of the Cossacks and peasants, Zinovy Khmelnitsky, who led the Ukrainian people in an uprising in 1648-1656, as they reacted against economic and religious oppression by the Catholic gentry.

These two noble characters, Khmelnitsky and Vishnevetsky, who had studied at the same Jesuit college, both of whom were full of merit, talent and wit, and whose achievements on behalf of the Rzeczpospolita were not to be scoffed at, now found themselves in opposing camps. The Rusin nobleman Vishnevetsky had adopted the Catholic faith, and the Rusin nobleman Khmelnitsky was orthodox. Khmelnitsky did not have the break-up of the Rzeczpospolita as his objective: he merely wished to defend the rights of the Rusin orthodox gentry. Ieremiah Vishnevetsky, meanwhile, who was an extremely wealthy magnate, and owned vast swathes of Ukrainian land, spoke out for equality between the Rusin gentry and the Polish gentry.

It was not to be however: the "party of war" won the day in Poland – a party which was not prepared to make any compromises and was demanding that the rebels be put down at any cost.

The rebellion which followed the long and bloody battle ended in the formation of a Cossack state led by Khmelnitsky, on part of the Ukrainian lands on both banks of the Dnieper. This leader's authority was so great that the people gave him a new name: Bogdan, i.e. *danniy Bogom*, God-given. Bogdan Khmelnitsky demonstrated the qualities of a great politician, diplomat, general and state-builder, and his memory was honoured by every subsequent generation of Ukrainians.

The truth of the matter was that the Cossacks never had the opportunity to create a sovereign state. The reason for this is simple: the most common form of power in the 17th century was the monarchy, in which power was inherited. In Poland the monarchs were elected, but all the candidates were members of royal families. As far as most of the leaders of Europe's nations were concerned at the time, Khmelnitsky was no more than a rebellious army officer.

There was not a single European nation which would have recognised a Cossack state.

As for Poland, she characterised the Ukrainians' rebellion as a revolt by a rabble against the sacred institute of the monarchy. Khmelnitsky, a wise man when it came to politics, was perfectly aware of this.

In an attempt to find support, and with the aim of protecting the newly-formed state, Khmelnitsky made overtures to Moscow's tsar, and in 1654 he signed an agreement which saw the Cossack state becoming a protectorate of Russia – and being afforded a considerable amount of autonomy.

Alas, after the death of this outstanding leader in 1657, the Ukrainian people proved incapable of handling his legacy correctly and with due care. To put it simply, they began to fight amongst themselves. Many refused to recognise the hetmans who were elected, and the latter were overthrown and killed. The country, which was not particularly big in any case at that time, was split into two parts along the Dnieper. Understandably, the country's neighbours – the Rzeczpospolita, Muscovy and the Ottoman Empire – were quick to get involved in this infighting, always pursuing their own ends, of course, when they did so.

This period of mutual destruction, which later came to be known as the age of 'Ruin', went on for thirty years, and the Hetman's mace (the symbol of power) changed hands fifteen times between leaders of varying degrees of merit. Some of them aligned themselves with Moscow, others with Warsaw, and others still with Istanbul. There were some outstanding politicians and generals among them, such as Ivan Vygovsky and Pyotr Doroshenko. Even the efforts of these men, however, were to prove fruitless.

The outcome was the same as it always is in such situations. Russia and Poland signed a peace agreement and carved up the Ukrainian land: the land on the left bank of the Dnieper was given to Russia, and the land on the right bank – to Poland. This meant that part of the Ukrainian people were now ruled by the tsars in Moscow and the rest was ruled by the Poles, and Ukraine's prospects for acquiring independence as a state had been lost. On the right bank of the Dnieper the Ukrainians were subjected to constant pressure and attempts to have the Polish nationality and the Catholic religion imposed on them. On the left bank the tsars in Moscow gradually began to erode the autonomy of the Cossack state.

UKRAINE'S SECOND ATTEMPT TO GAIN INDEPENDENCE

The period of Ruin came to an end with the election of Ivan Mazepa, an outstanding warrior, diplomat and state-builder, as hetman in 1687.

He attempted to pull Ukraine free from Muscovy's grasp right at the start of the 18th century. This attempt was made during the war between Russia and Sweden. As one might expect, Mazepa was declared a traitor by the tsar, and the Cossack capital and Mazepa's residence, the town of Baturin, was razed to the ground, and its citizens beheaded. A year later, the Swedish forces and the Ukrainian supporters of Mazepa, who had helped the Swedes, suffered a crushing defeat at the hands of an army led by the young Peter I, in the environs of the Ukrainian city of Poltava.

This story is not as simplistic as it might seem. Why is it that in present-day Ukraine, Mazepa is seen as someone who fought for the independence of the Ukrainian people, rather than as a traitor?

Ivan Mazepa was a vastly experienced politician; he was a well-educated, cultured and wealthy man, a landowner who enjoyed the full trust of the Russian tsar. It was obvious to him, however, that Peter the Great was bent on a policy of restricting Ukraine's autonomy and depriving her of any independence whatsoever. As it turned out, Mazepa was absolutely right.

Preoccupied with the Northern War against Sweden, the Tsar refused to assist Mazepa against Poland. Peter ordered that the towns on the right bank of the Dnieper, which had been captured during the rebellion against the Poles by the Cossack generals Gurko (Palii) and Samus, be returned to the Polish crown. Mazepa was forced to arrest Palii, who did not want to submit to the Tsar's orders and return the land which had been conquered at the expense of Cossack blood. Moreover, the Moscow tsar had concluded an everlasting peace with the Polish king August II the Strong. The peace between Moscow and Poland could be seen, however, as merely the latest carving up of the Ukrainian land. Hetman Mazepa had every reason to consider Peter's actions as a violation of a sovereign's duties towards a subject state, something which entitled him to seek the patronage of a different sovereign; the ruler Mazepa chose was the King of Sweden, Charles XII.

Mazepa was in the same situation as the one Khmelnitsky had faced. From the point of view of feudal rights, he could leave the sovereign, thereby failing to fulfil his obligations, but his only option would be to join a different sovereign. The King of Sweden was a suitable choice because Sweden was a long way away, and, whilst formally a protectorate of Sweden, Ukraine would acquire far more autonomy than it would under Russia.

Since history is always written by the victors, and the Northern War was won by Russia, one can understand why the Ukrainian hetman was slandered as a traitor for the next three hundred years. In independent Ukraine, by contrast, there are streets named after him in the big cities and he is depicted on one of the Ukrainian banknotes.

Prior to the Battle of Poltava, the Ukrainian Hetmans enjoyed a certain amount of independence. After Mazepa was defeated, the Tsar of Moscow Peter I decided that Ukraine was too wilful and must be ruled over far more brutally. For the next two hundred years, therefore, Ukraine was divided up into separate governorates, which were ruled by governors appointed by the monarch.

The Ukrainian Cossacks still bear a grudge against Peter I from those times, in their historical memory, over the fact that thousands of Cossacks were forced to dig the Ladoga Canal, north-west of Russia's new capital, St Petersburg. Many of them died of disease in the process. Digging the land was a humiliating task for these Cossack warriors.

The Ladoga Canal was of great importance to the Russian Empire: it was supposed to provide safe passage for merchant vessels on an important trade route from the Volga River to the Baltic Sea. The Canal was built extremely badly, because some Dutch engineers hired to assist with the project made some miscalculations. But many lives were lost. There is a view that is fairly widely held in Ukraine that the labour of Ukrainian Cossacks was the decisive factor in the construction of the Russian Empire's new capital – the city of St Petersburg. It is said that St Petersburg was built "on the bones of Cossacks". Such talk is probably inspired more by works of literature than by historical facts, however. But as for the idea that the Ladoga Canal was dug by Ukrainian Cossack regiments – that is a fact.

THE LEFT BANK OF UKRAINE UNDER RUSSIAN RULE

In the years following the Battle of Poltava, the Ukrainians had to fight for survival. The country had been ravaged by war and by an epidemic of the plague.

Russia brought a constant state of war to the Hetman's territory (the left bank of the Dnieper), Russian generals took charge of Cossack regiments, and the hetman was appointed by order of the tsar. Russia's policy in relation to Ukraine became distinctly colonial. Handling of all domestic and foreign issues was transferred to the Little Russia Collegium, which had been set up in St Petersburg. In 1720, a ban was introduced on the printing of books in Ukraine. Restrictions were imposed from all sides on Ukraine's foreign trade ties.

Be that as it may, even the Hetmans appointed by order of Peter I – Ivan Skoropadsky, Pavlo Polubotok and Danilo Apostol – tried with all their might to defend the Cossacks' political and economic rights, but were unsuccessful. Polubotok was arrested and died in a torture chamber in the Peter and Paul Fortress outside St Petersburg. Danilo Apostol was also arrested, and only survived because Peter I died and the Hetman was released from prison.

In 1734 the post of Hetman was abolished altogether. Several years later, Peter I's daughter, Elizaveta, restored this post, not without the influence, of course, of her morganatic spouse, the Cossack from Zaporozhye Alyosha Rozum (also known as General-Field-marshal Aleksei Rozumovsky), and appointed his brother Kirill as hetman.

Kirill Rozumovsky, a courtier from St Petersburg and the president of the Russian Academy of Sciences (he had received an outstanding education in Europe, incidentally), who was appointed to the post of Hetman by the empress, remained a Cossack in spirit and tried with all his might to restore the autonomy of the land controlled by the Hetman (and even considered, it is said, becoming a Ukrainian monarch). His efforts did not meet with success. After Kirill Rozumovsky, the Russian monarchs refused to countenance the idea of Ukraine getting any autonomy, holding firm to a policy of assimilating the Ukrainian people and merging them with the Russians.

THE RIGHT BANK OF UKRAINE UNDER THE RZECZPOSPOLITA

The right bank of the Dnieper, meanwhile, was ruled by the Polish gentry and the Catholic Church. Here, on top of the economic and political oppression, there was also religious oppression. Attempts to introduce Catholicism in Ukraine went on continuously from the moment this territory was included in the Rzeczpospolita[10]. These attempts came up against fierce resistance from both the orthodox population and orthodox priests.

Against the backdrop of this religious persecution, the orthodox population of the Right-bank of Ukraine looked on life as a Russian protectorate as the best possible means of existence.

The numerous insurrections by the Ukrainians against the Polish gentry and the Catholic Church were all put down, and crushed, but those Cossacks who refused to be subjugated left for the north, where they were closer to the Russians who shared the same faith as them. Throughout the 15th to 17th centuries there was a constant movement of Cossacks, peasants and churches to the present-day Kharkov, Sumy and Donetsk regions.

For Russia, this territory was on its southern border, which needed to be protected against invasions by Tatars from the Crimea and the Nogai. The Tsar's government therefore encouraged the settling of these areas by these sons of Ukraine: he exempted the settlers from having to pay taxes, allowed them to distil spirits[11] and enabled them to engage in profitable

---

[10] The most effective campaign to bring Ukraine into Catholicism's orbit was undertaken in 1596, when a number of orthodox bishops in the Kyiv metropoly recognized the supreme standing of the Catholic Pope and signed an agreement with the Catholic church on Unii. The new church was named the Greco-catholic church and, in the time when Poland ruled Ukrainian land, enjoyed all manner of exemptions and privileges as a counterweight to the church of the Byzantine rite (Orthodox). During Russia's rule it was subjected to all sorts of persecution and oppression. It nonetheless survived, and retained followers in Ukraine, and, in my own personal view, is one of the most dynamic, modern and democratic churches in our country. Judging by the number of young people who attend the events it organizes, this faith has a bright future ahead of it.

[11] In the main territory of Russia vodka was leased – as we would put it today, licences were issued for spirits, and the licence was expensive. The flow of money coming in from the leasing of vodka

trades (such as salt mining). The settlers owned a certain amount of free land, and retained their Cossack privileges and self-governance. They also brought with them orthodox spiritual faith. A large number of orthodox monasteries were built here.

The resistance put up by the Ukrainian people against the Rzeczpospolita at this time took on the character of guerrilla warfare. For 70 years, from the beginning of the 18th century, there was a movement of Gaydamaks, who carried out attacks on the estates of the wealthy gentry and enjoyed serious support from the local population.

On more than one occasion the Gaydamaks were at the heart of anti-Polish, anti-Catholic insurrections. The largest of these took place in 1768, on the Right-bank, at Koliyivshchyna. The rebels' wrath was directed at the Polish noblemen and the Jews.[12]

The Koliyivshchyna uprising came into being in completely different historical circumstances to those pertaining at the time of the revolt led by Bogdan Khmelnitsky. The Rzeczpospolita was greatly weakened by internal fighting. Koliyivshchyna was itself provoked by the actions of those involved in the so-called Barskaya Confederation. In order to counteract the decisions made by King Stanislav Ponyatovsky, who had been elected under direct pressure from Russia's diplomats and army, and who decreed that Catholics and followers of the orthodox church should enjoy equal rights, conservatively-minded magnates and nobles entered into an alliance (the agreement was signed in the small town of Bar, not far from the present-day regional centre of Vinnitsa).

The confederalists' political motives hardly concerned the Ukrainian population at all. They mocked the Orthodox priests, however, putting them in stocks and pelting them with stones, putting thorny laurel wreaths on their

---

accounted for a large share of the money coming into the Russian state budget.

12   Forced out of England, France and Spain, the Jews lived in the Rzeczpospolita in large numbers, though not as a majority, where they had been invited to settle by the Polish king Boleslav III. In Ukraine they engaged in trade and owned drinking establishments. Quite a lot of them were hired as managers on land owned by Polish magnates, or became leasers of land. The state machine of the Rzeczpospolita did not always operate smoothly on Ukrainian territory. The Ukrainians are an extremely insubordinate people. Collecting taxes regularly was a troublesome and difficult operation. It was far easier for a Polish magnate to give his estates to renters and leasers, on condition that they received a guarantee payment from them. As for how much the leaser collected from the people, that would on his own personal ambition and ruthlessness. The richest Jews in Ukraine in later times were descended from these leasers of land. One can well understand what motivated the leasers. The attitude of the Ukrainian people towards them is self-explanatory, too. Each time there was an insurrection against Polish rule, therefore, the Jews became the primary objects of revenge on the part of the rebellious population. This was also the case in the time of the Khmelnichchina (1648-1656), when a quarter of the Rzeczpospolita's Jewish population was killed by the insurgents or died of epidemics. The same thing happened during the Koliivshchina, as well.

heads, throwing them down wells or putting the burning cole in their boots top of burning coals.

    The rebels' actions were decisive and fairly successful. Their leaders, Maksim Zaliznyak and Ivan Gonta, expected to get help from Russia. When they arrived at the rebels' camp, however, the Russian forces, far from providing assistance, seized the leaders of the revolt, disarmed their units and handed them over to the Poles as prisoners. Thousands of Ukrainians were subjected to brutal, medieval torture and corporal punishment.

AN ASSOCIATION OF UKRAINIAN LANDS INSIDE THE BORDERS OF THE RUSSIAN EMPIRE

The Russian empress no longer needed the Ukrainians' help in the battle against Poland. Any genuine military danger on the part of Poland had disappeared, and there soon followed a series of carvings up of Poland, and in the late 18th century this powerful state which had so covered itself in glory disappeared from the political map for two hundred years.

The entire territory of Ukraine was incorporated within the Russian empire, and remained subject to the system of government and laws that were common throughout the entire empire until 1917. It was divided up into eight governorates: the Chernigov and Poltava governorates – the former Hetmanshchina; the Kharkhov governorate – the former Slobozhanshchina; the Ekaterinoslav and Kherson governorates – so-called Novorossiya; and the Kiev, Volyn and Podolsk governorates – the Pravoberezhe (Right-bank). In addition, the northern part of the Tavricheskaya governorate can also be considered part of Ukraine, from an ethnographical perspective. There were a fair few Ukrainians in the border towns of Bessarabia.

Having been brought into the main body of the population of the Russian Empire, the Ukrainians quickly found their place in it. The Cossack leaders and their descendants became land-owners and hereditary nobles. Unlike the Catholics and the Jews, Orthodox Ukrainians faced no restrictions, either in terms of their rights or their place of residence, and they not only took up all the positions on local government bodies on Ukrainian land, but also held a substantial number of positions in the empire's administrative machine, right up to the most senior positions. Ukrainians held some of the highest-ranking positions in the Russian Empire. The younger brother of the Empress's morganatic spouse, Aleksei Razumovsky, field-marshal Kirill Rozumovsky, was in charge of the Russian Academy of Sciences for fifty years; chancellor Alexander Bezborodko, who was born in the Ukrainian city of Glukhov, was in charge of the Russian Empire's foreign policy under two monarchs – Catherine II and Paul I – in the late 18th century; and both Troshchinsky, the minister of justice, and Kochubei, who was minister of the interior, then chair of the State council and the Cabinet of Ministers, were both Ukrainians.[13]

Russian military historians have observed that a disproportionately large number of senior roles in the army were held by Ukrainians, and have posited the theory that this occurred due to "a tendency towards military affairs inherited from their ancestors, whose lives had involved a continuous series of battles."

In 1812, when the French invaded, Ukrainian Cossacks were quick to join regiments of the Russian army as volunteers, and played a prominent role in the military action, going as far as Paris with the army. Some memoirs from the time refer to attempts by Napoleon's agents to break up the population of Ukraine and persuade the people to defect to the French side. The instigators of this 'special operation' were Poles – landowners from the Pravoberezhe. The Ukrainians saw the Catholic Poles as their sworn enemies, however, and therefore refused to listen to their propaganda. The propaganda was no more successful among the landowners descended from the senior figures in the warrior class. The agents were captured, flogged and handed over to the police. Unlike the Poles, who, taking Napoleon at his word when he promised to restore the Polish state (something which he did indeed do, albeit under the crown of the Duke of Saxony), were against Russia, the Ukrainians categorically refused to side with the French emperor.

In 1831, in anticipation of a large-scale war against Turkey, several regiments of Cossack volunteers were formed, just as had happened in 1812, but they were not required to fight, since the large-scale war never materialized. Thereafter no territorial (or national) military units were formed among the population of Ukraine, and Ukrainians were conscripted to the Russian army on the same terms as the rest of the Russian population.

In spite of the fact that the Russian Empire had taken under its wing Ukrainian land on both banks of the Dnieper, there was still a difference in

---

13   Ukrainians often held prominent positions in other countries too, incidentally. The French may recall Grigory Orlik, a general and diplomat loyal to the French crown in the 18th century. Grigory was the son of Philipp Orlik, a loyal follower of the hetman Ivan Mazepa. Philipp Orlik, incidentally, was the author of a document entitled 'Constitution'. This was an agreement, drafted in 1710, on the mutual rights and obligations between the Hetman, a position which Orlik held, and the Cossacks. In 2011 the administration of the Khersonsnk Region received a letter from Samuel Inigness of River College, Sacramento, in which the American linguist described Philipp Orlik's constitution as "the first truly democratic constitution" and "a prototype for the Constitution of the United States". Shall we take that to be true?

social status between the peasants on the right bank (Pravoberezhe) and those on the left bank (Levoberezhe).

In the Pravoberezhe, when this territory came under Russian power, the Poles held onto their property and rights, and Poland's feudal practices were preserved, so the peasants found themselves in a particularly harsh position. The landowners there were all Poles, who looked on their orthodox peasants as slaves with no rights whatsoever, and treated them accordingly. The Tsar's government deemed it necessary to preserve this social order. All landowners were given the rights and privileges of the Russian nobility, several Polish laws to which they had become accustomed were left in force, and the Polish language was used in the courts. There were no free Cossacks in the Pravoberezhe at all: Poland had converted all of them into serfs.

In the Levoberezhe they did not succeed in making serfs of the Cossacks. Only 35% of the peasants were owned by private individuals, and the rest of the agricultural population were either free Cossacks or state peasantry, who worked on land owned by the state and paid their taxes in monetary form. The southern regions of present-day Ukraine (Kherson, Zaporozhye and Odessa), which had recently been annexed to Russia following a triumphant battle against the Crimean Khanate and the Ottoman Empire, also opened up favourable opportunities for the Ukrainian population of the Levoberezhe. As they strove to conquer and colonize these territories as quickly as possible, the empire's government encouraged Ukrainian Cossacks, peasants and, interestingly, Jews, to settle there, in every way possible. The latter played a huge role in building up a system of economic relations and external trade relations with the southern part of the Russian empire. Naturally, as always happens when a place is colonized, various types of exemption, freedom and, most importantly of all, plots of land were provided. Here only 25% of the population were serfs, and the quality of life was better than in other parts of Ukraine.

By the early 19th century around 7% of the population of Ukraine lived in cities (civil servants, merchants and artisans); the main bulk of the people worked in agriculture. According to data collected in 1860, when preparations were being made to abolish serfdom, only 40% of the population of Ukraine were serfs. In Russia this figure was far higher, and in some areas stood at 100%.

In 1861 the Russian empire abolished serfdom at long last. It was the last of the European nations to do so. This formally meant that the great mass of the agricultural population now had equality in the eyes of the law. This mass was not, of course, homogenous in terms of its social make-up. In Ukraine, alongside Cossacks who owned tens, sometimes even hundreds of hectares of land, there were also peasants who owned very little land or, in some cases, no land at all. The latter became hired hands at major capitalist agricultural firms, or left for the cities, where plants and factories were being built at a rapid tempo. Capitalist firms developed more quickly in Ukraine than in the rest of the Russian empire.

The sugar and distillation industries, iron ore and coal processing, the flour industry, vast amounts of grain for export – all this attracted more and more new capital, and gradually transformed Ukraine from an exclusively agricultural area, with an extensive culture of production, into a wealthy region with rapidly growing industry and the most intensive forms of agriculture in the Russian empire.

As I see it, this period contributed to the differing outlooks of the Ukrainians and the Russians, just as it also contributed to the traits of their national characters. In Ukraine, at the time serfdom was abolished, there were a lot of free landowners. The working class which formed on its territory, containing people who worked in manufacturing and at the plants and factories, was formed in large part as a result of the flow of people from Russia, who had been released from the bonds of serfdom but had no land and no money. A few decades later, the industrial proletariat, which had nothing and was therefore prepared to do whatever it took to get something, was eager to follow the political force which had promised it a share of the national wealth – the Communists. And the native tongue of this section of the population was Russian…But as for a peasant with land, a house of his own, and cattle, who had accumulated his wealth through hard work, and would pass it on to the next generation, here in Ukraine – such a peasant spoke Ukrainian. This explains the furious resistance of the Ukrainian landowner to the efforts of those who had seized power in Moscow to impose a social structure which was not to the Ukrainians' liking.

This resistance was crushed through the use of a terror of a kind hitherto unseen in the civilized world. Yet the socio-political component of these processes merged willy-nilly with the ethnic component. Terror had been given a human face, and the language it spoke was Russian.

Despite the constant targeted pressure from the imperial rulers in Moscow, aimed at crushing the Ukrainian's people's sense of identity, at the adoption by the Muscovites of the name 'Russians', which, as explained earlier, did not belong to them, and at attempting to portray the Ukrainians as some sort of 'junior' nation, one that had been broken off but then 'reunited' with its 'elder brothers – the great Russians', the differences between the Ukrainians and the Muscovites could not but be immediately obvious to anyone looking at the facts objectively. When members of the Russian intelligentsia visited

Ukraine, they were quite surprised to realise that the people here were wholly different from the people living in Russia.

In the mid-19th century, the Russian philosopher, Western sympathizer, literary critic and publicist Vissarion Belinsky wrote in a letter to his wife: "30 versts from Kharkov I caught sight of Little Russia, although there were still some dirty Great Russian buildings mixed in. The huts of the *khokhol*[14] are like little farmers' huts: they are indescribably clean and beautiful. Just imagine it, borscht here in Little Russia is nothing other than green soup (only with chicken or lamb added, and with a bit of fat added for extra flavour). They make this soup extremely tasty and impossibly pure. And that's the men! Their faces are different, they look at you in a different way. The children are very cute, whereas I can't bear the sight of Russian children – they're worse than pigs, and more disgusting."

The Russian writer Ivan Bunin, who is well-known in the West and spent time in Ukraine in the late 19th century, wrote in one of his stories: "I took a liking to the *khokhly* from the moment I first laid eyes on them. I immediately noticed the stark difference which exists between a Great Russian and a *khokhol*. Our men are, in the main, a haggard people, who wear homespun coats, sandals and leggings with holes in them, with gaunt faces and shaggy hair. The *khokhols*, by contrast, make an agreeable impression: they are strapping, well-built and muscular, their gaze is steady and affectionate, and they are dressed in clean, new clothes."

Another well-known Russian philosopher, the writer and publicist Alexander Herzen, described the relationship between Russia and Ukraine as follows: "A Little Russian, even one who has become a member of the nobility, will never sever his ties with the people as abruptly as a Russian. He loves his fatherland, his native tongue, and his loyalties to Cossackhood and the Hetmans. Ukraine defended its independence – a wild and warlike, yet republican and democratic independence – for centuries, right up until the time of Peter I. The Little Russians, tormented by the Poles, the Turks and the Muscovites, and bogged down in an everlasting war with the Tatars in the Crimea, were never able to lay down their arms. After voluntarily joining up with Great Russia, Little Russia won considerable rights for itself. Tsar Aleksei swore that he would abide by them. Peter I, on the pretext of Mazepa's betrayal, left only the shadow of these privileges. Elizaveta and Catherine brought introduced serfdom there. The unhappy country protested, but was

---

14   Malorosses (little Russians) and kokhlys were names for Ukrainians used by Russians. The term 'khokhol' came from the Cossack custom of shaving their heads, leaving only a long pony-tail or toupet at the back. In the time of Kievan Rus, a khokhol such as this was a mark of membership of a noble family, and later it was a standard haircut for a Ukrainian Cossack.

she able to hold her own against this fateful landslide, which rumbled from the north to the Black Sea, covering everything that carried the name of Russian with the same icy desert of slavery?"

If I had cited some of the Ukrainian authors, you might suspect me of being biased and subjective. The words I have quoted came from thinkers who made a huge contribution to Russian-speaking, Muscovite culture. These men cannot possibly be accused of being Russophobes.

Russia's policy today is so similar to the actions of the Muscovite Tsars of 300 years ago that it is simply astounding. All one can do is recall Herzen's words: "The Little Russians have never been able to lay down their arms."

THE FIRST RENAISSANCE OF UKRAINIAN SELF-CONSCIOUSNESS

It is no secret that the people at the very top of Ukrainian society were quick to find their feet in the Russian-speaking environment and culture. Their native Ukrainian tongue, national customs and awareness of their ethnic 'distinctness' lived on in the hearts and minds of the masses, however. As long as waves of warfare and the Gaydamak revolts rolled across Ukraine, there was no opportunity to engage in culture and national traditions, and they were therefore only able to survive at 'grass-roots' level.

From the late 18th century onwards, though, interest was awoken in the Russian Empire in the historical events which had taken place on Ukrainian soil, and in Ukraine's culture and language. Literature in Ukrainian emerged, and a good deal of works were printed in Russian but about Ukrainian subjects. Ukrainian-speaking writers and poets produced works which were to become classics of Ukrainian literature. These works effectively recreated the Ukrainian language, which at the time, due to the vicissitudes of our people's historical fate, was only kept going at the level of day-to-day life, folk tales and conversation.

Russian-speaking writers wrote about Ukraine and about the Cossacks. The Russian intelligentsia reacted with empathy to this 'Ukrainophile' movement.[15]

---

15   A very well-known story by the Ukrainian poet, writer and artist Taras Shevchenko. A young serf blessed with extraordinary talent, who was owned by the landowner Engelhart, a Swiss and one of the richest men in Ukraine at that time, Shevchenko was talent-spotted by some artists and art historians of Ukrainian descent living in St Petersburg. They introduced him to some people with influence in the court of the Tsar, and in 1838 arranged for him to be bought out of serfdom. The landowner was given 2500 roubles in exchange for Shevchenko's freedom. By way of comparison, that sort of sum could buy 400 cows at the time, or 250 horses, or 1.9 kg of pure gold. After obtaining his freedom, Taras Shevchenko studied painting in Petersburg, completed a large number of paintings, wrote poetry in Ukrainian and prose in Russian, and carried out research into history and ethnography. He was an excellent engraver, and at the end of lifetime achieved recognition of his talent and was given the title of an academic of engraving. An

Since Kiev was considered a province at that time, and the centre of the empire was Saint Petersburg, Ukrainian societies and circles, whether of an educational or political bent, were often formed in the empire's capital city. Nonetheless, continually operating Ukrainian theatres were set up in Kiev, Odessa, Poltava, Kharkov and Nezhin in the early 19th century. Processes such as this were evidence that the Ukrainians were gradually acquiring an awareness of themselves as an authentic people, one that was in no way lost or on the periphery, as the historical doctrine of the Russian empire would have it at the time (and still maintains today, incidentally).

All the manifestations of the Ukrainians' national authenticity were only permitted by the empire up to a certain point, however. This approach was adopted by Russia on several occasions in later epochs, too: to take a little bit of pressure off Ukraine, but then dramatically reverse the direction of the national policy completely. There was a straightforward explanation for this strategy: to calm the volcano that was the Ukrainians' sense of identity as a nation, which was on the point of erupting, but not to allow them, under any circumstances, to start to think about the creation of an independent state.

It is fairly widely known that a Circular was published in 1863 by the Russian empire's minister of internal affairs, P. Valuev, in which he prohibited the publishing of religious books and academic literature in Ukrainian. The thing that prompted the publishing of this document was nothing

---

anthology of his collected works in Ukrainian, 'Kobzar', was so popular in Ukraine that it was seen as a must-have work in every household. Children would learn how to read using this book. In 1846 he fell in with a group of Ukrainian intellectuals who had set up a secret political society, whose aim was to liberalize cultural and political life in Ukraine. Shevchenko became attached to its most determined, revolutionary wing. Two years later the Tsar's police got wind of the secret society, and Shevchenko was arrested. When his home was searched, the police found poems which were so critical of the monarchy that he was given the harshest punishment of all the members of the society. This poet and artist was sent off to join the army as a rank-and-file soldier at the Orsk fortress (on the border with Kazakhstan), and banned from painting or writing. This was genuine torture for an individual as creative as Shevchenko, and he refused to submit to this draconian ban. Whilst in exile, he continued to write poetry in secret, and to draw his surroundings. The senior officers were aware that Shevchenko was a famous artist, so when two expeditions were arranged to the Aralsk Sea, he was forced to come along on the expeditions: they needed someone to put down on paper whatever was discovered and investigated during the expedition. The Tsar, who had imposed the ban on Shevchenko painting, was three thousand kilometres away, and cameras had not yet been invented. Taras Shevchenko's pencil and paintbrush therefore provided an excellent service during these missions. On being set free ten years later thanks to petitioning by his friends, Shevchenko returned to Petersburg with his health worn down by his time in exile, and died three years later at the age of 47. The famous cultural figure in 19th century Ukraine Panteleimon Kulish wrote of Taras Shevchenko's funeral: "The church wasn't big enough to fit all the people in. People from all nations and walks of life came to his funeral, because in Shevchenko the people saw a poetic figure of national freedom." After spending 24 years in captivity as a serf and a further ten years in exile, Taras Shevchenko nevertheless managed to create works of such significance to the Ukrainian people that he became a truly symbolic figure, who lived long in the memories of Ukrainians and came to embody their national spirit.

more than a request to translate the New Testament into Ukrainian. Valuev justified the ban by saying that all those living in Little Russia, as he chose to describe Ukraine, could understand the language of Great Russia. There was thus no need to publish religious books in the "little Russian dialect", all the more so given that the printing of works deemed to be "*belles-lettres*" in Ukrainian was permitted. There can be no doubt whatsoever that the underlying reason for the publication of the Circular was an idea which was neatly put into words by another high-ranking imperial civil servant of the day, Nikolai Annenkov: "If they managed to obtain…a translation into the Little Russian dialect of the Holy Scriptures, the supporters of the Little Russian party would achieve…recognition of the independence of the Little Russian language, and then, of course, they would not stop there and, relying on the fact that they had a different language, would start to lay claim to autonomy for Little Russia." This was spoken honestly and unequivocally: if they had a language that was considered to be on equal terms, then they would have a nation that was on equal terms, and then there would be grounds to start talking about the sovereignty of that nation.

In 1905, the celebrated Russian philologist and historian Aleksei Shakhmatov gave a speech at a general meeting of the St Petersburg Academy of Sciences, in which he demonstrated how, in a gradual process, without any laws being adopted but by means of secret circulars, Ukrainian publishing, science, music, theatre and national education had been suffocated. "Removing from educated people the right to write in their own language," the report said, "amounts to an attack on what these people is as dear as life itself, it is an attack on the very life of this people, for how else is this life expressed, if not through words, which conveys thought, expresses feeling, and embodies the human spirit?"

The story of the rebirth of Ukrainian people's national sense of identity in the 19th century would not be complete if we failed to mention a book published at the turn of the 19th century. It was entitled 'The history of the Russes, or Little Russia'. The author's name was not stated, and various people are credited with having written it.

In this book the history of Ukraine was described in the manner of the Greek epics. And it matters not the slightest that it was more like a novel than an academic work. It matters not that the historical events described in it did not, in fact, take place quite in the way it says they did. This book painted the history of Ukraine-Rus in romantic and fantastical hues. The author describes a special people: the Cossacks, who have nothing whatsoever in common with other peoples and were the forefathers of the Ukrainians.

To a man they were absurdly courageous, honest and noble, bursting with all possible merit and without a single character flaw. And this special people, who had their "freedoms and privileges", as a result of the circumstances which had arisen, was forced to subordinate itself to the general order which applied to the whole of Russia. But the descendants of their leaders, rather than being heroes and leaders of heroes, and tearing across the battlefields with their sabres, had been transformed into "sowers of buckwheat…"[16]

The ardour of this author, who was undoubtedly blessed with a gift for the poetic, influenced a huge number of Ukrainians. In the 1820s and 1830s, the History of the Russes achieved great fame, and was ready eagerly by the descendants of the Cossack elders, the landowners of Little Russia, who had grown weary out of boredom and doing nothing at their estates, and particularly by those who had not succeeded in making a career for themselves and who were therefore forced to sit at home at the country farms they had inherited. How pleasant it was, whilst reclining on a divan, to ruminate about the warlike history of your people, thinking of yourself as somehow special and dreaming of re-enacting the glory of your forefathers. Some even began to have thoughts of a political nature, such as the idea of coming out from under the wing of the Russian empire.

The increase in the Ukrainian people's sense of national identity in the late 19th century led to a split among the Ukrainian intelligentsia. The older generation favoured solving the 'Ukrainian question' through cultural and educational activity, their reforms amounted to nothing more than moderate reforms, which would have brought an end to the national and cultural restrictions imposed on Ukrainians in the Russian Empire. They pinned all their hopes on the democratization of the political regime in Russia.

The main ideologist behind this movement was Mikhailo Dragomanov, a Ukrainian historian, philosopher and publicist, and a member of the Dragomanov clan, a family of educators and cultural thinkers of great renown. The main idea behind this movement was that of 'autonomism'. Giving a brief description of their idea, its supporters wanted to achieve a little more cultural independence for Ukraine, along with an acknowledgement that the objectives of Ukraine and of Russia were identical. The movement became a mass movement, incorporating not

---

16 A word or two about buckwheat, incidentally. It is one of the most popular gain cultures in Ukraine, and is consumed so often in the form of *kasha* that it is comparable only with the porridge eaten in Britain. The accusation that they had been transformed into "sowers of buckwheat" amounted to a criticism to the effect that the descendants of warriors had become tillers of the land.

only the 'intellectual' section of the Ukrainian nation, but also the broader masses.

Young people of a revolutionary inclination were attracted by the ideas and ideals of socialism. They felt that national liberation could be achieved by means of social liberation, by means of a battle in conjunction with other nations against the existing social order in Russia.

The 'autonomism' movement was crushed following the defeat of the popular uprisings of 1905-1907 in the Russian empire. The reasons for these uprisings were a famine, countless violations of workers' rights and the low level of civil freedoms. The number of uprisings by the peasants, particularly in Ukraine, could be measured in the thousands. The crushing of these uprisings led not only to the establishment of a brutal regime for governance of the empire, but also to an unprecedented rise in Russian nationalism.

At the start of the 1890s, however, another trend emerged within the Ukrainian national movement, whose slogan called for state independence for the Ukrainian nation. The pioneer of this movement was Nikolai Mikhnovsky, a lawyer, publicist and revolutionary descended from an ancient Cossack clan. This uncompromising campaigner for the independence of the Ukrainian nation remained true to his ideals to the last, though his contemporaries did not support him and his descendants all but forgot him.

THE UKRAINIANS UNDER THE RULE OF AUSTRIA-HUNGARY

At this time, the Ukrainians living in the far western territories, which came under the control of Austria-Hungary after the carving up of Poland, benefited from an unexpected change of fortune as a result of a historical twist of fate.

In 1846-1848 there were uprisings in Galicia and Hungary against the Habsburg Empire.

Galicia, though (Lvov, Peremyshl, Ternopol, Stanlislav (present-day Ivano-Frankivsk)) – an area populated with Ukrainians and governed by Poles – was given to Austria-Hungary with an inherent system of interaction between the different layers of the population which had been shaped over the course of centuries. And in social terms, the population could be roughly divided into two parts: the masters (the landowners and the intelligentsia) – these were mostly Poles; and the tillers of the land – these were Ukrainians and Rusins, or 'Rutins' as they were known in Austria-Hungary. The component parts of the revolutionary movement therefore had completely different objectives from one another. The Poles wanted the restoration of Poland, but in no way favoured the abolition of serfdom. The Ukrainians and Rusins wanted the abolition of serfdom and also wanted land, but as for the restoration of the Polish state…I simply can't say. It seems to me that the Rusins' historical memory did not have the fondest recollections of the era under the control of the Rzeczpospolita. In my opinion, relations between the peasantry and the gentry were pretty tense. In any event, one provocative rumour in 1846 sufficed for the Rusin peasantry to kill members of the Polish gentry and burn down their estates. If one adds to this the fact that the Austrians paid money for every member of the gentry killed, it becomes clear that the Habsburg Empire and the Galician peasants had formed a pact based on the blood of their enemy. The revolutions were crushed (the Hungarian uprising was put down directly, with a decisive role being played by an expeditionary force from Russia), but the peasantry of Galicia were liberated from the chains of serfdom and given land.

Thenceforward a period of demonstrative support for the Rusins began in Austria-Hungary. The fact remains, though, that over the subsequent decades the Ukrainian language and culture had more opportunities for development in Austrian Galicia than in neighbouring Russia – there can be no argument at all about that.

I have no doubt whatsoever that the favourable conditions created in Austria-Hungary for the Galician Ukrainians in the late 19th and early 20th centuries affected the mood and expectations of the people when this land was captured by German forces at the start of the Second World War. These expectations ended in bitter disappointment, since the rulers of Hitler's Germany had set aside for the people of Ukraine the role of slaves, and the mass mobilization of Ukrainian youth to work in Germany served as clear confirmation of their intentions.

Without doubt, the Habsburgs too acted not out of love for the Ukrainian national idea; it was rather the case that, firstly, they wished to make allies of the Rusins against the unruly Poles, and, secondly, they foresaw a conflict with the Russian Empire and hoped to attract onto their side the Ukrainians living to the east of Galicia's borders.

Such a conflict did indeed break out. It was called the First World War.

THE EVENTS OF THE FIRST WORLD WAR IN THE TERRITORY OF UKRAINE

At the start of the war, the Russian army, during the course of the Battle of Galicia in 1914, captured Austrian-controlled East Galicia and almost all of Bukovina, and established on this land a Galician general-governorship. The Russian army's entry into Galicia was followed by an unprecedented campaign of Russification. The Russian administration was actively aided in this by the Muscophiles in Ukraine, who were counting on Russia's help in their battle against the old enemy – the Poles.

All periodical which were published in east Galicia in Ukrainian were closed down, Ukrainian typographies and bookshops were shut down, and so were libraries, museums and academic institutions, even agricultural schools. The activities of the Shevchenko Academic Society were brought to a halt, and the main constitutional privileges which the Ukrainian population of Galicia had enjoyed were abolished. A ban on the Ukrainian language was imposed in the schools.

The new Russian authorities began to persecute the Uniate faith, systematically exiling Uniate priests to remote governorates of Russia and inviting Orthodox priests to take their places. The Metropolitan, Andrei Sheptitsky, was arrested. The same policy was also implemented by the Russian authorities in Eastern Ukraine at this time. Printing in Ukrainian was banned here, as well, and the famous historian and public figure Mikhail Grushevsky was arrested and exiled.

The invasion by the German and Austrian forces in 1915 led to Galicia falling once again under the control of the Central states. After the Russian Army's retreat, the Muscophiles in Eastern Galicia were crushed. Russophile organizations were banned, and their resources and property were handed over to the Ukrainophiles. In 1916 the Russian army attempted an attack, moving the front-line several dozen kilometres to the west. The war ripped through Ukraine like a hurricane, first to the west, then to the east, and on each occasion the Ukrainians found themselves on the receiving end of this hurricane.

Towards the start of 1917 the armies of both of the warring sides began to feel extreme fatigue, and in the Russian empire, where discontent with this seemingly unending war was manifested sooner and on a larger scale, the revolutionaries saw that their opportunity had come.

And in 1917 Ukraine was given yet another opportunity to obtain independence.

THE THIRD ATTEMPT TO OBTAIN INDEPENDENCE – AND THE MOST LIKELY TO SUCCEED?

On 23rd February (8th March)[17] the revolution began in Petrograd, the capital of the Russian Empire. The mass strikes, protests and demonstrations against the war taking place that day grew into a universal strike, and then units from the capital's garrison began gradually to side with the demonstrators.

The monarch abdicated. The new Russian government, in an attempt to strengthen the internal situation in the country, had begun an attack in the summer of 1917 which ended in total defeat. The ensuing counterattack by the Austro-German forces forced the Russian troops to leave Galicia, and to withdraw even further than they had done in 1915.

News of the change in the central power reached Kiev on the 3rd (16th) of March and was reported in the local newspapers on the same day. Demonstrations supporting the revolution were held in a number of Ukrainian cities. The recognized leaders of the political forces active in Ukraine did not, however, lead the country into a campaign to establish and strengthen an independent state. The fiery campaigner for Ukraine's independence, the uncompromising Nikolai Mikhnovsky, and his comrades were the only ones to call for a declaration of independence, the establishment of bodies of power and the creation of Ukrainian armed forces. Alas, the other political leaders, respected, distinguished figures in the national movement with a large amount of authority – Vinnichenko, Doroshenko and Grushevsky – opted instead for a strategy of declarations, assemblies and speeches, a tactic of waiting things out and being moderate. The only form in which they could envisage Ukraine's future was as part of a federation with Russia.

---

17   A short time after this, the Bolsheviks, after seizing power, decided to switch the country to the Gregorian calendar, and many dates from this period are therefore recorded in two different ways – in the old style and in the new style.

On 4th (17th) March a social body was formed, something akin to a pre-parliament, known as the Central Rada, which attempted to perform the functions of state power. The Central Rada sent congratulatory telegrams to Petrograd in which it spoke of its desire to enter into a federation with the new, free Russia. And, significantly, it arranged for the memorial to Pyotr Stolypin to be destroyed, in a ceremony which took the form of a piece of theatre[18].

The Central Rada positioned itself as a territorial body which had introduced, in the territory of Ukraine, a policy of "revolutionary Interim government" (i.e. the type of government which was laying claim to power throughout the whole of the Russian Empire).

In May 1917 an 'All-Ukrainian military congress' was held in Kiev, which was instigated by organizations led by Nikolai Mikhnovsky. This congress adopted a demand for the immediate declaration of Ukraine's national and territorial autonomy. Once again a clash occurred within the Ukrainian national movement between the advocates of two different strategies on how to move forward: those in favour of full independence and those who advocated autonomy within Russia. Whilst the former group called for the immediate establishment of national administrative and military structures, the latter felt that the dominant movement in Ukraine's historical development ought to be not revolution, which would be necessitate bloodshed, violence and destruction, but evolution and the path of peace.

It is important to bear in mind that the First World War was still raging at this time.[19]

---

18   Pyotr Stolypin was an individual whom I cannot pass over in silence. Stolypin became Prime Minister of the Russian Empire in 1906, at the insistence of the monarch. The situation faced by the empire was very difficult: after the defeat in the war against Japan, the country had been hit by a wave of strikes, armed uprisings and terrorism. Alongside the political parties calling for the liberalization of the regime, some openly terrorist organizations were also being activated. Stolypin introduced a series of reforms designed to remove the causes of discontent among the population and set the empire on a path towards progress in industry and agriculture, and put all his efforts into bringing law and order to the country. He succeeded in completing the tasks he had been set, but, as has often been the way throughout history, the result of this was hatred on the part of the reactionary forces within the establishment, the liberals, and the revolutionary extremists. He survived 11 assassination attempts and was killed in Kiev by an agent of the Tsarist government's secret service. The authorities in the new Ukrainian state thus made the statue of him a form of scapegoat, and a valve with which to release the pressure of the "revolutionary energy of the masses".

19   Let us quote a few figures which illustrate the pressing need and unique opportunity to create Ukrainian national armed forces, and thus create a sovereign state, as quickly as possible. This opportunity was hopelessly wasted by the 'democrats' and those who were all talk, with disastrous results for the Ukrainian nation. At the time, Ukraine was the site of the south-western front and part of the Romanian front. The South-western front consisted of 3.3 million soldiers and officers, of which 1.2 million were Ukrainian. There were 1.5 million soldiers and officers on the Romanian front, 30% of whom were Ukrainians. Of the 6.8 million servicemen in the Russian army and the 2.3 million reservists, Ukrainians accounted for 3.5 million. Ukrainians also made up 65% of those serving in the Black Sea fleet.

The Central Rada, under pressure from those who advocated independence, drew up a Memorandum in which a series of demands were made of the Interim government in Petrograd, including the requirement a demand that ethnic Ukrainians be put in separate units within the Russian army. There was no response from the interim government to these demands.

The Central Rada, hurt by this, passed a legislative act which was known as the '*First Universal*'. It contained a unilateral call for national and territorial autonomy for Ukraine, *within Russia*. A delegation from the Interim government promptly arrived in Kiev, and the senior figures in the Central Rada were given "an offer they couldn't refuse". Before long the '*Second Universal*' was published, which stated that "we, the Central Rada, ...have always been in favour of not dividing Ukraine from Russia." The Government in the Central Rada – the General secretariat – declared itself to be "a body of the Interim government", and announced that the Rada was firmly against an unauthorized declaration of independence by Ukraine.

The mass increase in the national sense of identity, meanwhile, led to a situation in which the more radical groups of Ukrainian servicemen continued to make the demands which had put the leaders of the Central Rada in such an awkward position. One of the attempts to put pressure on the Central Rada and force it into taking more decisive steps was an armed exercise by infantrymen which took place in Kiev in early July.

The regiment had been formed in Chernigov and been on the receiving end of an extensive propaganda campaign led by supporters of Nikolai Mikhnovsky. The soldiers demanded that the regiment be included in an army corps which was to be peopled exclusively with Ukrainians. They spoke out for the immediate creation of a Ukrainian national army and expressed their consternation about the passing into law of the Second Universal (and the annexation to Russia).

The Central Rada refused to back this requirement, since it had no wish to have organized armed men "under its wing", speaking on behalf of those who supported genuine national independence. The regiment's soldiers stormed a number of military facilities in Kiev, and several other Ukrainian regiments came to help them. When the Central Rada sent in a Ukrainian regiment which had remained loyal, however, to crush the uprising, the rebels refused to turn their weapons on their brothers-in-arms, and laid down their guns.

In Petrograd, meanwhile, the Interim government was following a policy of limiting the powers of the Central Rada and its General Secretariat (the government). The activities of the Ukrainian 'government' were not financed, the state institutions ignored it, and the taxes, as before, were paid into the

Russian coffers. This last point, as you will appreciate, is what determines the real state of affairs.

The Interim government itself, however, suffered one defeat after another. Failures at the front, a tired army, a people who had been incited by the extremists' calls to take everything from the rich and divide it up equally among the people...

The upshot of all this has of course been well-documented.

On 25 October (7 November) 1917 there was an armed coup in Petrograd, and a group of people came to power who called themselves the 'Bolsheviks'. This political force acted decisively and coherently. Amid the ruins of the Russian empire, as a result of monumental efforts and sacrifices, they created a new, Communist empire, which stood for 74 years and had a decisive impact on the fate of the world in the 20th century.

The new Bolshevik government in Petrograd – the *Sovnarkom* (Council of People's Commissars) – immediately showed signs of being hostile towards the Central Rada. But the Bolsheviks were excellent tacticians. They sent a letter to the Central Rada, in which, although they put forward a host of complaints and accusations (such as accusations of bourgeois behaviour and of departing from Socialist ideas), they nonetheless recognised the right of the People's Republic of Ukraine to be separate from Russia.

The Central Rada, overjoyed, adopted the Third Universal on 7 (20) November, which talked about the creation of a People's Republic of Ukraine which would be federally tied to the Republic of Russia, the nationalization of land,[20] the introduction of the 8-hour working day, the establishment of state control of production, the expansion of local governance, the provision of freedom of speech, of the printed word, of religion, and freedom to form assemblies and unions, and hold strikes, the inviolability of the person and his residence, and the abolition of the death penalty.

The liberal leaders of the People's Republic of Ukraine felt as though they had achieved their goal. They had a poor understanding of what sort of people the Russian Bolsheviks really were, though. The Bolsheviks were brutal, insistent, merciless when dealing with any signs of disagreement, and yet at the same time flexible politicians and outstanding agitators. The idea of giving Ukraine independence never even crossed their minds.

The Bolsheviks forcibly broke up the Founding assembly at which Russia's system of state governance was to be determined, and the leaders of the party

---

20   This was probably the most serious mistake of all – the nationalization of land in the Ukraine of that time. A land of agriculture and peasants, and the embodiment of a man's life-long dream – to own a plot of land of his own. And then all of a sudden the land is nationalized. Why would I want independence if I've had my land taken away from me?

of constitutional democrats were killed on the spot, and those demonstrating in support of the Founding assembly in Petrograd and Moscow were shot. The Bolsheviks withdrew the Russian army from its operations, by issuing directives to its military units to sign peace accords with their opposite numbers on the enemy's side. Through this act Russia withdrew from the First World War, abandoning its allies. However the Bolsheviks enjoyed unprecedented popularity among the soldiers, who were suffering from deadly fatigue as a result of a war they couldn't understand.

The government of the People's Republic of Ukraine decried the Bolsheviks' actions, describing them as irresponsible. In December 1917 the Sovnarkom made a series of ultimatum-style demands on the Central Rada, but since the Central Rada had received support from the All-Ukrainian Congress of peasant, worker and soldier deputies, which had convened to determine the future fate of the country, these ultimatums were rejected.

At that point the Bolsheviks brought into the Ukrainian city of Kharkov trains full of soldiers who were loyal to them, disarmed the 'Ukrainified' regiments, convened an alternative congress in Kharkov under their control, declared Ukraine to be a republic of Soviets and announced the abolition of the Central Rada. It was only after this, in January 1918, that "our hope and support", the Central Rada, passed the Fourth Universal, in which Ukraine was declared to be the "independent, free, sovereign state, dependent on no-one, of the Ukrainian people."

This newly declared sovereignty needed someone to protect it, however. This was something that our leaders were not quite able to do.[21] At a time (January 1918) when Bolshevik troops were carrying out an attack right across Ukraine on the formations of the White movement,[22] achieving victories and capturing Ukrainian cities one after another, all the Central Rada was able to do was announce that the regular army had been disbanded. Just six months prior to this, 300,000 servicemen had sworn their allegiance to the Central Rada, but now the Ukrainian government had fewer than 15,000 soldiers left in the whole of Ukraine.

Naturally, the Bolsheviks could not let such an opportunity slip, and began an attack on Kiev, and the government of the PRU was unable to put together any sizeable force to resist them. At the same time as their attack on the Arsenal munitions plant in the centre of Kiev, the Bolsheviks stirred up an insurrection against the Ukrainian government, which all the troops which remained in the hands of the Central Rada were called upon to crush.

---

21 The leader of the Bolsheviks, Vladimir Lenin, said: "Revolutions are only ever worth anything if they know how to defend themselves." The Ukrainian national revolution proved unable to defend itself.

22 A politico-military movement against Soviet power, led by the senior officers in the Tsar's army

Consequently the last bastion before Kiev, next to the railway station of Kruty, was defended against the Bolsheviks by a 400-strong force, most of whom were students from Kiev, with inferior weaponry, poor training and limited stocks of ammunition. These young men are spoken of as heroes today, with statues put up in their honour and streets named after them. They were indeed heroes, who gave their lives to protect the idea of the Ukrainian nation. But who had put the People's Republic of Ukraine in a position in which it was unable to protect its independence?

At the end of January the Bolshevik forces occupied Kiev and for three days brought 'red terror' to the city, hunting down and shooting officers, cadets from military academies and well-off citizens.

THE OCCUPATION OF UKRAINE BY AUSTRO-GERMAN FORCES

At the same time a delegation from the Central Rada in Brest-Litovsk[23] held talks with representatives of Germany and Austria-Hungary on the signing of a separate peace. Understandably, the Ukrainian delegation found itself negotiating from a very weak position.

The separate peace agreement between the Central states and the PRU was the first peace agreement in this world war, and probably the most unsuccessful. Other than a nominal declaration of the PRU's independence (Ukraine's ethnic borders, incidentally, were not restored), it did not give Ukraine anything, but imposed obligations on it to supply a large amount of raw material and foodstuffs to Germany. Naturally, when the Bolsheviks, on behalf of Russia, signed another separate agreement with Germany and Austria-Hungary a short time thereafter, Ukraine was simply used as a makeweight and came under the jurisdiction of the Central states.

By the end of April the Bolsheviks had withdrawn from Ukraine, and the Austrian and German forces had occupied the country, since it is much easier to control supplies of foodstuffs from occupied territories. The Bolsheviks, however, protected their gains stubbornly, refusing to give them up without a fight. In February 1918 the Bolsheviks arranged the declaration of the Donetsk and Krivoy Rog Republic in the south-east of Ukraine and tried to organize resistance against the advancing German forces.

In March 1918 the Central Rada came back into being in Kiev, but the people of Kiev felt that it now existed on the back of German bayonets, and this was indeed the case. The authority of the Ukrainian leaders therefore fell

---

23   A city in the south-west of present-day Belarus; in 1918 it was chosen as the site of negotiations between the governments of the Central states (Germany, Austria-Hungary, Turkey and Bulgaria) and Soviet Russia on the issue of the cessation of military action. Despite the fact that the emissaries from Russia's Bolshevik government tried to speak on behalf of Ukraine as well, they were not recognised as representing the Ukrainian people by the other party in the negotiations. Thus the delegation from the People's Republic of Ukraine spoke at the negotiations independently.

below zero. The former members of the Central Rada had all been sacked, and as for the new ones...

The PRU undertook to supply the Central states with 60 million poods of grain (3,750,000 tonnes), 400 million eggs, and other agricultural produce. And this was to be exported whilst battle raged throughout the land.

By the end of March 1918 the German and Austro-Hungarian command and diplomats had become convinced of the hopelessness of trying to cooperate with the Rada, since the Central Rada did not have any genuine levers of influence over the people it was endeavouring to represent. And, most importantly of all as far as the occupying powers were concerned, it was unable to ensure that foodstuffs were imported to Germany and Austria-Hungary. Members of the Central Rada were therefore arrested and put in prison, and at a specially convened 'All-Ukrainian congress of grain-growers', the 'Hetman of Ukraine' was elected, a former lieutenant-general from the Russian Imperial Army and adjutant to Emperor Nikolai II, Pavlo Skoropadsky, who was supported by the German high command (a fact which is hardly surprising given that it was the Germans who put him forward for this post).

Though the Ukrainian state under Hetman Skoropadsky was recognised by 30 states, and there were permanent representative offices of 10 states in Kiev, with the state itself having diplomatic missions in 23 countries, history did not grant the state more than six months of existence. Ukraine did not embrace Skoropadsky. The anti-Hetman uprisings which broke out were put down with the direct involvement of the occupying forces. It seemed as though an army was starting to be formed, along with state bodies, but it was all too late, too late...

Skoropadsky had been propped up by German and Austrian bayonets, and by the autumn of 1918 it had become clear that the Central states were facing inevitable defeat in the First World War. Against this backdrop, Hetman Skoropadsky appointed a new cabinet on 14 November 1918, consisting almost entirely of Russian monarchists, and announced the Act of Federation, under which he undertook to unite Ukraine with the future non-Bolshevik Russian state in a federation. Yet again, a Ukrainian leader was once again looking towards Russia for a master.

In November 1918 there was a revolution in Germany, Germany withdrew from the war and the German and Austrian forces pulled out of Ukraine.

ANOTHER ATTEMPT TO CREATE A UKRAINIAN STATE

The former leaders of the Central Rada, after gathering in Belaya Tzerkov, a small town outside Kiev, attempted to seize power once again, and organized a new government – the Directorate – and advanced on Kiev. Many divisions of the Hetman's troops moved over to the side of the Directorate. In late November the Directorate's forces, led by Symon Petliura, laid siege to Kiev. The Germans fled Kiev for their homeland unimpeded, and Petliura's men slaughtered the Ukrainians, i.e. the officers and soldiers of Hetman Skoropadsky's army.

The passing on of power in Ukrainian territory from one group to another led to anarchy, a complete lack of law and order and pogroms against the Jews. Supporters of the Bolsheviks robbed Jews, on the grounds that "they're all bourgeois", and the army of the monarchist Denikin spread terror against the Jews on the grounds that "they are all Bolsheviks"[24].

As a result, the time of the Civil War was related to countless sacrifices on the part of Ukraine's Jewish population.

---

24 Pogroms against the Jews are sometimes associated with the name of Symon Petliura, which is undoubtedly a historical inaccuracy. Petliura had taken control of a completely powerless state, and in spite of all the attempts not to allow violence against the Jewish population, he was unable to take control of the situation. Samuel Schwartzbard, who assassinated him in Paris in 1926, allegedly did so by way of vengeance for anti-Jewish pogroms, and specifically for the death of his own family. There were also those who suggested that the murder was arranged by the Soviet secret police, although there is no documentary evidence for this.
One thing we can be sure of is that being an intelligent and humane person with no anti-Semitic views whatsoever, Symon Petliura was unable to deal with the anarchist, fanatical free-for-all which broke out in Ukraine, whose leaders had formally declared their units to be at the service of the Directorate, i.e. subordinate to Petliura, but in fact were often involved in acts of hooliganism and theft, with no nationalist rationale to them whatsoever. The person of Petliura nevertheless began to be associated with the idea of a force which was not overly subordinate to him, for which he later paid the price.

THE UKRAINIAN PEASANTRY TAKES UP ARMS

The unrest which always accompanies frequent changes of power, the inability of successive rulers to get to grips with the situation in the country, and the ordinary Ukrainian peasant's natural desire to want to protect his home, his family and his future, contributed to a situation in which the population was increasingly taking steps to organize itself and protect itself. It is for the reader to decide whether or not this was a consequence of the effect of the genes inherited from the Ukrainian Cossacks, but the following is beyond doubt: it was with weapons in their hands that the Ukrainian people sought to safeguard their ideas about the best possible future they could have, and there were times when events took on an epic dimension. Unfailingly, it was the leaders who came from among the ordinary people that put themselves forward for the most prominent roles. One need only cite such colourful historical figures as atamans Grigoriev and Makhno.

The first of these, a staff captain in the Tsar's army, served in the forces of the Ukrainian People's Republic, later teamed up with Skoropadsky, before switching allegiance to the Directorate and then moving to the side of the Red Army. In the end he led an uprising against the Bolsheviks, and suffered a crushing defeat. A fervent anti-Semite, he was responsible for numerous pogroms against Jews which took place in Ukraine at that time.

The second individual, Nestor Makhno, was a dyed-in-the-wool anarchist, revolutionary and rebel leader, who was in charge of a mass armed movement among the Ukrainian peasantry. His army played a decisive role in disrupting the attack by Denekin's Volunteer Army on Bolshevik Moscow. He was a man who typified the Ukrainian national character. He was nicknamed *batko* by his companions in arms, a word which, in the Ukrainian Cossack tradition, signifies acknowledgement of a high level of authority, trust and reliability. Ataman Grigoriev was shot on Makhno's orders, and among the things he was accused of were anti-Semitism and pogroms against the Jews. Makhno fought for the Red Army against the White Army, and then, once he had become aware of what the objectives of the Communists in Moscow actually were, instigated an uprising against the Bolsheviks.

The outbreak of an armed peasant uprising in Ukraine was inevitable. Just think about it: how many armies of various 'shades' had torn across Ukraine in 1918-1919 – both known and unknown. And it was the Ukrainian peasants who had had to provide food for all these armed people. Whoever came to power, they always demanded the same thing of the peasants: give us bread, give us foodstuffs. The Germans came and grain was carted off; the Bolsheviks came and food began to be confiscated by special armed divisions of soldiers. And the peasants had just a hard a time of it when the White Army troops came into their village. Small wonder that the Ukrainian peasant, in an effort to protect home and hearth, jumped on his horse, rifle in hand, and tried to fight them all off. Peasant leaders such as the atamans Grigoriev and Makhno brought together such mighty forces under their command that they were able to capture one city after another and swing military campaigns in favour of whoever's side they were fighting on.

FRENCH TROOPS IN UKRAINE

Following their victory in the First World War, the nations in the Triple Entente – as custom dictated, and without asking anyone's permission – carved up the territory of the former Russian empire into fields of influence. Ukraine fell into the zone of French 'responsibility'. In early 1919, therefore, a French expeditionary force landed at Ukraine's southern ports – Sevastopol, Odessa, Kherson and Nikolayev. The Entente nations backed the White movement, and gave them military and technical support. Political change within France herself, however, coupled with the fact that the French soldiers did not wish to interfere in a civil war in Russia, and – according to some reports – the buying off of certain members of the French high command by Bolshevik agents, resulted in the hasty evacuation of Entente troops from Odessa and the occupation of it by ataman Grigoriev's militia forces in April 1919. Before long the Entente forces had left the other ports in South Ukraine as well.

THE ACT ZLUKY
(THE ACT OF UNIFICATION)

In January 1919 an event took place which, without any exaggeration, could genuinely be described as being of historic proportions for the Ukrainian people: the unification of the western Ukrainian territories and the rest of Ukraine was proclaimed. The people of West Ukraine, who had been left without a sovereign ruler due to the vicissitudes of the First World War, proclaimed the establishment of the West-Ukrainian People's Republic (WUPR). The newly proclaimed state had an army at its disposal almost immediately – divisions of ethnic Ukrainians from the Austro-Hungarian army – the Ukrainian Sechevye Streltsy. The Polish Rzeczpospolita, which was being resurrected on the embers of the Russian and Austro-Hungarian empires, regarded the territory of the WUPR as its own. The Ukrainian Sechevye Streltsy engaged in a battle with the Poles over Lvov, the vitally important centre of Galicia, but were unsuccessful and had to retreat. Troops from neighbouring states moved on the WUPR from all sides, cutting it to pieces. The Romanians occupied Chernovtsy, the capital of Bukovina. Czechoslovakia took the most important city in Transcarpathia, Uzhgorod. Unable to stand up to the pressure being exerted on it from outside on its own, the WUPR, as one would expect, sought to form an alliance with a more powerful force, and the most desirable association of all was an association with its brothers from further East, the Ukrainian People's Republic.

The delegation despatched from the WUPR to see Hetman Skoropadsky reached Kiev when Skoropadsky had already been toppled. The act of unification between the UPR and the WUPR was thus signed under the guidance of the Directorate. For the first time in many centuries, the territories which cover the entire spread of ethnic Ukrainians were brought together into a formal association.

THE RED ARMY IN UKRAINE

As the old saying goes, man plans and God laughs. Nowhere is this demonstrated to a greater extent than when applied to the geopolitical landscape.

In January 1919 the Bolshevik Red Army invaded Ukraine, and the city of Kharkov was captured. In February, Kiev was taken. In March it was proclaimed, for the second time, that Soviet power had been established in the country.

By May 1919 the entire territory of Ukraine, within the borders it had under the Russian Empire, was controlled by the Red Army. A Communist dictatorship was established – and it took the form of so-called 'military communism', which entailed nationalization of the economy, the end of commodity-money relations, the introduction of requisitioning (enforced confiscation of food from the peasants), national service for all, equal pay for labour, militarization of society, and the abolition of communal payments, payment for public transport and so on.

This was not what the Ukrainian peasantry had been hoping for, it goes without saying. In the spring of 1919, Ukraine was gripped by a wave of peasant uprisings. Often the Bolsheviks employed the tactic of burning down populated areas in its battle with the peasants. The 'Soviets of workers and peasants deputies' which they created brought in military sieges of villages and a hostage system, established the payment of monetary and material contributions, and deprived the families of the leaders of the uprisings of housing. It was finding itself unable to cope, however, with the mass rebel movement. By the summer of 1919 the situation had been exacerbated by the fact that the Bolsheviks were now up against such powerful guerrilla leaders as the atamans Nikifor Grigoriev and Nestor Makhno, who had previously supported Soviet power.[25]

---

25 Let us quote the fairly well-known words of one of the most important leaders of the Bolshevik coup, the leader of the Red Army during the Civil War, Lev Trotsky: "It is no secret that it was not

THE WHITE ARMY IS IN UKRAINE – YET THE RED ARMY TRIUMPHS. UKRAINE IS CARVED UP ONCE AGAIN

Now the White movement had gained a second wind, and began its attack on the Bolshevik forces. In June 1919 an attack spread across Ukrainian territory by the Armed forces of the South of Russia (the White Army), under the command of General Denikin. This assault had the aim of removing the Bolsheviks from power, and it was so successful that the Communist government in Moscow thought the game was up and made ready for a transition to an illegal position.

This gave Ukraine no grounds for hope, however, in light of the fact that the Whites' political credo was the restoration of a "united and indivisible Russia", in which there could be simply no room for the idea of national independence for Ukraine. As for the most pressing issue of all – that of the right to own land – the Whites proposed to resolve it via a return to the old imperial order. Figuratively speaking, they were bringing the big land-owners

---

Denikin who forced us to leave Ukrainian territory, but the huge uprising against us by the well-fed Ukrainian peasants. The Commune, the 'Chrezvychaika' [the emergency commission for the struggle against counter-revolution and sabotage], the food brigades and the Jewish commissars – the Ukrainian peasants hated these things to the depths of their souls. The free spirit of the Zaporozhskoe Cossacks and the Guydamaks, which had lain dormant inside them for centuries, was awoken. It is a frightening spirit, which boils and seethes like the terrible rapids of the Dnieper, and prompts the Ukrainians to achieve marvellous acts of courage. It is the self-same spirit of wilfulness which gave the Ukrainians inhuman strength throughout hundreds of years of doing battle against their oppressors: the Poles, the Russians, the Tatars and the Turks, and to achieve magnificent victories over them. It was only their limitless credulity and pliability, and their failure to recognise the need for strong and constant adhesion between all the members of the state, in time of peace as well as in time of war – that undid the Ukrainians' victories every time. It was for this reason that they lost their independence so early on, and have had to live by turns under Lithuania, Poland, Austria and Russia, constituting a very valuable part of these states. Any agitator who keeps these character traits of the Ukrainians in mind will be assured of success. Don't forget, either, that however we go about it, it is essential that we bring Ukraine back under Russian control. There can be no Russia without Ukraine. Without Ukraine's coal, iron, ore and grain, and the salt of the Black Sea, Russia cannot exist: it will suffocate, as will Soviet power along with it, and you and I.

of old – the landlords – back with them, in convoy. Yet the Ukrainian peasants had, by this time, succeeded in dividing up the land among themselves. So there was no way Ukraine could support Denikin.

In August 1919 the White Army took Kiev. Along with the remnants of the Red Army, divisions of the UPR and the Galician army, which had entered the city at the same time as Denikin's army, were forced out of the city. The Directorate was enraged by this and declared war on the "whites". In October 1919 Kiev was occupied by the Reds once again, but yet again they were forced out by Denikin's army. By November 1919 Ukraine was under the control of the white movement.

The leaders of the two Ukrainian people's republics, the UPR and the WUPR, in a naïve attempt to survive inside their own shells, betrayed one another. It is true what they say, that naivety in politics is worse than a crime. The leader of the UPR, Symon Petliura, opened negotiations with Poland, defining Ukraine's borders in a way that went against the interests of the WUPR. The leader of the forces of the WUPR, meanwhile – Miron Tarnavsky – signed an agreement on a military alliance with the Volunteer army led by Denikin (who, as we have already seen, would not have even dreamt of considering granting independence to Ukraine).

The course of history was changed by the aforementioned peasant leader and *batko*, Makhno. In extremely trying conditions, this talented general managed to put together a rebel army out of rag-tag guerrilla units, and dealt such a blow to the rear of the White army that Denikin was forced to turn his most battle-ready divisions to against the peasant ataman: this was eventually to determine the outcome of the battle in 1919, and ultimately led to a breakthrough in the Civil War in favour of the Reds.

As we can see, the Ukrainian peasantry managed on the one hand to drive the Bolsheviks out of Ukraine at the beginning of 1919, and on the other hand acted in such a way as to ensure that the Bolsheviks were victorious over the White movement at the end of 1919. When the Whites' last stronghold on the Crimean peninsula was destroyed, the army led by Nestor Makhno was the first to tear into the enemy's rear lines, and decided the outcome of the battle. The Bolsheviks immediately showed the Ukrainian leader how 'grateful' they were: he was declared a traitor, and his army, in spite of some desperate resistance, was ultimately destroyed by the reds[26].

The end of the Civil War did not bring the Ukrainian people the peace they had craved for so long, however. A huge conflict broke out between the

---

26   Makhno and a handful of his men who had survived the battle broke across the border to Romania, and, after getting through a series of arrests and spells in internment camps, reached Paris in 1925, worked as a carpenter at the Grand Opera and died in 1934 at the age of 45.

Soviets and the Poles, in which the theatre of battle was once again Ukraine. And once again it was interference from within (on this occasion on the part of the Entente nations) that made this conflict inevitable. The Entente had decided to create a buffer zone against Bolshevism. Poland was selected as the raw material for this protective zone. Having received support from the West, Polish troops invaded in March 1920 and on 6th May they took the long-suffering city of Kiev.

In June 1920 the Red Army undertook a counter-offensive and got as far as the outskirts of Warsaw, but was then crushed.

Ultimately the peace talks between Soviet Russia and Poland ended in the dividing up of Ukrainian territory. West Ukraine, including Lvov, Rovno, Stanislav and Kovel now found themselves ruled by Poland once again.

RELATIONS BETWEEN THE COMMUNIST POWERS AND THE UKRAINIAN PEOPLE

Soviet power, with its methods of forcible collectivization of crops grown by means of hard physical labour, and brutal crushing of any manifestations of incorrect ideology, was not something that the Ukrainian peasants could have taken to. Resistance to the oppression they suffered, followed by an upsurge in oppression in response to this resistance, were to go on for many years.

Still fresh in the memories of the Ukrainians was the history of the rebel state, the 'Kholodnoyarsk Republic'. A self-defence brigade formed in 1918 in order to protect an Orthodox monastery against thieves, this movement had evolved over time into a vast army containing 30,000 soldiers and controlling a sizeable area of land. It was twice as big as Lebanon and roughly the same size as modern-day El Salvador or Slovenia.

The rebels' slogan was 'Freedom for Ukraine – or death!' Within the territory they controlled they had set up agencies of power and governance, and the other props required of a state, and this guerrilla state was transformed into a centre of resistance against the Bolsheviks.

On 12th April 1920 the rebels' first leader, Vasily Chuchupak, and a small brigade of men were ambushed by red soldiers on the Kreseltsa Ridge. Most of the red soldiers were Chinese. It was not a fair fight. Surrounded by enemies, Vasily shot himself. He was just 26 years old.

The Republic kept up the fight against the reds for a further two years. It was defeated by means of deception and treachery. First of all the Reds' special services created a false rebel unit and, during a meeting with the Republics' leaders arranged for the purposes of 'joining forces', the leaders were all arrested and sentenced to death by firing squad. Next the Soviet powers announced an amnesty on the rebels: it said that none of them would be punished, and they could all go back to their labours in peace. Many Cossacks took them at their word: they wanted to do so, and longed to go back to their families and to peaceful peasant labours. Oppression against the people soon broke out, however. Families of rebels and peasants who helped the rebels were evicted. They had their property, equipment and stocks of food confiscated. All those who were fit to work were sent to militarized 'working' units.

The Cossack leaders who were arrested refused to simply lie down and die, and instead attempted one last hurrah, instigating an uprising in the prison in which they were held. Throwing themselves on the guards with nothing but their bare hands, they seized a handful of revolvers and rifles and kept the battle going for four hours. The last Cossacks left alive used their last bullets to shoot one another dead: rather that than surrender to the enemy. Wounded Cossacks captured by the reds had their heads chopped off with axes.

The story of the Kholodnoyarsk Republic demonstrates, in condensed form, the nature of the relations between the Ukrainian people and the Bolsheviks who had entered their territory from Russia. There were the Chinese soldiers enticed into the Red Army to fight the Ukrainian rebels; the methods of betrayal, direct deception, and the rebels' willingness to die in battle rather than sit and wait for death at the hands of their executioners.

One can understand why the leaders of Bolshevik Russia saw an unruly Ukraine as a huge threat to their rule, and the task of breaking the back of the freedom-loving Ukrainian peasantry was constantly among their plans.

In the early 1920s, however, the Communists' grip on power was not as strong as it later became. Moreover, the Communist doctrine was so much at variance with the people's ideas about how life ought to be organized throughout the country, and the resistance put up by the people was so powerful, that the Bolsheviks were forced to retreat. The peasants in Ukraine were not the only ones to rebel. In March 1921 there was a revolt at the naval fort of Kronshtadt, outside Petrograd. And these were the very same 'revolutionary sailors' who had played the role of the Bolsheviks' mighty fist when they seized power in 1917. They had been known as the 'heart of the revolution'.

The revolt was brutally crushed, yet it had become clear that Soviet rule was on the brink of collapse.

THE MANOEUVRINGS OF THE BOLSHEVIKS TO QUELL UKRAINE'S RESISTANCE

With great reluctance, the Bolsheviks announced the introduction, in July 1921, of the New Economic Policy (NEP). In place of the unrestricted requisitioning of grain, a system of taxation was introduced (these measures were introduced in Ukraine after a delay of a few months, so that there would be time for some additional requisitioning of grain to take place). The fiscal system was restored and all restrictions on savings were lifted; and fares for rail journeys, postage costs and so on, which had been abolished during the final stage of military communism, were reintroduced. In October 1921, industrial companies were granted the right to sell their products on the free market.

Another part of the NEP was the restoration of industry, and concessions to capitalism had to be made in this regard, too.

These were enforced, tactical concessions, however. In his essay, *The Communist Manifesto* – the Bolsheviks' Bible – the founder of Communist teachings, Karl Marx, wrote that the peasantry, like other 'petty Bourgeois' groups, was destined for destruction as heavy industry developed. All these groups were therefore conservative – reactionary, even: they were striving to "roll back the wheel of history". In the minds of the Bolshevik leaders, the idea by which they were governed was the view expressed by Lenin, to the effect that the peasantry begets capitalism and the bourgeoisie "constantly, every day, every hour and on a mass scale." This served as justification for the deep distrust in every layer of the peasantry, as a source of danger to the Bolsheviks. Every opportunity was used in order that, whilst relying on the workers in the cities, the peasants could be peasants could be forced into harsh, brutal frameworks within which the economic fantasies dreamt up by Marxist theoreticians could become a reality.

The Bolsheviks planned to neutralize the danger which emanated, in their opinion, from the peasants, by depriving them of ownership of land and the tools of their trade, and turning them into hired staff at agricultural enterprises controlled by the state, and to do so using methods which were to become typical of Soviet Russia: violence, scare tactics and terror. As Lenin once wrote to an associate: "It would be the greatest mistake of all to think that the NEP brought an end to terror. We shall return to terror again, including economic terror."

In 1921, however, the national movement among the Ukrainian peasantry was a serious problem for the Bolsheviks. It was the failure of the first few Communist regimes due to resistance from the peasants which forced those in power in Moscow to think seriously about the need to quell the enemy's hostility: the peasants were no longer oppressed for behaving like peasants, and Ukrainians were allowed to enjoy a certain amount of cultural autonomy. These concessions to the Ukrainian national consciousness, like the concessions to the peasantry, were dictated by the need to have a breather before the decisive attack.

The first Soviet regime in Ukraine was openly anti-Ukrainian and therefore met its demise amid a storm of hostility from the masses. The national policy of the second regime, though it was more cautious, nonetheless provoked strong resistance among the people. The Communists' third, successful attempt came up against serious resistance, but on this occasion it had been prepared more carefully, and not just in a military sense. Political steps had been taken to weaken the people's resistance. This was achieved by means of a more cautious and coherent national policy, i.e. a respectful attitude towards Ukrainian national feelings and towards those Ukrainians who did not appear to the victors to be complete lost causes in terms of their hostility to Communism.

In December 1922, Ukraine, the Transcaucasian Republic and Belarus, which had hitherto been considered independent, became part of the Union of Soviet Socialist Republics.

In April 1923 the Communist party officially announced its policy of 'Ukrainization'. For the first time since the 18th century, a government with firm foundations in Ukraine had openly declared its intention to preserve and promote the Ukrainian language and culture. At a time when, within Russia itself, political figures from the pre-Bolshevik regimes were suffering merciless oppression, outstanding émigré academics and writers were returning to Ukraine, even those who had once expressed support for the Central Rada. Among them was the historian Mikhail Grushevsky, a former chairman of the Rada, and other ministers and ordinary members of the Rada.

The former chairman of the Ukrainian People's Republic, Vladimir Vinnichenko, was admitted to the Communist Party of Ukraine and became a member of its governing body, the Central Committee; he was even appointed deputy chairman of the Soviet People's Committee of Ukraine and commissar for foreign affairs. Vsevolod Golubovich, who replaced Vinnichenko in the role of premier, in spite of the accusations initially made against him, benefited from an amnesty and was employed in the capital construction department of the Ukrainian Council of National Economy until 1931.[27]

'Ukrainization' went further than the concessions made to nationalism in other regions. Representatives of Ukrainian culture, on returning to the country, genuinely hoped that Soviet Ukraine might become a theatre for national regeneration. Their poetry and belle-lettres, and their works on the study of language and history, were welcomed rapturously by every section of society, and the literature of the past was reprinted in copious quantities.

Ukrainian cultural organizations managed to find a route to the heart of the countryside, to the heart of the peasantry. Permitted by the Bolsheviks as part of their new strategy, these organizations consisted of people who, though they considered themselves Communists, were interested primarily in the history and literature of the Ukrainian people.

In early 1925 the restrictions imposed on the use of hired labour were lifted. As the country was put back on the path of product-monetary relations, a dramatic upturn in the economy began. The improvement in the situation was noticeable at once, and it occurred solely thanks to trade relations and peasant property. By 1925-1926 gross agricultural product had reached pre-war levels. That said, it must be acknowledged that the improvement was the result of tireless work on the part of people from the bankrupted countryside. There was hardly any draft cattle. The people ploughed the fields using cows or by harnessing themselves to the plough. Nevertheless, the success of the private sector in agriculture meant that the hardest-working peasants were able to flourish. Many of the peasants who had grown wealthy found that they were away from their home villages during the civil war, either fighting with the Red Army or with the guerrillas. These were people who often displayed exceptional initiative, and who came into collision with a different type of life and a different set of ideas.

At that time (by comparison with previous and subsequent years, of course) Bolshevik terror was scarcely noticeable, and was still at the lowest level by Soviet standards. An amnesty was even introduced for the rebellious peasants. An example was the emergence from their position in hiding in March 1922 of 126 partisan peasants in the small town of Lokhvits (in the Poltava region of Ukraine). The chairman of the government of Ukraine, Petrovsky, was personally in attendance when this took place[28].

---

27   Vinnichenko was fairly quick to sense how the situation might develop, however, and opted to go back to living in exile. Golubovich stayed in Ukraine and, after eight years of imprisonment, died in prison in Yaroslavl.

28   All those who had benefited from the amnesty died seven years later during a fresh wave of terror

THE BOLSHEVIKS SHOW HOW THEY REALLY FEEL ABOUT UKRAINE

All this was merely tactical manoeuvring, however. A secret circular from the Bolshevik secret intelligence agency, the GPU, in June 1925 contained the following passage: "We know that counter-revolutionary organizations and groups in Ukraine are well aware that the GPU is being forced, at present, to spend time being inactive, so to speak, and that this is dictated by the new economic policy, and also by government notions of a higher order. Each one of us knows that this is nothing more than a temporary state of affairs. The main secret police agency must not, therefore, lose the ability to expose our enemies, so that we can deal them a lethal blow when the time comes for this."[29]

---

29   In order that everything would be in place for this lethal blow to be delivered, "when the time comes for this", a list of individuals was compiled for Ukraine back in 1924 who were considered enemies and would be subjected to persecution.

This list included:
Political parties and organizations
1. All former members of pre-revolutionary bourgeois political parties,
2. All former members of monarchist unions and organizations,
3. All former members of the Union of voluntary grain-growers (from the time of the Central Rada in Ukraine).
4. All former representatives of the nobility and titled representatives of the old aristocracy,
5. All former members of youth organizations (the boy scouts etc.),
6. Nationalists of all kinds.
Bureaucrats and civil servants who actively served Tsarist power
1. Officials in the former Ministry of internal affairs: all members of the Okhranka (the secret police), the police and the gendarmerie etc.,
2. Officials in the former Ministry of justice: members of district and governorate courts, county court judges and prosecutors of every rank, judges from civil and criminal courts, court officers, the chairmen of district courts, etc.
3. All officers and junior officers, without exception, in the former Tsarist army and navy.
Secret enemies of Soviet power
1. All former officers, junior command and soldiers in the white movements and armies, Ukrainian Petliurite associations, and various rebel divisions and bands, who had been actively against Soviet power. **People who had been granted an amnesty by the Soviet authorities were not to be considered an exception,**

The main lethal blow that was planned was to be aimed at the peasantry, particularly the Ukrainian peasantry, which was the most hard-working and well-off. A new socio-political term was invented as an ideological basis for the justice that was to be dealt out to the peasantry: the 'kulak'. This term was used to define a hypothetical layer of wealthy agricultural farmers, who were making a living off the back of the labours of their fellow villagers, had accumulated great wealth and were the natural enemies of the socialist ideology.

In actual fact, peasants such as this simply could not have existed in the days of Soviet rule. In 1927, the most prosperous peasants had two or three cows and no more than 10 hectares of land, with an average family size of seven people. Income per head of the population, even among the richest group of peasants, was only 50-56% higher than the income of the poorest group. Only 3-5% of all peasant farms were in this richest group, but they produced approximately 20% of the total amount of grain.

The communists attempted to contrast the well-off peasant to the poor peasant. Poor peasants were given exemptions of various kinds, and promoted to the agencies of power. Yet this did not stop them from being peasant landowners, any more than they stopped being peasant landowners even though they had the help of the state, and had therefore been transformed into 'class enemies' of Soviet power. The Communists failed in their bid to sow hatred among the rich peasants and the poor ones. The wealthier peasants helped their less wealthy fellow villagers by lending money to them, and were respected by the community…

Something had to be done about the peasantry, particularly the Ukrainian peasants, who were unruly, able to defend themselves, and capable of fighting without having any pity either on themselves or on their enemies.

---

2. All civil servants in the departments and local offices of white governments, in the armies of the Ukrainian Central Rada, the police in the Hetman's state and so on,
3. All those who worked for religious cults: episcopal, orthodox and catholic priests, rabbis, deacons, church elders, church leaders, monks and so on.
4. All former merchants, stall owners and NEPists
5. All former landowners and major leasers of land (who had made use of hired labour in the past), major artisans and owners of industrial concerns,
6. All individuals related to people with illegal status or conducting an armed campaign against Soviet rule within anti-Soviet bands,
7. All foreigners, regardless of nationality,
8. All individuals with relatives or friends overseas,
9. All members of religious sects or communities (particularly Baptists)
10. All academics and specialists from the old regime, particularly those who have previously kept their political persuasion hidden,
11. All individuals previously charged with or suspected of smuggling, espionage etc.
All in all, a pretty sizeable chunk of the population!

In respect of the policy of Ukrainization, Bolshevik Moscow was also preparing to change the movement's direction radically. In doing so they showed no mercy to their own peers, who, one would think, had proved their loyalty to the Bolshevik leaders throughout the entire course of their lives prior to that point.[30]

---

[30] Ukraine's Minister for Enlightenment, Alexander Shumsky, who was an extremely active revolutionary – a Bolshevik and a Ukrainian by nationality, was removed from his post because, in the opinion of the leaders in Moscow, he had taken the policy of Ukrainization too far. He was later arrested, imprisoned in a GULAG and shot by a member of the secret service a few years later, without trial. As for the man who replaced him, Nikolai Skripnik – now there's a genuinely meritorious figure among the Bolsheviks. Ever since he was a young man he had been an active member of revolutionary, anti-monarchist organizations, actively taken part in their activities, and been sentenced by Tsarist courts to a total of 34 years' imprisonment and on one occasion to the death penalty. He escaped from prison and exile six times. He set up the Communist Party of Ukraine. In a word, he was a Bolshevik through and through. He held key posts in the government of Soviet Ukraine, was one of the leaders of the Bolsheviks' punitive wing – the Emergency Commission (ChK), and was extremely influential. He supported the policy of Ukrainization, and encouraged the development of national Ukrainian education and the development of Ukrainian culture, and criticized party functionaries who refused to speak Ukrainian. He suffered oppression organized by the party leadership in Moscow and, foreseeing the retribution that was inevitably going to come his way, committed suicide.

WHY DID THE BOLSHEVIKS IN MOSCOW HARBOUR SUCH HATRED FOR UKRAINE? A FEW THOUGHTS ON THE MATTER

How are we to explain the pathological hatred of the Bolshevik government in Moscow towards Ukraine as a whole and the Ukrainian peasantry in particular?

I shall not endeavour to put forward an expert view, but I shall attempt to provide a model of the Bolshevik leaders' though process. The Bolsheviks were, essentially, doctrinarians, blindly and pedantically following the path of implementing certain ideas which they had formulated themselves. These objectives and ideas changed numerous times depending on the situation, what's more – only for the new objectives to be pursued with the same stubbornness and with the same brutal oppression shown to those who did not share their way of thinking.

The Bolsheviks were obsessed with the idea of a global socialist revolution. When anti-monarchist movements broke out in Hungary, Czechoslovakia and Austria in 1918, just a year after the Bolsheviks had seized power, this was interpreted by them as confirmation of their belief that all developed countries would eventually go through a transition ending in socialism. As it transpired, however, this did not accord with how events actually unfolded. The Bolsheviks, therefore, having clung onto power at a cost of vast amounts of effort and huge casualties, nonetheless began considering a new war, aimed at spreading Communist rule beyond the borders of Soviet Russia.

If it was to do this, the country would need tanks and cannon, battleships and planes. It would need to manufacture all of this weaponry and machinery at its own firms, moreover, so as not to be dependent on any external supplies. Thus there was a need to build plants, factories and power stations, and to be quick about it. Huge resources were required, as a matter of urgency. How could such resources be secured? What could the country sell to other nations? Realistically, only raw materials and foodstuffs.

To tell the truth, the situation as regards agriculture in the Soviet Union was far from favourable. Just think: so many men had been lost as a result of the mass military campaigns which had gone on from 1914 to 1921, plus several years of adverse weather conditions (drought, then floods, which had caused failed harvests) – the threat of famine was constantly arising in one region or another.

Yet in spite of all this the decision was taken to effect a leap forward in the country's industrial development at a forcibly high tempo; and this leap forward was to be financed by pumping out resources from the agricultural sector. Ukraine, its people, its peasants, who had only just bid farewell to the shotgun, the helmet and the steed, was greatly impeding the implementation of these plans.

The gigantic frames of factories could be erected through forced labour, but how could these buildings be filled up with cutting-edge technological equipment? The equipment had to be purchased in exchange for hard currency in the West, and the only source of the resources required was to sell grain overseas. In the winter of 1927-1928, however, a grain production crisis had already taken hold (the peasants had refused to hand over their grain at prices which had been deliberately reduced, given the inflated price of industrial goods – the so-called 'pricing scissors').

The Stalinist leadership saw a way out of the crisis not in increasing the purchase prices for agricultural products, but in a return to the methods of 'military communism', the forcible confiscation of grain. Under threat of fines and confiscation of their property (amendments had been made to the Criminal code to cover these), direct requisitioning of grain began. Stalin and his entourage were becoming increasingly convinced that there was a need to convert the substantial number of individuals and private peasant farms (25-30 million throughout the USSR) which could not be controlled and were not answerable to the Communist Party, into enterprises which the authorities could manage and control, and whose role would be to become reliable suppliers of grain to the state (some 200-300,000 so-called 'collective farms' or *kolkhozy*).

In 1929 a long-drawn out economic crisis began in the West, which led to sharp fall in the price of grain. This meant that the Bolshevik leaders would be required to increase grain exports in order to obtain the currency it needed.

WHAT EXACTLY IS A "COLLECTIVE FARM"?

The Communist leaders decided forcibly to unite individual peasant farms into collective enterprises. These would take the form of a collective company, or a collective farm: the abbreviated form of these terms was the neologism *kholkhoz (collective farm)*. Yet the methods used to introduce this economic reform in agriculture were to endow this word with a frightening, lasting significance.

Ukraine, as the main supplier of grain, was given special standing: she was to set an example of how to go about organizing large-scale collective farms. For some mysterious reason, moreover, the model that was adopted for them was the *kibbutz* method, used by the socialist-Zionist settlers in Palestine. The plan for collectivization by means of kibbutz farms was devised for the settlers and was in full accord with the culture with which they were traditionally associated, since they had no intention of either creating a peasant farmstead or rearing cattle.

Collectivization in the kibbutz farms was taken to extreme levels, with no private property whatsoever permitted – the cooperative's members weren't even allowed to have lunch at home. The kibbutz farms set up in Palestine after the First World War proved themselves to be an efficient way of producing food (and remain so in Israel, for example, to this day). Obviously, the Bolshevik leaders were greatly impressed by the economic performance of this kind of cooperative, and used this ready-made organizational system without having any real second thoughts.

The instructions issued by the Communist leaders stated that collectivization in Ukraine was to be concluded by the spring of 1931. Such a rapid rate of collectivization could only be achieved through violence and the use of force. This effectively meant a declaration of war on any peasants who did not want to join a 'collective farm'. Although there was a formal procedure in place for joining a collective farm on a voluntary basis, peasants were in fact forced to apply to join, under threat of persecution. Those who refused to join a *kholkhoz* were deemed to be enemies of Soviet power and criminals.

It may be that you will get bored whilst reading about the events which unfolded thereafter. However I have deliberately endowed my narrative with a dry tone – otherwise I might break out into biased narration of these events, which would lead to doubts about my objectivity. To us, the Ukrainians, the facts and figures referred to signify millions of compatriots who died a torturous death. A large number of documentary reports have now been published which illustrate the situation.

One of the key parts of collectivization was the "elimination of the kulaks as a class". As I mentioned above, the term 'kulak' was thought up artificially by Lenin and interpreted by the totalitarian Communist powers however they saw fit to do so. The term was applied not only to describe those who made use of hired labour (though this criteria seems pretty dubious, given the seasonal nature of working in the countryside), but also to individual peasants who used a motor on their farms, or simply had a house with a roof made of metal sheeting. My grandmother once said to me: "It's a good thing my father died young. The roof of our house was covered with sheet metal. He would undoubtedly have been declared a kulak, and we would have suffered persecution." As it happens, the sheet metal on the roof of their house was torn off in any event by a local official – an alcoholic and parasite, who in spite of this (or perhaps because of it) was a 'property-less proletarian', and who supported the Communists.

Eventually, peasants classed as 'middling', and even peasants with very little property who did not wish to join collective farms were categorized as 'kulaks and their accomplices'. The 'elimination of the kulaks as a class' thus affected large sections of the population of Ukraine. Whereas in 1928 there were officially 71,500 kulak farms in Ukraine, by 1932 the number of farms which had been eliminated stood at 200,000. Peasants who openly resisted collectivization were either shot or sent to prison.

Peasants who were wealthier than most but had not been seen taking part in acts of resistance were deported to remote parts of the USSR (such as Siberia and so on). The statistics from the GULAG stated that in 1930-1931, 381,026 families were deported, making a total of 1,803,392 people, including 63,720 families from Ukraine. Less well-off peasants who did not wish to join collective farms were deported to other areas inside Ukraine.

As a result of the administrative measures, deportations and physical retribution, 70% of all peasant farm holdings in Ukraine had been collectivized by the end of 1932. The purchase prices for grain, vegetables, meat, milk etc. were exceedingly low. Moreover, the state had not set an upper limit on peasants' obligations, and this meant that almost all of the produce from the collective farms could be appropriated. The peasants had no material interest in the collective farm operating efficiently: their main means of subsistence proved to be the smallholdings. Yet the disproportionately high taxes forced the peasants to sell up and move from the countryside to the cities. They tried to find work at the factories and building sites. This did not fit in with the objectives of the country's communist leaders. In order to make it impossible for peasants to flee to the cities, in December 1933 a system of internal passports was introduced in Ukraine. Peasants were not issued with these passports, so they were effectively turned into serfs, deprived of the ability to move freely around the country.

In 1928-1931 the number of peasant farms in Ukraine fell by 352,000. All this led to degradation in the agricultural sector. The quotas for grain reserves were not reduced, however, since the cities needed to be fed, along with the construction workers and the army, and – most importantly of all – the industrial equipment that was being imported needed to be paid for.

THE CONSEQUENCES OF FORCING THE PEASANTS TO JOIN COLLECTIVE FARMS

In 1930 the USSR was in a state similar to the one it had endured at the time of the civil war. The country was getting by on rations and the budget deficit was being patched up through the printing of more money. A *record* amount of grain was produced in 1930 but it was exported to other countries, and the workers often went hungry. One of the ways in which the peasants resisted collectivization was to slaughter their cattle, so as not to have to give it up to the collective farm. As a result, the total number of cattle was halved. It took 30 years to make up for this dramatic reduction.

According to data from the Soviet intelligence services of the day (the OGPU), there were 6117 revolts in January – April 1930 against forced reforms in agriculture, in which a total of 1,755,300 people took part. Besides the revolts, resistance also took the form of acts of terrorism against the Communist leaders. In March 1930 alone, in Ukraine alone, 521 acts of terrorism were recorded (one can only speculate as to how many went unrecorded!). Over the course of 9 months in 1930, more than 1000 acts of terrorism were committed in Western Siberia, of which 624 were murders or attempted murders. And this was merely the tip of the iceberg – the crimes which were officially recorded. There was a dramatic increase in persecution on the part of the intelligence services, and the number of people imprisoned in camps rose from 180,000 in 1930 to 510,000 in 1934.

It should be noted that it was not just Ukraine that suffered as a result of 'collectivization', but also Belarus, Kazakhstan, the North Caucasus and the Volga Region. These areas suffered more than anyone else from the famine which resulted, firstly, from the elimination on a nationwide scale of 6-7 million of the best agricultural workers; secondly, from the peasants refusal to work in conditions when the fruits of their labour were simply requisitioned; and thirdly, from the unfavourable climatic conditions for growing crops. Given that the quotas for grain reserves for export, even in these conditions, were not lowered but instead *raised*, a huge mass of the agricultural population died of famine. This hunger was organized by the government in Moscow by means of confiscating the harvest from the peasants, and it was in Ukraine that the most brutal measures of all were taken. 1932 was the next year of intense social crisis. In many parts of the country, particularly in Ukraine and the North Caucasus, there was a miniature civil war, the outbreak of which called for forces, along with artillery and tanks, to be sent in against the peasants.

As a result of collectivization the spine of the self-sufficient Ukrainian peasantry was broken and its most hard-working layer was destroyed, with their incentive to work and their sense of ownership killed off.

In the period between autumn 1932 and April 1933, the population of the USSR fell by 7.7 million people. This included the loss of 4 million people in Ukraine and roughly 1 million in each of the following: the North Caucasus, the Volga Region and Kazakhstan. Understandably, the birth rate fell too: in 1933 the 'deficit' in the birth rate in Ukraine amounted to 1.5 million people. Ukrainians have every reason to believe that what took place was a policy of the genocide of their people. In terms of its factual results, this genocide meant the deaths of millions of Ukrainians, but its hidden agenda was to undermine the freedom-loving spirit of the Ukrainian people. It seems to me that to a certain extent this hidden objective was achieved.

In the 1950s, an American lawyer of Polish descent named Rafael Lemkin, who introduced into the theory and practice of international law the concept of 'genocide', wrote: "What I wish to tell you about may be a classic example of Soviet genocide, the longest and most large-scale experiment in Russification ever. It is the destruction of the Ukrainian people… For as long as Ukraine preserves its national unity, for as long as its people consider themselves Ukrainians and try to achieve independence, Ukraine is going to represent a serious threat to the very essence of the Soviet idea.

For the Ukrainians are not Russians and never have been. They have a different culture, a different temperament, a different language and a different religion. Whilst living very close to Moscow, they refused to accept collectivization, despite the threat of deportation and even death. It therefore became particularly important to force the Ukrainian people into the Procrustean bed of the ideal Soviet person.

It is a people too large to be totally wiped out. Nonetheless, the number of religious, intellectual and political leaders among the people is fairly small, and they could easily be dealt with, and therefore these groups fell victim to all the might of the Soviet machine, with its tried and tested methods: mass murder, deportation and forced labour, famine and exile."

If there is anyone that can do so, let him explain to me how, given the economic, political and social processes taking place in the Soviet Union in the 1930s, the Ukrainians were supposed to feel a sense of loyalty to the social order foisted on them by Bolshevik Moscow?

Nevertheless, it is important to have an accurate understanding of the circumstances pertaining in the USSR at that time. The Bolsheviks had always been known for their adept propaganda campaigns. Millions of people throughout the country felt inspired by the idea of building a socialist society. The policy of accelerated industrialization and enforced collectivization would never have ended in success were it not for the enthusiasm of the thousands of people who implemented collectivization and took part in industrialization –ordinary peasants, workers, engineers, scientists, and people employed in the field of culture, who interpreted the ideas of their communist leaders as their own and sacrificed themselves in order to strengthen the Soviet system. Had the rejection of collectivization and industrialization been total, the state would have collapsed and a new civil war would have broken out.

Although food was distributed based on vouchers up until 1935, over time the USSR paid off its debts, built its first tractor plants and despatched the new machinery to the collective farms, in order to lift farming to a higher level. However, as everyone now appreciates, these tractor factories were also used as tank factories. And the food crisis in the country had not been dealt with.

PARANOID STALINIST TERROR IN UKRAINE

In 1933-1934, when the Communist Party of Ukraine was led by a Pole named Kasior, and the central Kiev regional organization was led by a Russian named Postyshev[31] (in the circumstances, this meant that they were the all-powerful rulers of Ukraine), the state terror that they orchestrated led to all the brightest lights of the Ukrainian national rebirth, which had begun in the 1920s, being killed off. It was these men who were responsible for the draconian measures used in the policy of collectivization, the confiscation of grain from the peasants and the mass famine, and the deaths of millions of people, that this caused. It was these men who organized the persecution of Nikolai Skripnik, who committed suicide, and led the about-turn in the policy of 'Ukrainization'.

Their actions were fully accorded with the paranoid policy of Stalin, who was soon to commence the mass killing of his own supporters and henchmen in 1937-1938. The level of 'normality' exhibited by these people can be seen based on an assessment of the behaviour of Postyshev, who, whilst looking at a matchbox under a magnifying glass, managed to discover on it an image, in profile, of one of Stalin's rivals in the battle for power, Lev Trotsky, who by then had been exiled, then murdered by a Soviet secret agent. On this basis, a ban was introduced on selling matches. In a separate incident, Postyshev wanted to carry out mass arrests and killings of salesmen, because it had been reported to him that a swastika had been seen carved into a slice of smoked sausage.

---

31 Stalin, whose rule lasted for effectively 30 years, was probably particularly mistrustful of Ukrainians, recalling their resistance to the establishment of Soviet power at the time of the civil war. In Ukraine, therefore, the political and economic repression which was designed to ensure the submissiveness of the people in his own multi-ethnic country, was introduced with particular brutality. The very fact that the Bolsheviks never appointed as leader of their regional party administration in Ukraine someone from our country speaks volumes. Kviring, the German, Kosior, the Pole, Kaganovich, the Jew, and Khrushchev, the Russian, all led the Ukrainian wing of the communist party at various times before the Second World War, and none of them can lay claim to having represented the Ukrainian people. It was not until 1953 that a Ukrainian was appointed leader of the Communist Party of Ukraine for the first time…

People who were seen as embodying the ruling elite were arrested, thrown in prison or shot by firing squad, *en masse*. 50% of all the members of the Ukrainian Communist Party fell victim to this oppression, and Ukrainian writers and scientists were among those killed. During the terror of 1937-1938, 800,000 people fell victim to oppression in Ukraine. Why is it that it was only the Communist leaders who destroyed their fellow leaders so fervently – in exactly the same manner in which they killed ordinary people? It was probably an attempt to save their own skins, since the bloodthirsty Communist leader Josef Stalin was doling out retribution on the people who had until recently been seen as his comrades-in-arms without the slightest justification, merely on the basis of a suspicion of insufficient loyalty which was of his own invention. Marshals and generals were arrested and shot, as were senior figures in the party, directors of industrial concerns and teachers of Marxist-Leninist theory, engineers, teachers, agronomists, and ordinary workers and peasants.

As for the methods used to extract confessions from those who were arrested, we can form a good idea of them on the basis of what happened to Kosior, who was arrested a short time later and accused of being a member of an anti-Soviet 'Polish military organization', which was of course dreamt up by Stalin's intelligence services. Kosior denied all the charges, even when subjected to torture, until his 16-year-old daughter was raped before his very eyes. Kosior signed all the confessions, without looking at them. His daughter was released from prison. She threw herself under a train. It is easy to surmise what they might have done to Postyshev, given that he wrote a 'voluntary confession' about how he had been working as an agent of the Japanese intelligence services for twenty years.

The chairman of the Ukrainian government at that time, Panas Lyubchenko, on hearing that he stood accused of Ukrainian nationalism, and foreseeing that he would inevitably be arrested and tortured, shot his wife then turned the gun on himself.[32]

If we are to tell the full truth of it, it must be acknowledged that Stalin succeeded in turning the population of the Soviet republics into a great mass of slaves; many of these slaves, moreover, were not aware of the position they were in. They felt happy, and believed that Stalin and the Communist party which he led were the epitome of wisdom, and knew the only true path for

---

32 It reached a point where the only member of the Ukrainian government left alive was the director of the intelligence services, a man named Leshievsky, about whom nothing is known, since before long he too was arrested and shot. After the intelligence agents had finished going about their dirty work, Stalin decreed that the agents who had carried out this terror at his behest were to be shot as well

future development. And in order that people did not have the opportunity to compare their lives with the lives of people living in other states, the 'iron curtain' descended.

People in the next generation who were born under Soviet rule were genuinely proud of the fact that they lived in a country unlike any other, which was setting an example to other peoples of how to construct a perfect human society. And as for those who took the liberty of having doubts about whether this dogma was undeniably true, or whether the 'father of the peoples', comrade Stalin, was indeed so perfect…see above.

UKRAINE BEFORE THE SECOND WORLD WAR

Soviet propaganda has always, and in that period in particular, exerted a huge amount of effort in order to convince the people of the hostility of the surrounding world towards the Soviet Union. The country was portrayed as an island of freedom and as a just way to organize society, which might at any moment come under attack, either from the West or from the East. The people were called upon to work selflessly in the name of creating industrial potential, in the name of strengthening the military might of the state. Thanks to the selfless efforts of many millions of ordinary people who were sacrificed, the peasantry, who were rendered penniless, and an effective system of totalitarian enforcement and control, compounded by insistent and skilful propaganda and the promise that a society of prosperity for all, industry sectors which were fairly advanced by the standards of the day were successfully established within a short space of time. The Soviet Union relieved itself of the need to import machine tools and equipment, and harvests of agricultural products began to flourish. Industrial complexes and power stations were built on Ukrainian soil, and these became the nucleus of the Soviet economy.

The army was proclaimed as the people's favourite son, and military service was declared the prestigious duty of every citizen.

The way global events were unfolding served as confirmation of the Stalinist leadership's propaganda ideas. Italy had strangled Ethiopia's independence, and was then trying to repeat the trick in Greece. Germany, under Hitler, was becoming increasingly aggressive, seizing more and more territory from its neighbours with the connivance of some Western states. Japan was attempting to satisfy its military ambitions in China and Manchuria.

Both Hitler and Stalin understood that a war between the two of them was inevitable, and tried to outsmart one another. They even entered into a secret agreement in which they divided up their spheres of influence. As a result of this pact, at the start of the Second World War the Soviet Union was able to steal from Poland, which was suffering a devastating invasion, the territories in West Ukraine which had been lost through incompetence after the defeat by the Poles in 1920. The Soviet and German officers shook hands with one another when they met in occupied Poland, and held joint parades in Polish cities.

Another force was also active in West Ukraine by that time, however. It was called the Organization of Ukrainian Nationalists (OUN). This organization, created in Vienna in 1929 and led by the famous Ukrainian military leader from the time of the Ukrainian People's Republic, Yevgeny Konovalets, set as its goal the spreading of the idea of nationhood throughout Ukraine. In the first instance it was only able to operate in the parts of West Ukraine which were not part of the Soviet Union. Konovalets sincerely believed that there were forces in the east of Ukraine which would fight for its independence as well. It was for this reason that he died at the hands of a Soviet agent[33], who passed himself off as a representative of the underground nationalist movement in Soviet Ukraine and was able to gain Konovalets' trust. The leaders of the OUN could not even have imagined how comprehensively Stalin's terror had weeded out any green shoots or embryos of a national Ukrainian self-awareness. The accusation of nationalism was the most commonly cited justification for retribution against Ukrainians during the oppression.

In West Ukraine, the OUN was securing an increasing amount of support from the people. The founders of the OUN, who were led by Konovalets and subsequently – after his death – by his successor and long-serving associate Andrei Melnik – took the organization down the route of political struggle, planning their activity for the lengthy period of time required in order to acquire weight and win power. The younger generation of nationalists, however, who had elected Stepan Bandera as their leader, in their efforts to achieve their objective more quickly, opted to carrying out acts of political terror, aimed mainly at the Polish officials who had been following an anti-Ukraine policy. In the end, the organization broke apart and was split into more moderate and more 'revolutionary' wings.

---

33   The agent in question was Pavel Sudoplatov. Were it not for the fact that history is always written by the victors, Sudoplatov would be considered a legend of Soviet intelligence, and the man who organized its most successful operations, specifically operations against Hitler's Germany during the Second World War. Whilst still a general, Sudoplatov led an operation in 1950 to seize the commander of the URA, Roman Shukhevich, which ended in Shukhevich's death. After Stalin's death, the new Soviet leadership brought charges against him which led to him spending 15 years in prison. He suffered three heart attacks whilst behind bars and lost his sight in one eye. The case of Sudoplatov exemplifies the methods employed by the Soviet leaders. A man who had put all his strength and intellect into serving a particular idea, and who had been honoured and received awards, now found himself humiliated and trampled upon, and declared a criminal, because there had been a change at the top. I would highlight the fact, incidentally, that the idea itself had *not* changed, and it is a fact that the allegation that he murdered Konovalets was not put to Pavel Sudoplatov.

The Polish government was at that time implementing a policy whereby Poles settled Ukrainian land. One can understand why they would do so: nothing has such a strong grip on an area of land as a landowner, who has 'grown into' the land and is willing to protect it. The objective was the complete assimilation and Catholicization of the Ukrainian people. As is becoming clear, conflict between the Ukrainians and the Poles was a recurring theme throughout history.

The organization of Ukrainian nationalists tried to organize resistance to this policy, and they used violent methods to do so. For the record, it should be noted that the OUN simply had no other methods at its disposal. The Poles responded by carrying out campaigns designed to 'pacify' the people in the Ukrainian territories, which they introduced by bringing in collective responsibility among the population for acts of resistance. The OUN was responsible for the murder of the Rzeczpospolita's Minister of the Interior, who was in charge of the operations designed to 'pacify' the Ukrainian population. I am not going to go into these events in any great detail here.

When the Red Army occupied territory in West Ukraine in 1939, the people initially welcomed it with open arms. The Ukrainians imagined that a time had now come in which they would enjoy liberation from Polish oppression and union with their brothers in the east of the country. The Red Army were greeted with flowers, triumphal arches and 'khlebo-sol'.[34]

Next to arrive in West Ukraine after the rank and file soldiers, however, were the forces of the NKVD[35], the people Stalin used to inflict punitive justice. The towns and villages began to be purged of 'undesirable elements'[36]. From late September 1939, according to NKVD files, some 73,000 people were arrested, including Poles, Ukrainians, Jews and Belarusians. The best fate they could expect, on being arrested, was to be exiled to Siberia.

The policy of arrest and exile continued in 1940. The people of West Ukraine realised that their country had been occupied all over again. Support for the Organization of Ukrainian Nationalists therefore surged, and the organization began preparing for armed resistance.

---

34   The ancient tradition of giving guests whom you respect, and who have been eagerly awaited, a loaf of fresh bread with some salt on top of it. The loaf, placed on an embroidered towel, was usually brought in by beautiful women in ceremonial dress. The guest would break off a hunk of bread, dip it in the salt and eat it. This custom was an expression of the highest degree of hospitality and faith in the guest.

35   A state agency in the USSR at the time, which focused on carrying out a wide range of functions in state administration, including political spying and punitive measures.

36   The reader will recall the list of undesirable elements cited above.

THE SECOND WORLD WAR AND UKRAINE

It was not my aim to describe the events which took place on Ukrainian soil during the Second World War. A huge amount has been written on this subject by professional historians, those individuals who, as Bismarck put it, "govern history". I shall, however, cite a few special facts concerning Ukraine and its people, given that they have either been passed over in silence by our official historians, or interpreted in the spirit of the ruling communist ideology.

After commencing military action against the USSR on 22nd June 1941, the German forces advanced across Ukrainian territory over the days that followed. Within a few days West Ukraine was under German occupation.

Supposing the Ukrainians' worst enemies – Poland and the Soviet Union – to be defeated or on the brink of defeat, the leaders of the OUN's radical wing, led by Stepan Bandera and Yaroslav Stetsko, attempted to declare the creation of an independent Ukrainian state. On 30 June, in Lvov – a city from which the Red Army had withdrawn, but into which the Germans had not yet set foot – the rebirth of the Ukrainian state was announced. Let's be frank, this act was a naïve attempt to force Hitler into a situation in which he had to reckon with a Ukrainian state in Europe.

Hitler had other ideas, though, and Bandera was therefore arrested a few days later and sent to prison, and then to a concentration camp, where he remained until 1944.

THE UKRAINIAN REBEL ARMY

In 1943 armed divisions of Ukrainian nationalists, known as the Ukrainian Rebel Army (URA) began operating on Ukrainian soil. It is a favourite pastime of historians nowadays to argue that there were two Ukrainian rebel armies, one led by Bulba-Borovets and the other under the command of Shukhevich, and to claim that these armed units fought against three lots of enemies, and against one another.

In actual fact, laying aside for a while personal ambition and political differences between the Ukrainian political leaders of the day, there were three forces in 1943 which could justifiably be seen as enemies.

First of all there were the German occupiers. The Ukrainian nationalists tried to convince the Germans of their importance as allies in the fight against the Bolsheviks, and to this end they joined all sorts of military organizations, police units and auxiliary units which had been set up by the occupying forces on Ukrainian territory. It very soon became clear, though, that the Ukrainians were not viewed as fellow followers of Hitler, as partners, but merely as puppets. The Nazis adopted a policy of extermination against the Ukrainian people, and stole all they could from the Ukrainian land (even exporting the topsoil from the Ukrainian steppes to Germany); they expelled the young for use in forced labour (a total of 500,000 people suffered this fate), and took punitive measures against peaceful citizens when they discovered acts of sabotage organized by special groups within the Red Army, which were sent behind enemy lines (i.e. they followed the same principle of collective responsibility as the Poles had done not long beforehand).

Secondly, there were the Soviet powers, who, in 1939-1941, managed to carry out such mass terror, in the Stalinist spirit, to the West Ukrainian regions, that any attempts to restore the Communist regime were interpreted as hostile acts in Lvov, Lutsk, Stanislav and Ternopol. The Soviet guerrillas, therefore, who were fighting against Hitler's men, but had proclaimed Soviet rule over the parts of West Ukraine liberated from the Germans, were also seen as enemies by the Ukrainian rebels.

Thirdly, there was the ethnic conflict between the Poles and the Ukrainians before the Second World War: when the Polish authorities forced the Ukrainians from their centuries-old heartlands, it made the guerrilla units in the Polish nationalist movement enemies of the URA.

The Soviet guerrillas saw the diversionary movements against the rear of the German forces as a way of helping the Red Army, and therefore carried them out on communications lines (blowing up railway lines and bridges), and attacked the occupiers' military facilities (fuel, munitions and food stores), and made sure their actions coincided with the Soviet troops' operations. No attention was paid at all to the victims among the local population, following reprisals by the German occupiers: these were in fact seen as a positive factor, since they ought to make the Ukrainians more inclined to support Soviet power.

For the Ukrainian nationalists, the guerrilla struggle was a form of armed self-defence by the Ukrainian people on the occupied territory. The objective of it was to protect the rear, and accumulate strength and resources in order to prepare an armed uprising by Ukrainian nationalists at a convenient time, which, they believed, would come after the Wehrmacht and the Red Army exhausted one another in mutual destruction. The Ukrainian rebels therefore steered clear, as a rule, of railways, military headquarters and commanders' offices, and areas where military vehicles and machinery was based and concentrated. In most cases the rebels did battle with German units in order to protect the local populace.

Moreover, the URA hindered the activities of the Soviet guerrillas in certain circumstances, since the operations it carried out to undermine them provoked mass persecution against the people, whom the Ukrainian nationalists considered it their number one duty to protect. There were a lot of cases of collaboration with the occupying forces, and of Ukrainians serving in auxiliary and police units. Service of this kind was seen as military training, which was essential if a Ukrainian national army was to be formed in the future.

Let us bear in mind that history is written by the victors. This is why all the cases of collaborationism with the occupying German forces, as well as all cases of resistance to the Soviet guerrilla forces, later served as grounds for accusing the URA of having fought on the side of the Nazis, which automatically gave the members of the Ukrainian national-liberation movement the status not only of outlaws, but also of traitors.

It begs the question: what, exactly, were they betraying? Who were they betraying? Who would dare to try to answer this: the descendants of the people who organized confiscation of food from the Ukrainian peasants in

1929-32, causing the deaths of millions of people from famine? Or perhaps the descendants of the people who carried out mass persecution in West Ukraine in 1939-1941? As I mentioned earlier, the Ukrainians had no reason whatsoever to show loyalty towards the Soviet powers. Nevertheless, Ukrainians played an active part in the Second World War in the Red Army, and there were some senior officers among them.

Those who stayed in the territory occupied by the Germans, however, saw Kiev's beautiful central street – the Kreshchatik – blown up and ablaze. The retreating Red Army had laid tonnes of explosives under buildings in the city (as if it had no intention of ever coming back to Ukraine?), and five days later, when the Germans had arrived, they began to go off. The explosions went on for a week, and the tarmac melted. (It was announced after the war that it was the Germans who had blown up the centre of Kiev – another reminder, lest we forget, that history is written by the victors).

I think you will understand me when I say that events such as these stick in a nation's genetic memory. It might be prohibited to talk about them, and the official propaganda can try as much as it likes to amend its version of events. But everyone has a grandmother and a grandfather, and they in turn had a grandmother and grandfather too. And things that people have seen with their own eyes are bound to be passed down from one generation to the next, even it is only in a whisper.

It must be acknowledged that the Nazis had no intention of discriminating between the Ukrainians who were fighting for national independence and the guerrilla groups organized by Soviet agents. If diversionary operations were carried out on the territory occupied by the Germans against the administration or the army, the Ukrainian people, who had nothing whatever to do with these actions whatsoever, suffered mass persecution. The URA had decided that its main goal was to protect the people from terror. When the Soviet guerrillas carried out diversionary operations against a German military facility, therefore, the Germans would carry out reprisals against the local population, and the Ukrainian Rebel Army tried to protect this local population.

In the summer of 1943 the Germans carried out large-scale operations against the URA using tanks and planes. The fact that the operations were fruitless meant that the operational administration was forced to repeat the attempt in the autumn, but on this occasion too it was unable to destroy the rebel army operating at the German rear. Then the Nazis brought in a sweeping propaganda campaign, accusing the rebels of helping the Bolsheviks – this is a typical example of the deceptive nature of all propaganda: history has shown that the Ukrainian nationalists were the most implacable enemies of the Bolsheviks in Moscow.

In July 1943 one of the biggest battles of World War II took place: the battle between the German and Soviet armies outside Kursk. It involved more than two million people, six thousand tanks and four thousand planes. After the defeat of the German army outside Kursk, the course of the war changed radically, the Red Army shifted its strategy to one of attack, and the German army adopted a strategy of defence. Over the next four months, after a series of extremely difficult battles, the Red Army reached the Dnieper and prepared to storm Kiev.

300,000 young Ukrainian men from the towns in the left bank of Ukraine, which had been purged of Germans, were called up for military service. There was no time either to dress them in military uniform or issue them with weapons, let alone try to give them military training. They were immediately sent in to storm the German positions.

The famous Soviet general Grigory Zhukov, when he was reminded that the Ukrainian conscripts had no weapons or uniforms, declared: "Why are we bothering ourselves about this, my friends. Why the hell should we arm and issue uniforms to these *khokhols*? They're all traitors! The more of them we drown in the Dnieper, the fewer of them we'll have to exile to Siberia after the war." And young lads in civvies and boots, with no weapons, were forced to swim across the Dnieper, with German machine-guns firing at them. Of these 330,000 conscripts, 270,000 died. For many days thereafter, piles of corpses floated down the Dnieper.

What role exactly were these young Ukrainian lads playing in this battle? Were they liberating their homeland from the German invaders? What sort of feelings ought the Ukrainians to feel in relation to the Red Army command? I think the fact speak for themselves here.

As the front line came nearer and the regular divisions of the Red Army gradually took control of the parts of West Ukraine occupied by the Germans, divisions of the URA ceased their battle against the German Army, but actively impeded the activity of the German occupying administration in terms of the economic exploitation of Volyna and Polesya, where the materials base of the Ukrainian liberation movement was situated.

After 1944, when the Red Army, having broken through the German defences amid heavy fighting, burst into the West, the Ukrainian Rebel Army was preparing to do battle against the Communist powers whilst under occupation by the Bolsheviks.

What could they hope to achieve?

On its own, the Ukrainian Rebel Army was unable to offer any resistance, in spite of its size (by this time it contained 100,000 soldiers), and the fact that it was well-organized, disciplined and armed, had the support of the people, and the URA's soldiers were deeply committed to the idea of Ukraine's national independence and willing to sacrifice themselves. The most likely scenario of all is that the leaders of the OUN and the high command of the URA believed there would inevitably be a conflict between the USA and the western democracies, on the one hand, and the Soviet Union on the other. Yet again they had to attempt to survive whilst being caught between two fires, and having to try to take advantage of a conflict between more powerful rivals.

The course of history was to turn out rather differently, as we now know. The Soviet Union was on the winning side in World War II – indeed, it was one of the most important and authoritative victors. In Poland, which was occupied by Soviet troops, pro-Communist ruling agencies were established. The resettlement area for the Ukrainian people was divided up by Stalin and his Polish allies as they saw fit in the light of political considerations. An exchange of people began between the USSR and Poland: Poles left for the West, whilst Ukrainians moved inside the borders of the USSR. Several regions which had historically belonged to the Ukrainians, such as Lemkovshchina, Kholmshchina and Posyanie, were now inside Polish-controlled territory. Armed units of the URA continued to operate in these areas, and the Poles were unable to handle them. General Sverchevsky, the commander of operations against the URA, was killed. The Polish government could find no better way out of the situation than to forcibly resettle all Ukrainian and mixed families from the places where they lived, mostly to parts of the USSR. This operation was conducted in 1947 and dubbed operation 'Visla'; the result of it was that the Ukrainian rebel movement ceased to be loyal.

The URA's military actions continued throughout Soviet Ukraine for many years. The Moscow government appointed people to all the leading positions in West Ukraine whom it had sent in from the east of Ukraine or from Russia. Administrative, educational and scientific organizations were filled with people who had been relocated from the east, as well as the communist party agencies. For all the positive personal qualities these people may have had, their mentality, culture, language and ideology were all different, and alien to the local population. As a result, the people in West Ukraine felt as though they were living under enemy occupation. On top of this a ban was introduced in 1946 on the Ukrainian Greco-Catholic church, which was very popular in these districts, and its priests suffered persecution. One can begin to see why there was a spike in support among the people of West Ukraine for the rebel movement.

As time passed, though, the large-scale military operations, the use of provocation, the payments to traitors, the amnesties which were declared on numerous occasions and the mass persecution led to the activities of the

OUN and the Ukrainian guerrillas being to all intents and purposes crushed. In a period of five years (1944 – 1949) some 500,000 people were arrested and exiled to Siberia after facing charges related to the URA. For West Ukraine at that time, this was a huge number: it was around 10% of the population.

The Soviet ideologues always sought to portray the Ukrainian armed resistance as scattered, rag-tag outfits, consisting of Nazi enablers. In actual fact, the reports of army group leaders and the heads of the security services in the USSR from that time cite cases instances when large groups of soldiers were ordered to fight the URA, and these reports refer to numbers killed or taken prisoner in the tens of thousands. I have read press reports which said that there were between 400,000 and 700,000 people fighting in the Ukrainian resistance movement in total. When we add to this the half a million Ukrainians who were exiled to Siberia for supporting the URA, it starts to become clear that the scale of Ukrainian resistance to the communist powers was extremely large.

Many hundreds of thousands of Ukrainians who were sent to Stalin's Gulag camps, including warriors from the Ukrainian Rebel Army, kept up the struggle against the Soviet regime there as well, leading prisoner revolts and organizing and inspiring resistance to the inhumane practices. The administration's attempts to send criminals to these camps, who served their time in the same camps, invariably had disastrous consequences.

They took the fight to the guards, who carried machine-guns, with nothing but their bare hands; but the hundreds of thousands of lives which were sacrificed, along with the lives of the Lithuanians, Poles and other prisoners who had been their allies, and who were classed as 'political' prisoners, ultimately brought down the Gulag system.

THE POST-WAR PERIOD. WHAT CHANGED FOR UKRAINE?

We must acknowledge the courage of the soldiers who fought in Normandy, outside Monte-Cassino and in Iwo Jima. We know a great deal about this, and it would be a very good thing if people in other countries were aware of what took place here, in our country, during the Second World War. The world is obliged to remember the 418,000 US troops, 380,000 British troops and 250,000 French soldiers who gave their lives to liberate the countries of Europe and Asia from the Nazis and the Japanese. The losses suffered by China were huge (2.8 million fatalities). The numbers cited here do not include all the civilians who died.

At the same time, it must be recognised that in terms of the number of soldiers mobilized, areas affected and human casualties, the war of 1941-1945 between the Soviet Union and Germany constituted the largest component part of the Second World War. In this battle, Ukraine was the scene of bitter and bloody fighting.

What damage had been done to Ukraine by the time the war came to an end?

714 cities and towns lay in ruins, as did 28,000 villages, 16,000 industrial concerns (81%) of pre-war industry), 18,000 healthcare institutions, and 33,000 schools and institutions of further or higher education. The total amount of damage to the republic's economy and population was in excess of 1.2 trillion roubles[37].

Ukraine suffered terrible loss of life. It is extremely difficult to try to put a figure on the number of lives lost. In any event, the statistics indicate that the population of Ukraine was 40 million in 1940, and that in 1944-1945 it stood at 30 million. It is impossible to say, however, how many millions of Ukrainians

---

[37] I attempted to convert this figure into dollars. This was quite easy to do, since the Soviet rouble was tied to the dollar between 1937 and 1950. Based on the exchange rate in effect at the time, this was equivalent to $240 billion. If converted based on today's gold prices, this was approximately $1.6 trillion.

were deported to eastern regions of the USSR when the Germans invaded, how many millions were deported to Germany when the country was under occupation, how many people were living in the western areas which were annexed to Ukraine in 1939, and how many people died in conflict. Ukrainians took part in these military operations on both sides of the fence, moreover, and the winning side then persecuted those who had fought on the losing side during the war.

Six million Ukrainians fought in the Soviet Army, and three million died. Compare this figure with the population of your country.

Untold manpower was put to work to restore the ruined cities and industrial concerns. Heavy industry was the first thing to be restored. The Soviet Union had urgent need of a military-industrial complex as a guarantee that socialism would defeat capitalism.

In Ukraine, the coal mines of the Donbass had been restored to working order within a few years, as had the thermal power plants and the pride of the hydro-electric power industry: the Dnieper hydro-electric power plant in Zaporozhye. By 1948 there were more engineering enterprises operating in Ukraine than there had been before the war. It must be acknowledged that such an astonishing rate in terms of restoring heavy industry in a war-torn country could only be achieved by having victims in other areas. These victims were ordinary people, because agriculture, light industry, science and culture were having to eke out a pitiful existence.

In 1946, following severely adverse weather conditions (a drought), the grain harvest collected was very small. It is remarkable that the people managed to harvest at least something. At the collective farms there were no more tractors, horses or men (besides those who had returned from the war having lost limbs or with other crippling injuries). Everything had gone up in smoke when the fire of war had raged. The women and children dug the earth, putting harnesses on the cows in the fields or attaching the harnesses to their own backs. In the winter of 1946-1947 a famine began which was to cause the deaths of more than 800,000 people in Ukraine.

The main cause of the famine, without question, was not the drought but the position adopted by the state and the Communist party. The quotas set for grain production were unreasonably high, and grain and livestock products were exported overseas in large quantities. The USSR gave a lot of support to the countries of Eastern Europe, which had set off down the route of "building Communism". In 1946 the USSR exported 1.7 million tonnes of grain. Meanwhile, in the same year, hundreds of thousands of peasants from Ukraine and the other republics in the USSR died of famine. The famous political figure from the Soviet period Nikita Khrushchev, who took charge of the Communists in Ukraine after the war, was a staunch Communist and Stalinist. Yet not even he was able to bear the horrors which were brought about in Ukraine by the central leadership in Moscow. He asked Stalin on numerous occasions to send at least some part of the food supplies to Ukraine. Stalin replied: "You're a softy! You're being lied to, they're playing on your sentimentality. They want us to waste our state reserves."

In 1946 Nikita Khrushchev was brought back from Ukraine, and replaced by one of Stalin's closest associates, Lazar Kaganovich. Kaganovich's response to complaints of any kind was to persecute the people and tighten the screws.

West Ukraine was at that time going through the phases of Sovietization at accelerated pace, and this included peasants being forced to join collective farms. The mass popular support for the guerrilla Ukrainian Rebel Army needs no explanation.

In West Ukraine industrial concerns were set up, a system of universal primary education was introduced, and higher education institutions were created. Was this a progressive state of affairs? Of course it was. But all the teaching at the academic institutions was done in Russian.

Do you remember what was said earlier in this book about how *surzhyk* came into being? That same imperial ideology was present here, too. Do you want to get an education and make something of yourself? If so, you'd better speak Russian. Ukrainian is a second-class language, destined slowly to become extinct. Indeed the Ukrainian people, as Moscow envisaged it, ought to disappear, and merge with the "great Russian people". The slightest departures from this chosen course were punished mercilessly.

There are all sorts of examples I could give you, both large and small. Let's consider one of them: there once lived in Ukraine the famous poet Vladimir Sosyura[38]. There is no doubt that he was of Ukrainian nationality, although he himself said that his father had French roots and that his mother was from Croatia. In 1944, whilst working as a war correspondent, he wrote a poem called 'Love Ukraine'. This is a poem that I know well, and it contains nothing that is anti-Communist: it is a call to the poet's fellow countrymen

---

38   In 1918, Vladimir Sosyura, like many Ukrainian writers and poets whose works can be considered classics of 20th century Ukrainian literature (Petro Panch, Andriy Golovko, Boris Antonenko-Davidovich, Oleksandr Kopilenko and even Yury Yanovsky, then aged 16) had fought on the side of the Ukrainian National Republic against the Bolsheviks. Pavlo Gubenko (Ostap Vishnya), Pavlo Tichina and Yury Smolich were state servants of the UNR. As you will appreciate, the intellectual part of the population always embodied the quintessence of the national consciousness. This was why the Bolsheviks were particularly fervent in their destruction of the Ukrainian intelligentsia.

Sosyura was one of the few people before the Second World War to write intimate poetry, which was seen as somewhat suspicious in the Soviet Union in the 1930s: poets were supposed to be singing the praises of the great feats of young people in the construction of factories and power plants, rather than writing about love.

to love their native land because of its beauty. For writing this poem, Vladimir Sosyura was accused of Ukrainian nationalism and suffered persecution at the hands of the party leaders.

I have read works by other Ukrainian writers and poets who were subjected to ideological persecution in the post-war years. I can well imagine the motives of the NKVD, whose persecution had led to the suicide in 1933 of the founder of Ukrainian post-revolutionary prose, Mykola Khvylovy. Khvylovy openly made the following rallying cry: "Away with us from Moscow – Europe is what we want!"

In the works of Maksim Rylsky, Yury Yanovsky, Yury Smolich and Pavel Gubenko, however, there was no "propaganda designed to undermine" at all – honest to God. Could it be that they were punished because they wrote in Ukrainian, and all their protagonists were Ukrainian?

And on what grounds was the music teacher, composer and virtuoso pianist Konstantin Dankevich accused of nationalism? Was it that his fingers were pressing down on the keys of the piano in the wrong way from an ideological point of view?

Despite the intense ideological pressure, the Ukrainians did not want to merge with the Russians and form a single people. This resistance to the imperial policy adopted by Moscow could not fail to be taken into account in the decisions taken by the Communist leadership. When the United Nations was set up, Stalin succeeded in making sure that Ukraine (and also Belarus) were among its founding members. There are many who believe he simply wanted to increase the number of votes he would have under his control within the organization. That may be true. To me, though, it is abundantly clear that by returning some of the characteristics of independence to Ukraine, such as a Ministry of Foreign Affairs, he was attempting to show the Ukrainian national liberation movements that their accusations to the effect that Ukrainian no longer had any sovereignty were unfounded.

THE PERIOD WHICH BECAME KNOWN AS THE 'THAW'

After Stalin's death, the struggle for power among the ruling Communist elite was won by a coterie led by Nikita Khrushchev. This period would later become known as the 'thaw'. Under Khrushchev the punitive nature of the Soviet regime weakened slightly, the GULAG was destroyed, and people who had been condemned on political grounds began to be rehabilitated.

Management of large industrial concerns on Ukrainian soil was gradually transferred from Moscow to local Ukrainian administrative agencies. Over the next ten years several hundred new concerns were built, and there was intensive industrialization in six Western regions. In the Lvov and Ivano-Frankov regions, natural gas extraction complexes were constructed, and these still provide gas for everyday use to the local population to this day.

Purchase prices for agricultural products were increased: grain became 7 times more expensive, potatoes were 8 times more expensive, and livestock products were 5.5 times more expensive. For the first time, agriculture became a profitable enterprise.

Intensive construction work began on housing for the people. Apartment buildings were built using simplified high-speed technologies, the apartments were not particularly large and had fairly low ceilings, and no lifts were put into them, so they were never more than 5 storeys high. Nonetheless, in the space of ten years, 18 million Ukrainians moved out of their cellars, huts and 'communal flats' – where the toilets, kitchens and bathrooms were shared by all the residents – and into an apartment of their own: and that meant a lot. Let's not forget, however, that in Soviet times housing was given out for free in most cases.

This policy led to significant changes in the mind-set of the peoples living in the Soviet Union. I would characterise these changes as 'inspiration'. After the prison-like stagnation of Stalin's regime, in which there was a sense of universal treachery, fear and uncertainty about tomorrow, there had come a time of universal faith in a bright future. And it should be observed that the results of this faith and inspiration were not just spiritual, but also material. When Ukraine's gross income grew by 10% a year for 10 years in a row (as happened in the '50s and '60s), it is difficult to attribute this solely to the reforms brought in by Khrushchev. People began responding eagerly to the slogans and challenges issued by the Communist leadership. When Khrushchev decided that to increase levels of agricultural production grain would have to be planted on the virgin soil in North Kazakhstan, hundreds of thousands of young people, including a large number of Ukrainian students, voluntarily moved to the wild steppes and set up agricultural concerns there, working in very harsh conditions. They were in the grip of the romance of creating something new, and the country thought of them as heroes.

Don't forget that at around about this time (in 1961), Yury Gagarin became the first cosmonaut to complete a space flight, and this gave everyone in the Soviet Union something they could legitimately feel proud about.

A MOUTHFUL OF ETHNIC FREEDOM?

Khrushchev, without question, was neither an economic genius nor a confirmed democrat. On his conscience were the major administrative gambles which had brought the country to a food crisis, and the decision to fire on striking workers in Novocherkassk (in Russia's Rostov region) in 1962. Nevertheless Ukraine found she was able to breathe more easily during his time in office.

Moreover, there were signs of a more liberal policy in relation to the non-Russian nationalities – not for the first time, as you'll remember. In this period it became possible to discuss the problems associated with preserving the Ukrainian language, ground-breaking works such as The Ukrainian Soviet Encyclopaedia, The History of Ukrainian Literature and The Ukrainian Historical Journal began to published, and preparations began for the multi-volume History of the Cities and Towns of Ukraine. I think this speaks for itself: if the publishing of works about Ukrainian subjects, and written in Ukrainian, was seen as a breakthrough, then what must things have been like before this?

Today some Ukrainian authors, when writing about that period, attempt to demonstrate that in the Soviet Union the favouring of the use of Russian rather than Ukrainian was enshrined in the law. They often cite a law published in 1958 and entitled 'On the strengthening of the connection between school and life', and maintain that this document created conditions in which the Ukrainian language was forced out and Ukraine could undergo Russification. There is no doubt that this is a foolish assertion: it was clearly written by someone who was not very familiar with the law, before being copied blindly by everyone else. The Communist ideologues never operated in such a primitive fashion. The process of strengthening the position of the Russian language took place even as the authorities were proclaiming that the national languages and cultures would have freedom to develop. Yet the Soviet Union was a multi-ethnic state – it was thought that there were people from at least 100 different nationalities living there. How were all these people expected to communicate with one another? If they were to do so, some sort of common language was required, and Russian was chosen to do this job.

Thereafter all scientific and technical literature was printed in Russian, films were made in Russian, and the TV spoke Russian – so that everyone could everyone could understand. The best singers, musicians and actors were invited from Kiev to Moscow: it was there that they could earn more money, be given honorary titles, and achieve wider fame. And it was taken as read that you would converse in Russian and create your art in Russian.

Lessons were taught in Russian at institutes and universities from Uzhgorod to Donetsk and from Sum to Simferopol. Academics wrote their dissertations, striving to obtain degrees and fellowships. The value of their dissertations was determined and confirmed in Moscow, so budding professors had no choice but to write their dissertations in Russian.

At congresses and assemblies, at academic conferences and state institutions, it was not customary to speak Ukrainian.

There was a policy of universal conscription in the country: all young men who had reached the age of 19 were required to serve in the army for two to three years. And which language was spoken in the army? Russian, of course.

There are schools in Ukraine where subjects are taught in both Russian and Ukrainian, but more and more parents are sending their children to Russian schools, which promise a better future for them.

In 1958, 60% of all the books published in Ukraine were written in Ukrainian; in 1959 this figure stood at 53%, in 1960 it was 49%, in 1965 it was 41%, and so it went on, following a downward curve.

UKRAINE'S 'MEN OF THE SIXTIES'

At this time a plethora of talented young figures emerged in the arts, which had formed amid conditions of ideological liberalization. This group was dubbed the 'men of the sixties', since the dawn of these people's creativity came in the 1960s. In Ukraine, the 'men of the sixties' movement felt it was its duty to lift up the banner representing the rebirth of Ukraine, preaching freedom of expression and seeking new art forms and artistic styles[39].

The official powers did not remain impartial for long in relation to manifestations of free-thinking and national consciousness. The creative work of the 'men of the sixties' began to be subjected to criticism, the most dangerous of which, from their point of view, was the allegation that they had "departed from the principles of Marxism-Leninism", which automatically meant that it would be impossible for them to publish their works, perform in public or shoot a movie. The works of the men of the sixties were often passed from one person to the next in the form of books printed illegally, and handed from one reader to the next. As you can imagine, in the Soviet Union this sort of behaviour was deemed as activity intended to undermine the status quo.

As for the attempt to create any forms of Ukrainian political organizations, the authorities made short work of the people who founded them.

A case in point is the Ukrainian Workers and Peasants Union, set up in 1959 by a group of young Ukrainian intellectuals. According to the Union's manifesto, which was written by a young lawyer from Lvov named Levko Lukyanenko, the organization's main objective was the armed struggle for civil rights in Ukraine, for ethnic and cultural rights and for financial rights. The manifesto was founded – and this is worth emphasizing – on the principles of Marxism-Leninism. It asserted that "the study of the principles of Marxism-

---

39   Among the famous figures in this group were the writers and poets Ivan Drach, Lina Kostenko, Mikola Vingranovsky, Vasil Simonenko, Vasil Stus, Yegveny Gutsalo, Igor Kalinets; the artists Alla Gorskaya and Panas Zalivakha; the literary critics Ivan Svitlychny, Ivan Dzyuba and Yevgen Sverstyuk; the cinematographers Sergei Paradzhanov, Leonid Osyka, Yury Ilenko and many other remarkable, talented people (there really was a huge number of them, I wouldn't be able to provide an exhaustive list here).

Leninism reveals the insuperable gulf between contemporary Soviet activity and the ideals for which the proletarian classes in all countries fought, along with their leaders, Marx, Engels and Lenin."

In such situations, the Soviet authorities would immediately show their true face in relation to the issue of ethnicity, forgetting all its declarations and guarantees about the freedom of different peoples and ethnic cultures to develop. Levko Lukyanenko was sentenced to death. To a certain extent he got lucky. The death penalty was replaced with a 15-year prison sentence. His fellow party members were also handed similar sentences.

Whilst in prison, however, Lukyanenko, like the other 'men of the sixties', behaved in the same way Ukrainian warriors have always behaved in prison, throughout all time: you'll recall the uprising by the leaders of the Kholodnoyarsk Republic, who were taken prisoner after being deceived, or the rebellion by soldiers from the URA in Sevlag[40], which ultimately signalled the beginning of the end for Stalin's prison camp system. In other words, Lukyanenko protested, organized resistance, tried to engage the law enforcement agencies, and was once again incarcerated. After twenty-seven years of prison, camps and exile, Lukyanenko returned to his native land and became a member of parliament in independent Ukraine, ambassador, and Chairman of the President of Ukraine's commission on issues related to clemency. Many of the other Ukrainian 'people of the sixties' suffered an even more tragic fate: the poet Vasil Stus died in prison, Vasily Simonenko was beaten to death at a police station...The artist Alla Gorskaya, who was part of the 'men-of-the-sixties' movement, was, according to the official version of events, killed by one of her relatives, who for some reason committed suicide immediately afterwards.

The talented writer and journalist Matvei Shestopal – a hero of the Second World War, who won medals and badges for his courage, and who served as dean of the faculty of journalism at Kiev University, took the liberty of expressing the view, in public, that a person could not have two 'native' languages – Russian and Ukrainian – simultaneously, an idea that the Communist party's ideologues were trying to introduce into the people's consciousness at the time. He lost his job and his means of subsisting. Those of his friends who tried to help him suffered persecution by the intelligence services. To raise enough money to buy a hunk of bread, he was forced to

---

40 On 25th May 1953, the biggest rebellion in the history of the GULAG took place in Norilsk, at the so-called Gorlag. It was a response by the prisoners to the shooting dead, that same day, of a group of their fellow prisoners. According to various reports, 150 prisoners died during the uprising. Their actions were successful, however: one year later, in 1954, the Gorlag was closed down. And by 1956 practically all of those involved in the uprising who were still alive were living in freedom. 70% of the prisoners who revolted were members of the URA.

collect empty bottles from the rubbish bins and hand them in at recycling points.

Some members of the *men-of-the-sixties* generation reached a compromise with the authorities, and many continued to put up various forms of resistance. Some survived, and others met their demise.

The *men-of-the-sixties* were the kernel of the dissident movement in Ukraine, the source of a different way of thinking; they introduced the concept of human rights into Ukrainians' consciousness. After the mass terror, bloody war, and millions of lives lost due to the famine (in the heart of Europe, in the 20th century), and the totalitarian brainwashing of the people, the notion of 'human rights' sounded like something exotic, forbidden, and rather alarming.

In spite of the relentless pressure they were under, there were those among the new generation of Ukrainian intellectuals who stayed true to their opinions and went into direct confrontation with the authorities. In the end, it was these people who became the leaders of the national renaissance that is taking place today.

It is my view that the idealism, unselfishness, refusal to compromise and self-sacrifice of the *men-of-the-sixties* are all things that the ruling elite in Ukraine find unpalatable even today. It is telling that the death of one of the outstanding figures in the dissident movement in Ukraine, Vyacheslav Chernovol, is still being investigated today. A staunch, principled, dedicated fighter for Ukrainian independence, he was arrested several times by the Soviet authorities and put in prison under an article of the Criminal code that was entirely 'political'. On the face of it, he lived to see his dream come true: Ukraine became independent. He has been a member of parliament, he has come second in a presidential election…But then there was a strange car crash, following which some key witnesses died of heart attacks…What more can I add to this that is new?

Once Khrushchev had been removed from office in Moscow, the ideological pressure exerted on the Ukrainian people grew even stronger. The slightest manifestations of conscious nationalist thinking, or an incautious phrase could lead to accusations of Ukrainian nationalism, which, in the view of the ideologues at the Kremlin, was one of the most serious crimes against Communism and led to very real oppression.

Even high-ranking Communist civil servants, when facing allegations that they had not been decisive enough in the battle against nationalism, lost their jobs and were punished by their bosses in Moscow.

Allow me to cite as an example the fate of Pyotr Shelest. The leader of the Communist Party in Ukraine from 1963 to 1972, and thus the man who was de facto in charge of the country, he took advantage of the considerable authority he enjoyed among party bosses at the Kremlin. He tried to suppress the dissident movement and was a firm supporter of intervening in Czechoslovakia in 1968 to crush the Prague Spring.

Nonetheless Shelest promoted the development of the Ukrainian language in schools, facilitated the publishing of Ukrainian language books and newspapers, and defended the writers Oles Gonchar and Ivan Dzubu when they were accused of nationalism (an allegation for which, as I have already said, would lead to a person disappearing from public life). He was the instigator of the creation of an encyclopaedic work, The history of the towns and villages of Ukraine, wore Ukrainian national dress – including an embroidered shirt – and wrote a book called Our Soviet Ukraine, in which he defended the country's authenticity.

Pyotr Shelest was removed from all the positions he held and sent to work in a provincial town in Russia, in an insignificant technical role at an aviation plant. He was under surveillance by the intelligence services and banned from returning to Ukraine, and the entire print run of his book was confiscated from the bookshops and libraries.

THE 'PERIOD OF STAGNATION'

Under Brezhnev's rule it became clear fairly quickly that the resources available for growing the Soviet economy were running out. On top of this, the levers formerly used to exert ideological pressure – such as the oppression which took place under Stalin and the romantic hopes which grew under Khrushchev – had disappeared. For a while, the country's leaders tried to maintain the nation's wealth by exporting natural gas overseas. The money they made from this was soon swallowed up, though, and the country found itself lagging behind its economic rivals in terms of productivity, energy production capacity and mastery of the latest achievements of scientific and technical progress. After this, the 'oil boom' came to an end and the economic situation became extremely tense. Prices for consumer goods began to rise, and this was something the Soviet propagandists were utterly unable to explain. Throughout the preceding decades, when there had been a small reduction in prices for foodstuffs, for example, this fact was widely cited in the press as evidence of the efficiency of the Soviet economy. The people had grown used to the idea that as their socialist society continued along its chosen path of development, they would be better-off and enjoy a better quality of life – and then suddenly, out of the blue, prices for consumer goods started going up. Why was this happening?

As for the methods used in agricultural production, even explaining how they worked seems absurd these days. To give you an example: every year, hundreds of thousands of people from various sectors of industry, science and education were supposed to leave the workplace behind and go and do seasonal work collecting the harvest on neighbouring farms or in more distant agricultural districts[41].

---

41   When I was a schoolboy, I did some apple-picking and cherry-picking at some state-owned orchards 300km from home. When I was a student I picked tomatoes and cucumbers, and when I was an academic I collected potatoes in primitive buckets, removing the ones that were starting to go bad, and also looked after a herd of cows along with my colleagues at the science and research institute. By then some of us already held degrees.

It was declared in the country at that time that a period of stability had come, but it was later described as a time of stagnation. I am not going to go into the economic problems in any great depth. In terms of the regime's ideology, however, as I see it there was a certain loss of direction. On the one hand, attempts had begun to whitewash the regime of Stalin, who had previously been damned, and resurrect his methods of ruling the country. This period even came to be known as neo-Stalinism. On the other hand, the state's leaders strove to improve the totalitarian dictator's image somehow, tried to have an active policy in the international arena, took part in multilateral conferences on security and cooperation in Europe, and signed the final draft of the Helsinki Accords in 1975. As you may remember, these Accords established the principle of respect for human rights, as well as the principles of military and economic security. This in turn prompted a number of figures in the rights protection movement to set up a charitable organization in Moscow to 'facilitate the fulfilment' by the Soviet powers of the Helsinki Accords in relation to human rights. In November 1976 a similar organization, the Ukrainian Helsinki Group, was set up in this country as well. Since the concept of human rights had been interpreted rather differently in the Soviet Union to the rest of the civilized world, organizations such as these had no difficulty recording countless violations of the rights of individuals and cases of persecution on ideological and political grounds. Their founders and any new members were therefore soon decried as anti-Soviet agitators and thrown into prison on fabricated charges, or, in cases when it was impossible to arrest dissidents due to the authority they enjoyed in society or on the international stage, they were exiled from the country.[42]

It should not be supposed that the dissidents and people who 'thought differently', in the Soviet Union in general and Ukraine in particular, were somehow not satisfied by their position in society, or people on the margins or pathological anarchists and rebels. In fact, the people fighting for human rights in this country tended to be among the wealthier, and were often part of the establishment, with numerous awards for their services to the country. The first chairman of the Ukrainian Helsinki Group was Nikolai Rudenko – a former officer who had won medals and badges for his heroics during the Second World War, a well-known writer and journalist, and the former director of the Communist Party in the Union of Writers of Ukraine (a very prestigious and significant post in Soviet Ukraine at that time). Pyotr Grigorenko, another of the founders of the UHG, had been a general in the

---

42 Psychiatric hospitals were often used as a method of fighting against political free-thinking – dissidents were forcibly sent to them with the aim of breaking their will and turning them into submissive 'vegetables'.

Soviet Army. There were also academics, lawyers and teachers in the civil rights groups, and people who had enjoyed successful careers.

In the 1970s, the pressure on Ukrainians' sense of their national identity grew even stronger. The slightest, most harmless displays of national identity were punished. I recall an incident from the early '70s when a student from the Taras Shevchenko University of Kiev decided to lay some flowers next to the monument to Shevchenko on 22nd May, the day when Shevchenko had been buried at his final resting place. The memorial to Shevchenko is 50 metres away from the university. He was not allowed to lay flowers at the monument on 22nd May, however, because, as our ideological directors explained to us, "Ukrainian nationalists gather on that day, and use this date to promote nationalism." So a group of men came and put the young man into a car and took him off somewhere. I would suggest that it is not hard to guess what sort of men they were. He was later expelled from the university. The saddest thing about this story is the fact that it was true. What a tiny thing it was that the student was trying to do – and yet what serious consequences it had!

At the time my thoughts as regards this lad were as follows: "What a stupid person! Why did he perform such a demonstrative act of protest, disobedience and provocation?" I now realise that acts of protest and disobedience such as this, regardless of their scope and regardless of their significance, were expressions of continuous, deep-rooted, instinctive resistance to Russification and to the Ukrainians' struggle to preserve themselves as a nation.

The structure of the Ukrainian economy was moving increasingly towards the fuel and raw materials industries. Yet the country's economic potential was growing in such a way that it was putting the whole country under a serious ecological threat. Ukrainian territory housed 40% of all the Soviet nuclear power plants and more than a thousand chemicals plants, even though the products they made were not widely used in the country. Gigantic hydro-electric power plants were built here, and consequently the reservoirs which served them flooded the fertile areas suitable for agriculture. Production of cast iron and steel flourished here, and gigantic thermal power plants were built. Can you picture what a very big thermal power plant entails? It entails not only large buildings and high-voltage power lines, but also vast warehouses containing low-grade coal with a high sulphur content; tall chimneys through which clouds of smoke, of various colours, come billowing out both day and night; and waste water, which is pumped out of the cooling systems into bodies of water in the surrounding area.

Ukraine constituted 2.6% of the total territory of the USSR, yet it was on the receiving end of more than a quarter of all pollution in the country.

To be frank, an industrial policy such as this is considered, in the civilized world, to be colonial in nature.

In spite of the extensive amount of industrial construction work taking place, the rate of growth in Ukraine's national income slowed with each passing year, from 7.8% in 1966-1970 to 3.5% in 1981-1985. In 1990, for the first time in many decades, Ukraine's national income fell to 1.5%.

THE DISASTER AT CHERNOBYL

The culmination of the environmental damage taking place in Ukraine was, without question, the explosion which took place at the Chernobyl nuclear power station.

What were the consequences of this industrial and ecological disaster for the country?

The reasons for the disaster reflected the atmosphere in the country at the time in relation to safety, proper use of machinery and responsibility for one's actions. It became clear fairly quickly that the accident had been caused by the irresponsible actions of the staff, who decided, acting on someone's instructions, to conduct a risky experiment involving the nuclear reactor. To make matters worse, the team sent in to put out the fire at the nuclear power plant consisted of firemen and servicemen who did not have any anti-radiation equipment. 31 people died of radiation poisoning immediately after the accident, and 600,000 people who were involved in dealing with its consequences were exposed to various doses of radiation. Word got out that, in spite of the ubiquitous assurances of the official mass media to the effect that there was no risk of danger to the people of Kiev, high-ranking officials began evacuating their families from the city. Meanwhile, people in the city, who had not been properly informed of what had happened – students, schoolchildren, factory workers and teachers – were told to come out onto the streets of Kiev to take part in festive processions, at the very time when the city had been covered by a radioactive cloud. The fact that the Communist leaders were themselves present at these festivities didn't change anything. In this day and age, people are well aware of the difference in the effect of small doses of radiation on people aged over 70, as our Communist leaders were, and on children, newborn babies, schoolchildren, students, pregnant women and the rest of the healthy, forward-looking section of the population.

After a few days, advice began to come out to the effect that we should make sure windows were closed tightly, wash the floors more often than normal, and keep water from the pipes in glass jars for several days at a time, and use only the middle section of this water in our food (I'd like it if those advisers could demonstrate exactly how this can be done). And that was it. Did you suppose that they handed out anti-radiation pills of some kind? Nothing of the sort took place. They delivered cheap red wine to the shops, and put about a story to the effect that red wine was good at removing radionuclides from the body.

After the disaster at Chernobyl, trust in the Communist leaders among the people of Ukraine fell to an all-time low.

THE ATTEMPT TO MODERNIZE THE USSR

The Chernobyl disaster took place at a time when a group had come to power in the Soviet Union who intended to give a fresh impulse to the country's development by bringing in reforms in the political, economic and even ideological fields. This group, which was led by Mikhail Gorbachev, attempted to 'lift the pressure valve' slightly, and reduce the tension which had accumulated in society.

The country could no longer afford to pursue a foreign policy which relied on the use of brute force: tanks in Eastern Europe, tension on the border with China, attempts to export socialism to developing countries.

Whatever spin you try to put on it, the fact is that in Ukraine – one of the most developed parts of the Soviet Union – the average worker in industry was half as productive as their American counterpart, and the average agricultural worker was five times less productive. Inside the country there was growing discontent with the economic problems, and the monetary sums paid out in the form of salaries were not sufficient to pay for products. People no longer wanted to work out of the kindness of their hearts: there were no incentives for doing so. The dissidents – for all the authorities' attempts to throw them into prisons or psychiatric homes – could not be suppressed. Talk of the luxuries in which high-ranking Communist officials indulged left ordinary people bewildered. There was no sense whatsoever that the much-vaunted society of "universal wealth and wellbeing" – Communism – was approaching. Instead, there was corruption, the 'shadow' economy and organized crime. There was an obvious ideological crisis, and ideology has always been the foundation of all Communist states.

It was at this point that the leaders of the Communist party proclaimed a new policy direction: a course which would involve the restructuring, or *perestroika*, of the whole of public life. It was announced that the 'human factor' must play a crucial role in the growth of the economy. In other words, the authorities had at long last decided to encourage people who showed initiative, and get rid of the phenomenon of 'equalling out' which had been in place for many years, whereby your productivity at work had no real bearing on how much you were paid. The start of a campaign of *glasnost*, or 'openness', was announced, in which many of the taboos on obtaining information and expressing your personal opinion were removed.

But it was a case of shutting the stable door after the horse had bolted. Of course, the people behind the *glasnost* campaign supposed that it amounted to nothing more than permission openly to criticize some of the problems in society, and certain abuses by individual civil servants. This was supposed to improve society's health, and allow a bit of steam out of the system. In practice, it transpired that the Communist empire had simply run its course. *Glasnost* quickly turned into complete freedom of speech. The weakening of the role of the Communist party structure led to the abolition of article 6 of the Constitution of the USSR, which decreed that the country's political life was to operate on a one-party basis.

A NEW ERA APPROACHES

In Ukraine, this latest liberalization of the Communist system once again led to a desire to restore the country's own sense of identity. Things which people were forbidden to talk about, remember and discuss came back into public life. The works of the historians Kostomarov[43] and Grushevsky[44], and the writer Vinnichenko[45] re-emerged from oblivion, people began talking about the great famine of 1932-33 (the *golodomor*), about the persecution suffered in the past, the history of the OUN, and about the Ukrainian rebel army. A plethora of informal charities, environmental movements and anti-Stalin societies were set up[46]. Within the Communist party itself, critically-minded and nationally aware Communists created the so-called Democratic platform.

A movement for the restoration of the Ukrainian autocephalous Orthodox church came into being, along with another which campaigned for the Graeco-Catholic Church, which had been banned by the Communists, to be legalized.

The Ukrainian agencies of state power, finding themselves, which, on the face of it, were controlled by the Communists, were unable to resist the wave of national self-awareness which rose up in Ukraine at that time. In 1989 the Supreme Soviet of the USSR adopted the Law on languages, in which Ukrainian was declared an official state language.

In 1990 the Supreme Soviet in Ukraine adopted a directive on the procedure for registering charitable associations, and this marked the end of the Soviet system.

---

43   An extremely original character, who led a very unusual life rich in radical changes. His political credo in respect of Ukraine was reflected in the phrase: "Let neither the Great Russians nor the Poles describe as their own, lands which were populated by our people."

44   The first Chairman of the Central Rada of the Ukrainian People's Republic.

45   The first Chairman of the independent Ukrainian government in 1918.

46   This was important, since at the time of the Khrushchev 'thaw', a large number of those who had suffered persecution had not yet been 'rehabilitated', and not everyone had had their good name restored. The period of 'neo-Stalinism' which followed this curtailed the process of rehabilitation altogether.

The first party which amounted to a genuine alternative to the Communists was the Ukrainian Republican Party, which was created on the basis of the Ukrainian Helsinki Group. And then the floodgates opened: within a year, 20 opposition parties had been created, including the Greens, the Liberal Democrats and so on. Understandably, the new parties had neither experience nor any serious financing for their work, but they sped up the politicization of public consciousness, given that most of them were in favour of national sovereignty and Ukraine's independence. A central position among these newly-formed political organizations was occupied, of course, by the Narodyn Rukh Ukrainy. Set up back in 1989 at the instigation of a group of writers, the name of this organization, before it became a political party, originally had the suffix 'a movement to provide assistance for *perestroika*', i.e. cooperation in the policy introduced by Mikhail Gorbachev's group, who hoped to reform the Soviet Union. The Narodny (Peoples) Rukh brought together all manner of political objectives and views under one banner: from liberal Communists to extreme nationalists. However, Rukh quickly evolved, together with the change in the socio-political situation, from a moderate organization advocating a degree of democratization of the Soviet system, into an all-out anti-Communist movement.

In 1990, elections for the Supreme Soviet of Ukraine were held. The pro-democracy bloc led by the National Rukh of Ukraine, which included 43 political organizations and parties, won just 125 seats in parliament. The pro-Communist majority won 300 seats. The electorate had not yet worked out who was who, and over the course of 73 years of Communist rule it had grown used to the idea that politics was something the Communists took care of. But you can imagine what the political situation in Ukraine was like at that time, if you consider that in spite of those results, Ukraine's Supreme Soviet nonetheless passed into law a Declaration on the state sovereignty of Ukraine.

Against this backdrop it became clear that the Soviet Union could no longer go on existing in its former guise. And then, on 19th August 1991, a group of state leaders, representing orthodox, conservative forces and a 'Stalinist' way of thinking, attempted a coup d'état. It must be noted, incidentally, that the intended victim of this plot was Mikhail Gorbachev – the most senior Communist and the legitimate President of the USSR.

Of all the political forces in Ukraine, the Communist Party was the only one that supported this move.

After three days the attempted coup resulted in defeat for the conspirators, who had tried to return the country to a totalitarian regime. The scenario in which the Soviet Union would be preserved as a unified state was no longer on the table. The Supreme Soviet of what was still, at the time, the Ukrainian

Soviet Socialist Republic adopted the 'Act on the proclamation of Ukrainian independence'. A ban was imposed on the Communist Party of Ukraine.[47] On 1st December 1991 this Act was put to a nationwide referendum and was approved by 90.3% of Ukrainian citizens.

That same day, elections were held for the First President of independent Ukraine. Six candidates were put forward, and the candidate from the state apparatus, Leonid Kravchuk, received 62% of the vote. This is hardly surprising: events had simply unfolded too quickly. None of the alternative candidates, representing the nationalist and patriotic forces, had a genuine opportunity to hold an election campaign. At the same time, the state apparatus was represented to a man by former Communists, who had big opportunities to exert a positive influence in favour of their candidate, and the former ideologue of the Ukrainian Communists became the leader of an independent Ukraine. It should be noted, incidentally, that Leonid Kravchuk held the post of Chairman of the Supreme Soviet (parliament) of Ukraine, had been a fairly prominent figure in the political landscape, and he it was who presided over the vote in parliament in favour of a Declaration of the state sovereignty of Ukraine. During the coup in August, Kravchuk made a great show of giving up his membership of the Communist Party. By so doing he managed to satisfy a lot of people – both the activists in the banned Communist Party and the nationalist-democrats, who heralded the chairman of the Supreme Soviet as the 'father of independence'.

The aim of everything I have narrated so far was to explain to people observing the current reality of Ukrainian life from outside, who the Ukrainian people are, why we should not be grouped together with other peoples, and why we are pretty sensitive about any actions by our neighbours which, in our opinion, place limitations on our hard-won sovereignty. Yet the fact is that we are living in the present, and it is with the people living in Ukraine in the present that we must concern ourselves.

Let's spend a little bit of time examining the make-up of the Ukrainian population, from the point of view of ethnic background, religious faith, linguistic preferences and national character.

---

47   It was restored two years later, incidentally – after all, we were striving to build a democratic state in which all political forces are equally entitled to try and win over the sympathies of the electorate. Incidentally, today the restored CPU has a fairly large contingent of MPs in parliament, and advocates – don't be in any doubt about it – establishing closer ties with Russia.

THE POPULATION OF UKRAINE TODAY

Who currently lives within the borders of the state known as 'Ukraine'?

From an administrative perspective, the territory of present-day Ukraine took shape during the era of the USSR. To all intents and purposes it coincided with the ancestral homeland of the Ukrainian people, though not entirely. Today, there are certain hot-heads in Russia who would like to take away from Ukraine certain regions in which a significant portion of the population is of a different nationality, such as the Crimea and regions in the east of Ukraine, for example.

It must be said that Ukraine is currently very weak from a military perspective, and it is only able to preserve its territorial integrity thanks to the general conviction of the European community that it would be undesirable for there to be any military conflicts over land on European soil. On the other hand, however, the collapse of the former Yugoslavia, and then of Serbia, go to show that nothing ever lasts forever.

As it happens, the ancestral homeland of the Ukrainian people extends slightly beyond the state's current political borders. At any rate, when the Communists decided in the 1920s to demonstrate that their policy as regards nationality was different from that of the Tsarist government, they ordered that civil servants and party functionaries must only speak in the language of the local population. In respect of the Ukrainian language, this affected not only the territory of present-day Ukraine, but also Kuban, the Stavropol Krai and parts of the North Caucasus and the Kursk and Voronezh regions. These areas are currently part of the Russian Federation, and somehow nobody ever seems to remember that these areas were once inhabited by ethnic Ukrainians.

As of 1st January 2013, Ukraine had a population of 45.5 million people, of which around 31 million lived in urban areas and the rest lived in the countryside.

The passports and other official documents of people in Ukraine do not state the citizen's nationality. According to a survey of the people conducted in

2001, the breakdown of the population in terms of nationality was as follows: Ukrainians – 77% (the majority, except in the Autonomous Republic of Crimea), Russians – 17.3% (account for a significant part of the population in eastern and southern regions of the country), Belarusians – 0.6%, Moldovans – 0.5%, Crimean Tatars – 0.5%, Bulgarians – 0.4%, Hungarians – 0.3%, Romanians – 0.3%, Poles – 0.3%, Jews – 0.2%, Armenians – 0.2%, Greeks – 0.2%, Tatars – 0.2%, others (Azerbaijanis, Kazakhs, Uzbeks, Kyrgyz, Georgians, Tajiks, Latvians) – 1.2%.

Average population density is 77.3 people per square kilometre.

Estimates of the number of Ukrainian citizens living outside the country (in Canada, the United States, Romania, Argentina, Russia, Brazil, Poland, Kazakhstan, Armenia, Belarus, Georgia, Moldova, Kyrgyzstan, Hungary, Iran) range from 8 to 15 million.

Ukrainians are an eastern Slavic people by descent, and are considered the third biggest Slavic people after the Russians and the Poles.

Yet anyone setting out to describe the 'average' Ukrainian, or the 'typical' Ukrainian, is destined to fail. We are talking about a country which stretches 1300 km from West to East and 900 km from North to South, across which the great waves of huge movements of populations have rolled, to which warriors have arrived from the four corners of the globe, and in which one group of conquerors was succeeded by another, and entire peoples were forcibly resettled and later repatriated: a country such as this has, by definition, incorporated within its ethnic make-up a vast plethora of ethnic origins, bloodlines and lines of descent.

The population of Ukraine is falling steadily: in 1991 it stood at 52 million people, in 2011 it stood at 45.6 million, and between January 2012 and May 2012 it fell to 45.5 million. As of 1st June 2012, the population of Ukraine's capital city, Kiev, was 2.8 million.

Although there are fewer children in the country, it would appear that their prospects, in terms of surviving, getting an education and finding fulfilment in the workplace, are on the up. The average life expectancy for children born in 2011 was 66 for men, and 76 for women. For those born in 1991-1992, by comparison, average life expectancy was 64 for men and 74 for women. A small upward trend has been observed, primarily due to the fact that the infant mortality rate has fallen, and for this we have modern medical techniques to thank.

UKRAINIANS LIVING OUTSIDE THEIR NATIVE LAND

The Ukrainians have always been a very dynamic people, prepared to go in search of a better share of wealth, a higher salary and the opportunity to move away to distant lands. Keeping their native land in their hearts, they would set off to far-flung countries a long way from home.

The Ukrainian diaspora in Canada began when Ukrainians living in the Austro-Hungarian Empire decided to emigrate. The first Ukrainian settlers in Canada were Ivan Pylypiv and Vasily Yelenyak, who came from the village of Nebyliv in the Rozhnyatov district (in those days it was part of Austria-Hungary), who arrived in Canada in 1891. Pylypiv established the town of Edna-Star in the province of Alberta – this was the first, and the biggest, mass settlement of Ukrainians in Canada. Moreover, the man thought to have initiated the mass migration of Ukrainians to Canada is Dr. Josif Oleskiv, who encouraged and promoted the idea of emigrating to Canada from Western Ukraine, and also from Galicia and Bukovina, in the late 1890s.

After 1918, supporters of the Ukrainian People's Republic, who were unable to reconcile themselves to Soviet rule, began arriving in Canada. So too, after the Second World War, did supporters of the national resistance movements (the URA and so on), i.e. in all cases these were supporters of the countries or movements which were fighting against Tsarist Russia or the USSR.

As a result, the number of Ukrainians living in Canada shot up to more than 1.2 million people (3.9% of the Canadian population), and Canada now had the third largest Ukrainian population in the world (after Ukraine and Russia).

In the 19th century, tens of thousands of Ukrainians living in the Russian empire moved to the Far East of Russia, to Priamurye. The empire's borders had to be protected, and people had to be moved into the area to settle there. As always, the Ukrainians were deemed to be best suited for the job. To this day, some of the towns in these areas, which became known as 'Green Klin', still have Ukrainian names.

In 1926, one fifth of the people living in these areas stated that their native tongue was Ukrainian.

Small settlements of Ukrainians, known as 'klins', formed in other parts of the Russian empire too. Among them was 'Yellow Klin' (in central and southern parts of the Volga Region), 'Raspberry Klin' (in Kuban) and 'Grey Klin' (in southern parts of West Siberia and North Kazakhstan).

In the 1960s and 1970s tens of thousands of Ukrainians moved to the north of Russia to exploit the huge reserves of oil in the Tyumen Region. Needless to say, they had a hard time of it; the fact that this region had always been used by Russia and the Soviet Union as a place of exile for political opponents tells you all you need to know.

On the other hand, the money that could be made by experts and ordinary workers, as they exploited the oilfields and built new towns and cities, was far more than they could hope to earn on the banks of the Dnieper in their homeland.

After the collapse of the Soviet Union, the Ukrainian economy – particularly industry in independent Ukraine – were caught up in a process of intensive de-industrialization. By contrast with countries in the West, this process did not create a post-industrial economic way of life – an information economy, a service economy, a knowledge economy. In the mid-1990s, despite the population crisis, unemployment – particularly undisclosed unemployment – reached a very high level, and this led to a record wave of people emigrating in order to find work or make money. The labour migrants were, in the main, people from the regions (particularly West Ukraine), most of whom came from small towns and villages.

In an attempt to secure decent living standards for themselves and their families, a large number of Ukrainians moved to other countries to try and earn more money. It is estimated that there were some 4.5 million economic migrants in total. Of these, more than 2 million Ukrainian nationals work in Russia (the official figure is 169,000), there are 500,000 (officially 195,000) work in Italy, more than 450,000 (officially 20,000) in Poland, 250,000 (officially 53,000) in Spain, 75,000 (officially 45,000) in Portugal, 150,000 (officially 51,000) in the Czech Republic, 75,000 (officially 20,000) in Greece, 40,000 in the Netherlands, around 70,000 in the United Kingdom, around 500,000 in the USA and approximately 100,000 living in other countries. According to data from the Ukrainian centre for social studies, some of the main areas of employment of Ukrainians living abroad are the construction industry, agriculture and housekeeping.

Whereas agricultural workers from West Ukraine emigrate to the West, workers in East Ukraine opt instead to emigrate to Russia. The people who move to Russia tend to be those with a special professional education of some description. The Ukrainian workforce is fairly attractive to Russian business, not only because of how highly educated it is but also because of its good discipline, and because by taking on Ukrainians, Russian companies are able to get rid of undesirable employees who don't bother to abide by the labour laws. It is fair to characterize the schedules and working conditions endured by temporary employees as demanding. Most of the labour migrants who move to Russia are young or middle-aged men, most of whom come from eastern parts of Ukraine (particularly the Donetsk and Kharkov regions).

As the statistics quoted above reveal, many migrants from Ukraine travel to Russia or the West on an unofficial basis, and therefore often fall victim to the black market: human trafficking, the drugs trade, sex-tourism and so on and so forth.

Be that as it may, Ukrainian migrants who leave to make money in other countries make a significant contribution to the country's economy. In 2011 they sent back 7 billion dollars (4% of Ukraine's GDP) to their homeland, and in 2013 they sent back 7.5 billion dollars. It is hard to put a figure on exactly how much money comes into the country from Ukrainian migrants: whilst you can count the money sent by bank transfer or via international payment systems, no-one knows how much employees actually bring home in their pockets. The national bank estimates that this figure is in the region of 0.5 billion dollars a year.

RELIGIONS IN UKRAINE

We do not have a dominant religion in Ukraine. Most Ukrainians describe themselves as Christians, and a handful of Christian churches vie with one another over the congregations' wallets and over temples which in many cases were built two hundred, four hundred, or even a thousand years ago. These include the Catholic church, the Greek Catholic church, the Orthodox church – part of the Moscow patriarchate – and another Orthodox church, the Kiev patriarchate, which broke away from the Moscow leadership, who imposed treacherous ban on it, but which is nonetheless exists and is respected by many believers as a "the true church of Ukraine".

The wrath felt by the church leaders in Moscow with respect to the Kiev patriarchate is understandable: the fact that major dioceses broke away from the Russian Orthodox Church at the time when Ukraine obtained independence not only meant a fall in its profits, but also led to the loss of the channels used by Russia to exert an ideological influence inside Ukraine. The task of strengthening this influence was something that the church was constantly being set by the political leaders in Russia.

Incidentally, the breaking away of some Ukrainian Orthodox Christians (who are not to be confused with the Greek Catholics) from Moscow was the second time something like this had happened in history, because the first such incident took place after the February revolution of 1917 in the Russian empire. On that first occasion, the Ukrainian autocephalous church had been set up, and this church too was not recognized by Moscow. Ukraine did not manage to defend its independence, and became part of the Soviet Union. The Ukrainian autocephalous church therefore became the religious organization of the sizeable Ukrainian populations in Canada and the USA. Today this church also has followers within independent Ukraine.

Data about the number of adherents to one religion or another are compiled on the basis of surveys or databases from the Ministry of internal affairs about the number of people who go to church on major religious holidays.

The overall picture in terms of support for various faiths is as follows:

Traditional Christian churches: the Moscow patriarchate – over 6 million. The Kiev patriarchate – over 4 million. The Ukrainian Greek Catholic church – over 2 million. The Ukrainian autocephalous church – 250,000. The Roman Catholic church – around 700,000. Protestants – around 500,000. Islam – at least 500,000. 150,000 people describe themselves as Jehovah's Witnesses, and there are 300,000 Baptists. There are 30,000 Jews and the same number of Buddhists.

There is also a whole host of so-called 'charismatic churches', each of which also found support among believers in Ukraine[48].

---

[48] My theory is that the followers of the minor faiths, which are known as 'sects' here in Ukraine, are people who simply lost all sense of ideology after 1991. Believe me, I know whereof I speak. These people were brought up in an atheist environment. The transition from a condition in which everything was determined, decided and scheduled in advance, for many years down the line, to a condition in which nothing is certain and everything is changing - often for the worst - and it's every man for himself, and not everyone is strong enough to cope - this transition was that happened extremely abruptly.

Both manpower and creative minds were suddenly surplus to requirements. Not everyone was able to find their feet in this new world. An ideological vacuum had come into being - and suddenly huge groups of men in black robes and white collars came rushing into the country, who would start up conversations by asking: "Tell me, do you believe in God?"

People who felt utterly lost were promised support and training in how they ought to feel in a world in which they had lost their sense of direction, and people went to church services, taking their children, relatives and friends with them. Preachers and psychologists from America suddenly found they had a fairly large following here. Often people who were fairly well-off - and even those in high office - chose to follow these religions.

The religious communities which emerged are very efficient at collecting money from their followers. The pastors themselves lead a life of luxury. And scandals sometimes occur, too.

The memory is still fresh of a case in which a black pastor from one of these 'creative' churches urged his followers to take their savings out of the bank and invest them in a business run by his friend David, who had created a 'pyramid scheme' and a fraudulent wedding agency. They had a remarkable protector - than the mayor of Kiev at the time, who was a follower of this "charismatic church" (or a brainwashed member of this sect, if you will - he was described in various ways depending on the views of each news commentator). It all ended rather predictably: the 'friend' David was put in prison, but the money was never returned to the citizens who had been duped. One can only wonder at the gullibility and fatalism of some Ukrainians.

Having said that, the well-coordinated activities of the leaders of these religious communities enables them to install their members within executive bodies at various levels, and ensure they have a majority in 'social councils' created within the bodies of executive power (such as the Ministry of Foreign Affairs, for example). At one time, several of these 'non-traditional' churches even planned to "take power" in the capital.

LANGUAGES IN UKRAINE

I wouldn't say that there is a single language which dominates in Ukraine. There is an official state language: Ukrainian. In a state census, 67% of the people said that Ukrainian was their native tongue. At the same time, half the population of Ukraine uses Russian in everyday conversation, and does not experience any difficulties doing so. All the right conditions are in place for people to be bilingual in our country. The attempts made by some overly 'nationally oriented' political figures to put the Ukrainian language on some sort of pedestal are seen as a clear failure to understand the population. On the other hand, the calls being made from neighbouring Russia to protect the Russian-speaking population of Ukraine do not make sense to anyone here either: who are we supposed to be protecting it from? In our country, the Ukrainian language gets along in harmony with the Russian language. Bilingualism, whereby people are able to switch freely from one language to the other, without thinking of either as a foreign language, is widespread here. We speak whichever language we want to speak.

The Ukrainian language existed in the past, exists today and will continue to grow. I hope it is clear from what I have said above that the attempts to suppress Ukrainian, and turn it into something more akin to a provincial dialect, went on for several centuries. Today, the language's rich lexicon stems not only from the works of the older generation of Ukrainian writers and poets, written in the 19th and 20th centuries. A new generation of novelists and playwrights, actors and singers are creating, quickly developing, expanding and enriching Ukrainian speech, which is characterized by soft pronunciation and a melodic timbre. And I'm not talking about folk culture, but about contemporary artistic genres for mass audiences.

Without question, the Ukrainian language, after such a sustained period of 'suppression', has yet to regroup fully. During the stormy development of scientific and technological progress in the 20th century, Ukrainian was still being suppressed, and was unable to assemble the range of vocabularies which make all languages full-blooded, complete and resilient. As well as the literary and artistic languages, we also need technical Ukrainian, computer Ukrainian and scientific Ukrainian. Even the administrative and state Ukrainian, in which our laws are written, is far from perfect. This last language, incidentally, is heavily dependent on the level of literacy of the person writing the law, and in this regard we have a big problem.

Not all the citizens of Ukraine have complete mastery of the official state language. Some are fundamentally against the idea of speaking it. Many use a mixture of Ukrainian and Russian in their everyday lives, and this is known as 'surzhik'. Surzhik first came into being around 150 years ago, perhaps even longer ago. It caught on particularly well in Kiev. I recall that one Ukrainian linguist and academic proposed that 'surzhik' be defined as a 'Ukrainian-Kievan dialect', and put on a legal footing of some sort, for which he was criticized mercilessly by his colleagues.

The reason for its emergence is simple: people who originally came from the countryside, where they not only spoke Ukrainian but thought in the language, too, would go off to make their fortune in the big cities – the biggest of which was of course Kiev. When they arrived, they found that the state language was Russian, so if they wanted to make anything of themselves, they had to 'retune' themselves, from a linguistic point of view, pretty quickly. Russian was the language of authority, the language of education, the language of culture. As they sought to integrate themselves into their new surroundings, people tried to pronounce Ukrainian words in a Russian way, and Russian words were pronounced in an identifiably Ukrainian manner. 'Surzhik' exists only in the form of a conversational language, for use in everyday conversation. In written speech and in publications, the only languages used are Russian or Ukrainian.

I have often heard people say that Kiev has always been a 'Russian-speaking city'. This, of course, is the view expressed by people who turn their personal, day-to-day experience into an absolute truth. My question for them is: "What do you mean by 'always'?" A very long time is not the same as 'always'.

Prior to 1654, when Hetman Bogdan Khmelnitsky was forced to be a protectorate of the state of Muscovy, and all the changes related to this occurred, there was not a single Muscovite living in Kiev. Kiev was a Ukrainian-speaking city, since the Ukrainians were a people whose roots were in this land. Anyone who knows both languages (Russian and Ukrainian) will be able to take a view on the so-called *Lexis* (i.e. dictionary for schoolchildren), a work published in 1596 which was written by a famous teacher, translator and academic from that time named Lavrenty Zizaniy. In the left-hand column is a list of words which are clearly recognizable as

Russian words, and in the right-hand column are Ukrainian words. So this helps us to establish that there was a need for people who could translate from one language to the other even then[49].

At the Kiev-Mohyla Academy (a famous academic institution which dates back to 1615), lessons were taught in Latin and Ukrainian. Not until 1751, by decree of the Russian emperor, did the Academy start providing lessons in Russian language and poetry. In 1784 a ban was imposed on reading lectures in Ukrainian! And how are we to explain this if, as certain 'linguistic researchers' claim – echoing, incidentally, the arguments put forward by their imperial forefathers – Ukrainian is nothing more than a dialect from Little Russia, a spin-off of the language of Great Russia?

The Ukrainian language was forced out of Kiev and out of the big cities in general, and this was a deliberate, colonialist policy.

In the days of the Soviet Union, Ukrainian, though it was not officially banned, was taught in many schools throughout Ukraine (known as 'Russian schools') as a 'second' language, and pupils began studying it after they began studying Russian. It was therefore in Russian that a child would first learn to write, recite poetry, and speak in a sophisticated and grammatically correct way. All school subjects were taught in Russian, incidentally. Moreover, there was a law which decreed that a pupil's parents could declare that they did not want their child to study Ukrainian – and the child would duly be exempted from having to study it. Children were not allowed to be exempted from studying German or English, not to mention Russian, but if they wanted to get out of studying Ukrainian – so be it.

There were schools where Ukrainian was taught, admittedly, but there were fewer of them, they had fewer pupils, and most of them were concentrated in rural areas, which was inconvenient given that the higher education institutions and cultural sites were concentrated mainly in the cities.

After 1991, the situation changed for the better: now Ukrainian schools were in the majority, lessons were taught in Ukrainian at the higher education institutions, and, prompted by patriotic 'instincts', the boldest politicians proposed bringing in measures which would prohibit the use of Russian on Ukrainian soil. This was all fine, but for the last part: banning the language.

In general terms, our people are known for their high levels of tolerance. We are not fond of the word 'ban' – it provokes an immediate reaction and

---

49   It is quite amusing to see that in this ancient dictionary, the language which we call Ukrainian today is referred to as 'Russian'. This goes to show once again that the ethnonym 'Russians' was one that the Muscovites adopted, after taking it from another people. And this other people, not wanting to merge with them, and in an attempt to preserve their sense of identity, began calling themselves 'Ukrainians'.

resistance. You might speak Russian here and find that your interlocutor replies in Ukrainian; equally, you might say something in Ukrainian only for the response to be in Russian. In this bilingual country, people don't even stop to think about which language they're speaking, because they understand both languages perfectly well. In areas where the population speak mostly in Ukrainian, such as the city of Lvov, people react amicably and calmly on hearing Russian being spoken, and don't differentiate between their Russian-speaking fellow-citizens and the ones who speak Ukrainian. I deliberately wanted to highlight the phenomenon of Ukraine's linguistic tolerance, because in recent years there has been some hysterical speculation on the subject of languages, on the part of politicians battling to win votes from the Russian-speaking electorate.

At the end of the day, if my grandparents spoke Russian, and my parents spoke Russian, then what language would you expect me to speak? And if I'm to have the ability to use my native tongue forcibly taken away from me, this will cause me nothing but irritation and protestation.

Our previous parliament, which to a large extent represented the interests of the densely populated regions of Ukraine, where large numbers of people speak Russian, passed a law on regional languages, whereby, in areas in which a significant portion of the population did not speak Ukrainian, these people were allowed to use this other language as an official one, with the same standing as the state language of Ukrainian.

In this law there were overtones of political flirting with Russia, since Russian is in pretty good shape in Ukraine as it is, and did not really need any support in the legislation[50], whilst there are only three other languages which can lay claim to the status of regional languages – Hungarian in the Transcarpathian region, Romanian in the Chernivtsi region and Crimean Tatar in the Crimea.

Ukrainian will definitely hold on to its place in the sun, if it manages to create a critical mass of cultural values. In previous eras it did not have the opportunity to do so – and you will understand why that was after reading everything I have narrated in this book so far. Ukrainian must go through a transition from being an 'exotic' language to an 'ordinary European language'. If this is to happen we need good writers, poets, playwrights and actors,

---

50   Anyone who has read in detail the law I referred to earlier about languages in the Ukrainian Soviet Socialist Republic, from 1989, which is still in force today, would realize that in this law, Russian, like the other languages spoken on Ukrainian territory, besides Ukrainian, enjoyed a status in which it was afforded serious protection. The adoption of the new law was not actually brought about by necessity. But these were political games by the last administration under President Yanukovich: he kow-towed to Russia and in return received loans or low prices for gas.

followed closely by chemists, mechanics, mathematics and biologists who are able to create spiritual and scientific values in this language.

Indeed, attempts can be made to encourage the publication of books in Ukrainian by means of subsidies and exemptions, but if these are not attractive enough in terms of the way they are bound and their literary level, then the law of supply and demand, the law of the purse-strings, will prevent any progress from being made in any case. Similarly, no-one would want to come and listen to a rock group performing songs in Ukrainian if they couldn't sing for toffee.

I would hasten to point out, mind you, that our Ukrainian language rock groups are very good, so they tend to get a lot of listeners. Some outstanding authors are beginning to emerge who not only write in Ukrainian but make virtuosic use of the language. And if we are a little short of books by Ukrainian writers at present, we'll simply publish more English, German, Brazilian and Spanish literature, translated into Ukrainian. And if there's one thing I can say with absolute certainty, it's that our literary translators are superb.

In 1998 a law was passed which decreed that all foreign films had to be dubbed in Ukrainian. This was perhaps something that ought not to have been applied to films made in Russia, but for films from all other countries it was absolutely the right thing to do. Our film distributors are constantly lobbying for this law to be amended, and for the compulsory requirement for dubbing to be replaced with subtitles, since dubbing is a fairly expensive procedure. It's obvious that these attempts are aimed at bringing an end to the compulsory dubbing of Russian-language films.

I can nevertheless take pleasure in saying that the most popular Ukrainian artists are all getting involved in this work, and that a school of magnificent Ukrainian dubbing has taken shape, and we have grown accustomed to seeing Bruce Willis and Angelina Jolie speaking Ukrainian – or appearing to do so.

THE NATIONAL CHARACTER OF THE UKRAINIAN PEOPLE

They say that every people has its own national character traits, its own distinct national mentality.

There is a persistent belief that the essence of Ukrainian's mentality can be conveyed in a single word: *khutoryanstvo*. This word is derived from the word *khutor*, meaning a detached peasant farm-holding, a tiny little village located to one side of all the others, something akin to a ranch.

The owner of a *khutor* is more concerned about the state of his own affairs than the events taking place in the wider world. His core values are family values, the values of home and hearth. The wellbeing and good fortune of his own home is the *raison d'être* of the Ukrainian[51].

It should not be supposed that Ukrainians are individualistic and egotistical beyond all measure. History dictated that for the Ukrainian peasant, who was living peacefully and working in the countryside, public life was of great significance. The agricultural communes, which in this country were known as *gromadas*, had a huge impact and were an expression of collective strength.

---

[51] I can cite what was said by Lyubomir Guzar, the former Primate of the Ukrainian Greek-Catholic Church, someone whose wisdom is beyond doubt, who said that 'khutorism' was the reason why Ukrainians were unable to stand up for their freedom in situations when history has given them the chance to do so:
"I have heard from various people, on many occasions, that we, the Ukrainian people, are massive individualists. Once you've got your khutor, your family and your garden - and frankly, what more do you need, if you want to live without thinking about the outside world or the people beyond the fence? The land is so fertile that any farmer worth his salt will be able to construct something akin to his own little world. This created the unfounded illusion that we had freedom for all, and therefore didn't feel the need to fight for freedom for all.
As the historians put it: "Ukrainians worked the land first and foremost, and therefore the habit of working together is something that is a fairly inherent part of their character."
Ukrainians can be united for a while by a noble idea, a fine objective or a great struggle. For such things, many are prepared to give their last ounce of strength, go to prison, jeopardise their health or lay down their lives. Yet things that are less important, but ostensibly more prosaic and troublesome, aren't capable of arousing such passions, such blood, sweat and tears, such eagerness to sacrifice oneself in some way. We are capable of fighting for a clearly delineated heroic objective, but it is not in our nature to undertake comprehensive, everyday work in a collaborative way."

As an old Ukrainian proverb from the era of serfdom goes: "If the Gromada's made its decision, not even the Lord can intervene." Through its authorized representatives the *gromada* would resolve issues related to land ownership and breaches of the rules made by members of the commune, monitored the state of the peasant farm holdings and the use of public forests and pastures, kept an eye on how the *korchmas* (pubs) and fairs were being run, and monitored the state of roads, bridges and public buildings. Not a single event of any degree of significance took place in the village without it being involved somehow.

An extremely important function of the *gromada* was to organize collective mutual assistance for farm labourers when they were engaged in particularly demanding physical labour: the so-called *toloka*. If the need arose, all the farm labourers took part together in the work in the fields, the harvesting of crops, construction of housing and administrative buildings and so on. Collective work such as this was usually done in a mock competitive way, and was accompanied by much singing and joke-telling. The commune thought of this assistance in the fields as a matter of honour for every member. The agricultural *gromada* was more than just a body responsible for local governance; it was thanks to its efforts that folk customs and traditions were preserved and passed on from one generation to the next.

But what sort of young man envisages his future shut up inside a peasant courtyard, engaged in monotonous work, mostly for the good of his master, and in the local *korchma*? The dream, the ideal to aspire to, and the example to follow for peasant children and young people were of course those free men, who were warlike and successful – you've guessed it, the Cossacks.

And sure enough the Ukrainians, preferring freedom over a boring, mollycoddled life under their master, would become Cossacks, and set off for the South-West, to the wilds and the distant steppes, and build *khutors* there. They worked hard all their lives and were constantly involved in battles against the nomads, who had colonized these same Wild steppes from the South-Western side. Once or twice a year the Cossacks, led by a general elected for a temporary period, gathered to launch an attack on the opposite banks, where there task was not only to win but also, first and foremost, to survive and return home with their prey. One can see why, in conditions such as these, a *khutor* which you had built yourself and which you could defend in person became the centre of your worldview and your *raison d'être*.

To adopt a *khutorite* mentality is to fence yourself off from your surroundings, and this causes a certain social passiveness on the part of the bulk of the Ukrainian population. We do not easily get provoked into a nonsensical and destructive uprising, and we do not easily get carried away by the fantasies of political adventurists. Yet at the same time it is fairly hard to unite us. There will always be dissidents who have their own particular opinion and will never accept the opinion of the majority. One sometimes gets a strong sense that what the average Ukrainian longs for more than anything else in the world is to be left alone at last. He doesn't want to interfere, doesn't want to take part in any mass protests[52].

We are happy to curse the authorities whilst sitting around the kitchen table, but when we come into contact with the agencies of power, we strive to adapt, come to an agreement with them, or even pay them off if need be. And as far as the agencies of power are concerned, we find ourselves coming up against Ukrainians exactly like ourselves, so we are generally able to reach a compromise.

The inherent character traits of Ukrainians are caution, a peaceful nature, optimism, suspicion of all that's new, a distrustful nature and a certain social fatalism.

For all that, we cannot help but say a few words about Ukrainians' sense of humour. In the main, the jokes we tell are well-intentioned. We tend to poke fun at ourselves more than anything else, for being greedy and for our habit of drinking too much strong alcohol. We like to tell jokes about our determination to demonstrate the leading role played by Ukrainians in any world event you'd care to mention[53].

We are a little more acerbic when making fun of our government and our politicians, and jokes about them abound.

And however angry a president, minister or mayor might feel deep down inside, none of them have any choice but to accept that they are going to be criticized, mocked and parodied, not just on the Internet, with the freedom it provides, but also from the stages of the big concert venues and on the public's televisions. What's more, some of the political figures are man enough to sit

---

52   Any government which seeks to rely too much on Ukrainians' passive nature and detachment from politics would be risking a great deal, however. If the Ukrainian people's patience is tested too much, it could spark the all-engulfing fire of civil war, the emergence of a powerful, irreconcilable opposition movement, and the kind of civil unrest seen during the so-called 'Maidan' protests in recent times. In 2004, a 'Maidan' like this – i.e. a continuous protest lasting several days on the city's main square ('maidan' is the Ukrainian word for 'square') in the Ukrainian capital, Kiev, led to the annulment of the election results, which had been falsified to help one of the candidates, and to a re-run of the election. In 2013, another 'maidan' began due to the Ukrainian people's desire to see their country become part of Europe, whereas those ruling the country were trying – for the umpteenth time in our history – to throw Ukraine into Moscow's embrace, for the sake of egotistical business interests.

53   Let me try a little joke on this subject myself. You may recall that nomadic Sarmates wandered the territory of Ukraine immediately prior to the Slavic tribes arrived? Some modern-day British historians have suggested that a heavily armed unit of Sarmat cavalrymen, and their leader, who had served the Roman Empire and helped defend Armorica (as Britanny was known at the time), were the model on which the legend of King Arthur and his knights was based. Can you see how easy it would be to make the leap towards suggesting that King Arthur was Ukrainian?

OLEKSANDR SHYSHKO

among the audience at comedy shows and look on as a couple of thousand people laugh at how they are being portrayed on stage.

My thoughts on the character of the typical Ukrainian are fairly abstract in nature, of course. It is the same sort of thing as saying that all Englishmen are gentlemen, or all Italians would make good opera singers.

RELATIONS BETWEEN THE SEXES

I sincerely hope that feminism, in its European form, does not take hold in Ukraine. It is more likely that 'benevolent sexism', as feminists themselves define this phenomenon, will reign supreme here.

The definition they give for it is as follows: benevolent sexism "characterizes women as pure, fragile beings, who need to be taken care of, protected and admired, and whose love is essential to every man, in order for him to remain a man. The automatic assumption behind such idealization of women is that women are weak, and that they are required to perform traditional female roles." An important role in the rhetoric of benevolent sexism is played by references to motherhood. For example, the idea that a woman, as a mother or potential mother, requires special protection, is used as the grounds for the list of professions which women are forbidden from having.

I will now try to explain why it is that in Ukraine, the enemies of feminism include not just men but also women. Of course, some people might assert that feminism is correct, and that it is about equal rights for women. Equal rights in relation to what, though?

In our country there is a list of professions and types of work which are deemed to be extremely onerous, dangerous or harmful to a person's health. Employing women to do these jobs is strictly forbidden. Below are a few examples of the professions and jobs in question.

They are jobs connected with lifting and moving heavy loads by hand, felling trees using chainsaws, stump extraction, the manual slaughter of cattle, skinning animals, work related to explosives, the kind of work done by steeplejacks, work related to repairing high-voltage electricity cables, manual crushing of carbides, manual labour involving molten metal, the production of phosgene, mercury and phosphorus, compounds containing arsenic, cleaning the inside of aircraft fuel tanks and so on and so forth.

If feminists are of the opinion that preventing women from being able to do these types of jobs represents a violation of their rights, let them go ahead and do them in Europe. Our women would never be seen doing these jobs, they have a high regard for themselves. And indeed we would never let them do these jobs, because they are dear to us as they are – healthy and beautiful. This probably amounts to sexism – but in Ukraine it's the way we like things to be.

In day-to-day life, benevolent sexism manifests itself in what we tend to refer to as gallantry or noble behaviour. Feminists criticize traditional forms of behaviour, such as the requirement that men must give up their seat to women on public transport, open doors for them, lend them their coat or pay for them when dining out at a restaurant. They point out that small marks of attention such as this do nothing to improve women's lot in any tangible way, nor give them more power or resources, but rather reduce women's ability to offer resistance: benevolent sexism "not only describes women in a benevolent way, but also offers them the promise that male power is only going to be applied in a way that benefits them, if they support men's powerful position in society."

I do not even wish to discuss these conclusions by the feminists, which to me have the air of being somewhat made up. Let's take for example the woman who is the Chairman of the Board of Directors at the company for which I work. Women can be found in such senior roles everywhere you look here in Ukraine, incidentally. I am a little lower down on the ladder. Yet if I did not open the door for her, or did not let her go ahead of me when the lift arrives, she would be taken aback. And what this unconscious act shows is by no means a subconscious bit of kow-towing to my boss (I don't open the door for my male boss), but rather a display of my respect for women, which is ingrained in my psyche.

I have read that in some countries, the merest hint of behaviour towards women which suggests they are anything over than a sexless being – a nice compliment, a playful tone, small signs of attention – could be interpreted as sexual harassment. I sincerely hope that such fear-mongering is the invention of sensationalist reporters. Our women, who are often in a position in which they order men around or earn large salaries, and who are sometimes better educated than their male counterparts – indeed they might be a hundred times more successful than men in a social sense, yet the fact remains that they want to be treated as women, in other words they want people to give them compliments and show our concern for them in small ways. Our women want to be attractive, and it's for that reason that they put on nice clothes even when popping outside for a stroll. Our women love wearing heels. They know it's not very good for their legs, but since it makes their legs look more beautiful it's something they want to do. Our women expect to hear compliments from a man, because these compliments provide evidence that their efforts to be attractive have not gone unnoticed, and they also enable them to feel good about themselves. When I compliment one of my female acquaintances on her complexion or on a dress that suits her particularly well, no-one ever sees any hints of sexual harassment in what I say.

Men who refuse to give up their seat on public transport to a woman are seen as unsophisticated barbarians. This is particularly true of cases involving elderly women or women who are pregnant. Incidentally, the same expectation exists with respect to elderly men, or men with disabilities. It is customary for people to give up seats to mothers with small children, so that the kids have somewhere to sit.

In the summer months, when herds of girls in mini-skirts and barely-there tops appear on the streets, we men do not react to this as if it were an invitation to enter into intimate relations. Our country is a far cry from Saudi Arabia. If you're feeling lonely enough to want to go up to a girl in the street and get to know her, why not go up and tell her as much. She might just take a liking to you, and begin to get to know you. On the other hand she might tell you where to go, and turn the air blue in doing so.

I should point out that in previous decades there was no real need to emancipate women in our country. One of the principles of the Soviet way of life was that women should be involved in production for the common good. There were whole industry sectors in which women were the core component of the workforce: clothing and textiles, sweet factories and so on.

The number of women working in agriculture, as a percentage of the total workforce, was exceptionally high. At most schools, the vast majority of the teachers were women. There were quite a large number of female managers at the low and middle levels. The Communist party closely monitored the elected representative bodies to make sure that the quota of female members was met.

Many administrative managers rightly feel that in many cases women are preferable to men: they are more disciplined, take fewer smoking breaks, and definitely consume less alcohol, particularly during working hours[54]. Women do not allow themselves such breaches of discipline, even though men consider them to be standard practice, and this makes female members of staff even more valuable in the eyes of the management. Moreover, women are prepared to accept jobs with lower salaries, which men would never agree to. I can picture the feminists recoiling with horror after reading this sentence. But let's deal with this issue now, calmly and straightforwardly.

---

54   The consumption of spirits during working hours, which, it goes without saying, is officially prohibited, is something to which our society turns a blind eye all too often. Among the exceptions to this are professional chauffeurs, operators of nuclear power plants and similar institutions, for whom the slightest mistake could result in a catastrophe. Rest assured that people in these jobs never drink alcohol at work.

OLEKSANDR SHYSHKO

Everyone ought to receive equal pay for the same job. But are we to demand that women do an equal amount of work to men? Are we going to send women off to meld steel, drive tractors, put out fires or handle machine-guns?

I remember the days, under the Soviet regime, when the so-called 'women in orange jackets' used to work on the roads. These were road repair workers who used to work on the roads holding crowbars and huge shovels in their hands, struggling to breathe amid the toxic fumes of hot tarmac. What a wonderful example of equal rights that was, don't you think? That form of equal rights had its roots in the Second World War, when men went off to the front line and died there not in their thousands, or even tens of thousands – but in their millions. And it was women that took their places – in manufacturing, at the machine tools, in front of the blast furnaces – by women. For many years after the war, the colossal disparity between the number of men and the number of women meant that the latter had no choice but to take part in hard physical labour. But if we have the chance to rectify that today, then it is an opportunity we ought to take.

FINANCIAL RELATIONS IN THE FAMILY

According to an unwritten rule, tradition in Ukraine dictates that the man of the house is obliged to be capable of earning more money than the woman. There are exceptions to this rule of course, but they do not alter this principle. It is the man's duty to support his family. How can we expect women to have children, if we are to impose on them the burden of having to provide for the family? And once a child has been born, women are given up to three years' maternity leave under our laws, and do not lose their position at the company where they work. And this is a good thing: the children will grow up healthier, better cared for, better educated. Incidentally, men are also entitled to take paternity leave should this prove necessary or in the child's best interests. In such cases, the woman continues to work and the husband's company reserve a place for him until the child reaches the age of three.

In most cases, however, it is the woman who brings up the kids, and the man is required to make an effort to provide the kind of lifestyle that lives up to the couple's mutual expectations. The obligation on the man to make every possible effort to provide for his family, in Ukrainian society, is one that cannot be shirked. I know of some families in which the wife turns a blind eye to her husband's affairs, but I don't know of a single family in which the wife forgives her husband for failing to bring home the bacon. Our society looks on the failure by a man to fulfil his side of the 'social gender contract' as a serious crime, which may result in the most barbaric of punishments.

I would not want to probe deep into issues of domestic violence in Ukraine. Cases of such violence do occur in our society, although they are not common. Public opinion will always be on the side of the woman, so it is entirely up to the woman as to how she reacts to her husband's violence. There are some smart-alecks who will always try to justify such relations with the old saying: "If he beats you – it means he loves you!" The theory is that if the husband's feelings for the woman were not strong, and if he were not jealous of all other men on the planet, then he wouldn't hit her. You don't need a degree in psychology to work out that a man who hits his own beloved wife is not quite right in the head.

To tell the truth, some women are no less aggressive than their spouses. In these cases, interestingly, public opinion will once again be on the side of the woman. I can quite easily picture how events might unfold in a working-class family, not overly concerned about its reputation in the outside world, if the man of the house were to come home drunk and without the money he was supposed to bring home to his wife. Our Ukrainian woman, enraged by her spouse's behaviour, would try to teach him the error of his ways, and not just verbally but also with the help of physical means of altering his behaviour, such as using a rolling-pin for example: this has roughly the same effect as a baseball bat. What would the neighbours' reaction be, in such circumstances? I have no doubt that they would think ill of the husband and be understanding in respect of the actions of the wife.

So if you're planning to take a Ukrainian woman as a wife, be prepared to fulfil your side of the social gender agreement. If you want your wife to cook tasty dinners for you, look after your offspring, keep the house clean and tidy, greet you and your friends with a smile, let you go out on the town with your mates without the slightest hesitation, and so on and so forth – be nice and 'pay the bills'.

Who is the 'head of the household' in Ukrainian families, then? The days when the man was required to put on a coat of armour, take hold of his sabre and charge off to do battle with the infidels, whilst his loyal wife stayed at home wiping away her tears and waiting for her husband to come home safe and sound – and, better yet, bearing the spoils of victory – are long gone. The development of civilization and the achievements of technological progress have led to a situation in which male muscle-power could not be less significant for the wellbeing of the family. The head of the family nowadays is whichever of the spouses has the last word when it comes to drawing up the family's financial and economic strategy. I'm being tongue-in-cheek when I express it in such grandiloquent terms, of course. To put it more simply, the head of the family is the one in charge of the family's money[55]. In Ukraine it has traditionally been the woman that has disposed of the family's income[56]. If this were not the case, then the male custom of withholding part of his

---

55 I don't know how things work in billionaires' families, in this regard. I suspect that the same rule applies, though. As the old joke goes: "Can a woman make a man a billionaire?" "Yes – if he already was a billionaire when he met her."

56 I was once chatting to a Turkish manager, who was a director at a major retail firm. In my naivety I began to talk about how in the East, and in Turkey in particular, women have a lower, unequal status to men. In response to this he asked me: "Who do you give your salary to?" I replied: "To my wife!" "I give mine to my wife too," my Turkish friend replied. "So who's really the head of the family?"

income from his wife (known as 'stashing it away') for his own personal use – to go for a drink at the local bar with his friends, for example – would not have arisen. Incidentally, if the woman should happen to find this 'secret stash' whilst dusting the apartment, she's entitled to consider it her own, and her husband can do nothing but curse his luck.

There are, of course, families that are not like this, in which the familial relations are different. In some families the husband and the wife each dispose of their money independently, and come to an agreement on how to finance joint ventures. But what I'm talking about is the people's mentality, about what's hidden away, so to speak, in people's subconscious.

It is far from unusual for Ukrainian women to marry foreigners. They get married not only to Europeans, but also to Asians, Africans and Arabs. I have observed some very successful marriages indeed, in which the husband and the wife are respectful towards one another.

I once knew a Chinaman who married a Ukrainian woman, and who was forever complaining to me: "How awful these Ukrainian wives are! With a Chinese wife, whatever her husband does, she's fine about it. With a Ukrainian wife, whatever her husband does, she's not happy!" He had clearly ended up with a powerful spouse, who controlled the family with a firm grip. Yet they have lived together for many years in Kiev, have had children, and are happy here.

I am well acquainted with a mixed family in which the husband is a Frenchman and the wife is Ukrainian. The man's first wife did not want to have children with him (there's a real victim of feminism for you). The young man really wanted kids. He got married to a nice Ukrainian girl, and she has now given birth to two charming little children and cherishes them like a true Ukrainian mother. But her husband doesn't get a moment's rest now, and complies strictly with the social contract. He is thought of as the 'head' of the family. And yet his wife could be seen as the family's 'neck': whichever way she turns, that's the direction the head will be facing.

PROSTITUTION

We are aware of the fact that in the West, Ukrainian girls are seen as loose women. This view is not without a basis in fact, since many of our women offer sex services in other countries. But prostitution has existed since the dawn of time. It has been interpreted in different ways by different cultures. In our country, prior to the coup in 1917 prostitution was a legalized form of commercial activity; under the Communist regime prostitution was officially punished strictly, and its organized forms disappeared, although the provision of sexual favours for money has always existed.

One particular contingent in this industry was the so-called 'hard-currency prostitutes' – the women who sold their charms to foreigners for currency that they could convert. As anyone who has lived in the Soviet Union will be able to imagine, for the law enforcement agencies, getting rid of 'currency' prostitution was something that could have been got rid of in a day. Were it not for one small proviso. Nobody intended to get rid of it, because *every single* hard-currency prostitute was an informer for the intelligence services. Cooperation with the intelligence services gave these girls a free pass for the crimes they were committing by being prostitutes, and enabled them to keep their earnings in foreign currency. This played a cruel joke on Soviet morality. Hard-currency prostitutes enjoyed a far better quality of life than honest workers from the plants and factories.

There's a good topic for discussion as regards emancipation and feminism: one set of women, who enjoyed equal rights with men, were working their hands to the bone in manufacturing industries. Others, meanwhile, "humiliated and sexually exploited", were spending their days at restaurants and resorts, wearing the latest fashions and buying things that ordinary Soviet female workers could only dream about.

When an anonymous survey was conducted in the late 1980s among Soviet schoolgirls, therefore, hard-currency prostitution was seen by many of them as one of the most prestigious professions of all.

Prostitution exists in Ukraine today, too, despite being officially prohibited.

Conditions for prostitutes are less comfortable here than in the West, however. Here, it is a business controlled by criminal gangs. In the West it is safer, and the clients tend to come from a better background. That's why they come to your countries to make a living. Men travel to other countries from Ukraine too, of course, though not to brothels, of course, but to work at construction sites or collect the tomato harvest. Regrettably, talented IT experts, doctors, young academics and other workers of value to the country are also leaving the country. And they too are doing so in order to earn more money.

There are prostitutes all over the world, and there always have been. And yet I would advise against making sweeping generalizations about the rest of the country based on the impressions you've picked up of Ukrainian prostitutes.

UKRAINIAN MAIL-ORDER BRIDES

Every Cinderalla dreams of finding her Prince Charming, and this has prompted young women to be increasingly active in their attempts to find their other half with the help of the latest innovations in IT. Other factors which have prompted this have been the economic disorder in the country and the high level of unemployment in the country (it is a good deal higher than the official statistics would suggest). Men are becoming incapable of performing their side of the 'social contract' to which I referred earlier.

At a certain point, there came a time when it seemed to many Ukrainians that the future did not promise anything good. I would even go so far as to say that we somehow lost sight of our *raison d'être*, which in the past was provided by the Communist ideology. That particular *raison d'être* was an ephemeral one, such as 'building a bright future', yet social morality was built upon our efforts to achieve it: people were supposed to work hard for the good of society; there is work for all, as long as people were not too lazy to do it; those who refuse to work are feeding off the work of society like parasites and are society's enemy; drunkenness is a form of behaviour that is to be roundly condemned; infidelity in the family is a serious social crime; addiction to drugs is not a disease but a crime, and so on. The brief introduction to the rules of social morality, which was called 'The moral code of the constructor of communism', outlined the moral principles – for mankind in general as well as ideological ones – which are very similar to the ideas contained in the Sermon on the Mount.

Today there is nothing remotely like this. The principle of 'every man for himself' is being implemented in full measure. All the mass media seem to do is publish reports about the criminal past of an oligarch, or a member of parliament. The new *raison d'être* is to get rich at any price. Success is measured by what car you have, how big your house is, and whether or not you can afford to holiday in the Maldives. The code of behaviour and social morality have become very far removed from Communism and from the Bible. The country's President, when inviting foreign visitors to come and watch football's European Championships in this country, delivered the line: "Come and see how Ukrainian girls like to bare some flesh in the summer."

Against this backdrop, what are nice young girls from small towns to do? Some of them choose to sell what nature has bestowed on them. Photos of these girls abound not only on the chat forums but also on the news websites. Wedding agencies have sprung up like mushrooms after the rain has fallen, promising to find these girls a wealthy foreign husband.

The foreigners themselves are convinced that the girls who sign up to wedding agencies' websites are readily accessible and willing to sell themselves, too. These leggy beauties with heaving chests – beautiful, but poor – are willing to sell themselves to the first person they meet for a bowl of *borshcht*. In exchange for a meal out at a restaurant they'll marry you. And they'll be faithful wives – for in Ukraine the household is still run as in days of yore and the man is the God of the family: a far cry from the situation in the countries where feminism has won the day[57]. Tens of thousands of men from Europe and America come flocking to Ukraine, like so many moths to a flame.

We are also aware that some of these men genuinely long to find their life partner and better half here, but that more often they simply come here to have a bit of fun…

This is how you see all this as you observe Ukraine from the outside. But I would now like to tell you about how all this actually looks from the inside. The so-called 'Ukrainian wedding business' is a serious and dangerous animal. It is a business, indeed an incredibly profitable, popular and high-risk one at that. And if you tried to tell me that it's not controlled by organized criminal gangs, I would drop down dead with surprise.

Puppet brides and experienced matchmakers from wedding agencies fleece foreign 'princes' at will, as was demonstrated recently by the case of an American named Dolego, which caused quite a scandal. He came here to get married to a Ukrainian, lost all his money and was left to live among the paupers at Chernivtsi station…What's more he didn't come here with a view to marrying just one Ukrainian girl, but several – and yet it only took one of them for him to lose all his money.

On the free 'chat' sites there are unscrupulous fraudsters hiding behind the images of beautiful girls, or else automated computer programmes which trick visitors out of their money.

---

57 I have already written about the social gender contract and the rolling pin and about who is the head of the household. You don't have to believe me, but this contract, and the rolling pin, and the issue of who's in charge at home – these are in Ukrainian women's DNA, whatever you might hear from other people.

Meanwhile the 'professional brides' know how to be extremely convincing. The men involved are willing to break away from their lives and go straight off to meet up with them. How disappointed they are when, on meeting them, all they get from their impassioned beauty is a smile, and a few complaints about the harsh life she has endured. They use every trick in the book: you'll hear tales about a sick mother, who needs some cash for an operation, or about how the TV caught fire at home, or a pair of winter boots have been worn through.

One such 'professional bride', with the typically Ukrainian first name of Oksana, said to reporters in an interview: "People buy phones for me, and holidays and clothes. And we don't have intimate relations at all! After all, I'm an "honourable girl in search of the lover fate has chosen for me." But the conversation never gets as far as serious relations. And that's not because I'm so grasping, but because their expectations are so high. They're some of the baldest, fattest, greediest men around, yet they expect a model to come and throw herself around their necks."

A short while ago the British press whipped up quite a storm about the wedding industry in Russia and Ukraine, which delivers mail-order brides to British and American men who have been unlucky in love in their native land. As the Daily Mail reported, special romantic city breaks have been created for such customers – a form of 'wedding safari', the whole point of which is for the visitor to be able to meet as many women as possible. The market for acquaintances is unashamedly referred to as a 'cattle market'. Yet these lonely gents make no bones about it, and are willing to pay between £1500 and £3000 ($2300 - $7600) for a tour like this.

The key thing here is the sum of money involved. Can you sense that 'serious and dangerous animal' pricking up its ears and twitching its nose? The organizers promise foreigners that they are going to be in the company of "unsullied young beauties who believe in family values" practically all the time. The men receive fervent assurances that "in the space of 11 days they will meet more beautiful women than they would otherwise meet in five years." They have genuinely been given a passport to paradise – after all, there are generally ten times more women than men taking part in such meetings, and they tend to be half their age or younger.

Usually, during the course of such events there will be 15-25 clients meeting around 150-250 women, many of whom don't speak English, so they interact with one another with the help of interpreters. To make the task easier, each participant is given a name-badge to wear, or indeed a number – something that critics of the practice say is reminiscent of the slave trade. In the course of a day, a man will meet an average of five different women.

Anonymous surveys of the people who buy tours like this – and indeed of the employees of foreign social services – have found that in Ukrainian and Russian women, these men are seeking "traditional wives, brought up strictly and prepared to look after their husband like a mother; educated housewives who are devoted to their home and children." "What's wrong with that?" the men say, contrasting this type of woman with women from their native land, to whom Western civilization has given the gift of equal rights and independence. "'Soviet' brides have not been infected with all this feminine nonsense," the foreigners reflect, in a reverie.

Incidentally, in spite of the high expectations in the spirit of the patriarchate, these elderly, balding grooms insist on their woman of choice being 'sexy'.

On the Internet forums the discussion is heated. Many people express extreme disapproval, often in vulgar or uncensored terms, along the lines of: "How can they sell themselves to these fat old monsters? The mere thought that they'll have to sleep with them makes me want to puke!" Others defend the brides, saying that they're prepared to accept any terms as long as it means they can get away from their alcoholic husbands and poor quality of life. All I want to do is focus on one thing. If we go ahead and compare the 'bridal market' to a 'cattle market', then I can clearly see that there are some cows fit for being 'milked' at this market, who are caught up in the sweet illusion that they've found a wonderful bit of entertainment. It's similar to the way a young girl, when milking a cow on a farm, will start by caressing its udders affectionately. It helps the milk come out more easily. It's worth having a good think about which of the parties involved can ultimately be described as the 'cattle'.

I have to say that for a foreigner, marrying a Ukrainian woman can only be a good thing. But remember that male domination and 'patriarchal' relations have long since disappeared from our society. I would describe what we have now as the 'social gender contract'.

I like to express the idea behind this agreement light-heartedly as follows: "Men rule the world, and women rule men."

So if you come to Ukraine looking for prostitutes, don't worry – you'll find some. If you want to 'buy' yourself a slave – mind you don't end up naked and with nothing on your feet yourself, that's my warning.

But if you get lucky and a Ukrainian girl falls in love with you, all your friends will envy you. Be worthy of your chosen one – and in return she'll give you devotion, beautiful and clever children, and a long and happy life together. She too, after all, has the *khutorite* mentality, i.e. an understanding of the fact that nothing is more valuable than the family. Isn't that what you wanted?

A TOUCH OF THE EXOTIC: AGE-OLD TRADITIONS AND CUSTOMS

I feel compelled to give my narrative about Ukraine some sort of ethnographic and folkloric hue. For example, I'd like to tell you about some of the customs and traditions which have existed for centuries – some of which live on to this day. It is traditions and customs such as these that make each people unique and exotic to the outside world.

In former times, rites and ceremonies served as an unwritten way of organizing the lives of those who lived off the land. Special types of food, household and familial magic, the paying of respects to our forefathers, fortune-telling and divination – these extremely important events were accompanied by these actions both on working days and public holidays. As one would expect, it was all connected with the cyclical calendar governing agricultural work. The start of the ploughing and the sowing, driving the cattle out to pasture, and finishing the harvest: these things were all accompanied by special rites. In family life, rites accompanied every stage of human life: birth, weddings, and funerals. The performance of the rites was supposed to ensure prosperity and happiness in the home, provide a good harvest and fertile cattle, and ward off all sorts of evil. I have no doubt, though, that there are similar traditions among all the peoples of the earth, isn't that the case?

I shall describe some of the rites and ceremonies in Ukraine; it may be interesting to see to what extent they differ or are similar to the equivalent traditions in your country.

I am not going to talk about the really ancient traditions; after all, this is not an archaeological dig. It makes sense to talk about the customs and ceremonies which can still be observed to this day in some shape or form.

Let's take the ceremonies seen in the run-up to the celebration marking the Birth of Christ, for example. In this country, the preparations for the celebratory dinner have been transformed into a real ritual. As Ukrainians see things, all the objects which are related in some way to the ceremonial dinner table have assumed miraculous strength. For that reason, in order to make sure that the coming harvest is abundant, the home-owner would place 'didukha' – a ritual sheaf of rye or wheat, decorated with dried flowers from the fields – under the icons, in pride of place. On Holy evening (Christmas Eve) a set number of dishes would be prepared: 7, 9 or 12. A compulsory feature of Christmas celebrations was caroling, when groups of young people would walk around the yards of their home village singing special Christmas songs and wishing health and plenty to all the members of the family. A separate song of good cheer was sung for each member of the family. If there was a little child in the family who had taken a long time to say his first word, the child was given some water to drink from a small ceremonial bell. Girls, meanwhile, were supposed to give gifts of apples and nuts to each person for whom a song was sung.

In the big cities, of course, these ceremonies were not always observed, but in the villages people engaged in them a great deal.

New Year's Eve was considered the most suitable day for caroling and for making the most secret and intimate of wishes, and it was usually the young people who did this. This was a pagan ritual, of course, rather than a Christian one. But Halloween isn't a Christian festival either, of course, and yet half the world has fun carving eyes and a nose into a pumpkin.

On Epiphany, all the members of the family were sprinkled with holy water, as was the house, the yard, the well and all the domestic animals. It was believed that the holy water used on Epiphany had miraculous powers.

At the start of spring (late February to early March) the festival of Maslenitsa was celebrated – the arrival of spring. Throughout the week people made *blini* and *vareniky*, drank vodka and paid visits on one another. Young men and women who had not got married in the autumn (the most popular time for weddings for tillers of the land) were supposed to drag a block of wood or log along to Maslenitsa, and if they wanted to get out of doing so they were forced to pay a forfeit. This would of course lead to a great deal of laughing and joking. These days, of course, no-one is punished for not wanting to tie the knot – not even in jest. We live in a different age.

Maslenitsa is a celebration before *Veliky post* (Lent). We are a people that loves celebrating, and it makes no difference who among us is going to go on to observe Lent later in the year, and who among us does not intend to: at Maslenitsa, everyone eats, drinks and makes merry. In exactly the same way, at the end of Lent everyone starts celebrating, although, if I were to look at the one hundred people closest to me – my family, my close friends, my acquaintances and colleagues at work, and so on – then there would probably only be one of them who observed Lent. Yet we all, to a man and woman, celebrate the end of Lent.

At Easter people used to bake and sanctify *kulichi* (Easter cakes), paint and decorate *pisanki*[58], cook stuffing for smoked sausage and make other dishes. On public festivals, processions would be held in the main square, next to the church, which would go on for three days. On these days, everyone was allowed to ring the church bells. On the first Sunday after Easter people paid their respects to the dead, and went to the cemetery to visit the graves of their forefathers. This custom survives today and is observed by almost all Ukrainians. At Easter, both the Christians and the atheists celebrate, and in the same way (regardless of whether or not they are actually members of a religious community of some shape or form) everyone goes to church to 'sanctify' Easter cakes, decorated boiled eggs and home-made smoked sausage (all of which is very tasty, especially the smoked sausage).

The 'Green festivals' (the Trinity) celebrated the end of spring and the start of the summertime. On these days houses and administrative buildings were always decorated with green boughs. The Trinity falls on the fiftieth day after Easter, so people who don't enjoy observing Christian customs sometimes find it hard to follow the dates of movable church festivals. But as soon as you see women holding sheaves of sedge, which is used to decorate homes, on public transport, in the streets or at the markets, you know that the festival of Trinity has arrived.

On 24th June the festival of Ivan Kupala is celebrated. It is a pagan festival, of course, and it is an extremely old one, which marked the summer solstice. The Christian church has sensibly stopped trying to fight it, and instead tied it to the birthday of John the Baptist. The ceremonies, admittedly, are the same as they always were, pagan: jumping over fires, fortune-telling using wreaths and night-time bathing in open bodies of water. It was believed that jumping over fires purified people of their sins, and that wreaths of flowers thrown into the river were able to predict women's fate: how soon they would get married and whether or not their marriage would be a success. The young people in Ukraine still love to go out on the town to mark this festival even today. I think there are a lot of people who celebrate it: in Finland it is the festival of Juhannus, in Germany it is Midsommerfest and in Latvia it is known as Ligo.

As well as these ceremonies, the Ukrainians loved to use all manner of talisman: herbs and flowers, trees and shrubs, birds and natural essences and

---

58   A *pisanka* is a boiled egg, the shell of which has been decorated with a natural colouring, such as onion peel (this makes the egg turn bright-brown in colour). As time passed, however, people began painting patterns on the eggs, and Ukrainian experts have attained incredible levels of mastery in this regard. There are a lot of examples of *pisanki* that are housed in museums. Faberge eggs, when it comes down to it, are nothing more than the *pisanka* tradition taken to an absurd level (or to a fine art – depending on your point of view).

so on. As far as trees are concerned, Ukrainians have always had a particular regard for the willow-tree. They believed that a sanctified willow had magic powers, and therefore, in order to stop hail, for example, they used to throw willow twigs into the yard. In spring, they would use a rod made of willow branches to drive the cattle out to pasture, so that the animals didn't pick up a disease. Ukrainians believed that a willow filled with spring sap would give a person health and vigour.

In the spring, when the buds start appearing on the willow's branches – grey, fluffy balls – many Ukrainians even today take willow twigs home and put them in a vase with some water, so that these grey lumps first of all start to get fluffed up, then push out a little areola, and then some sticky green leaves appear from underneath them. Whilst this is happening, winter might well still be lingering on outside, with its snow and freezing temperatures. Meanwhile there is a vase on the table, and inside it there the buds are, proof of the irresistible approach of spring.

The symbol of girls' beauty, love and loyalty is the viburnum. The viburnum shrub was used as a lucky charm, i.e. constantly providing protection against 'impure forces'. For this purpose, the viburnum was planted next to the home, necklaces were made out of its berries, and its stems were used to decorate the trains of wedding dresses and the bridal wreath. The viburnum has generally come to symbolize Ukraine, in the same way that the maple leaf is the symbol of Canada, the lily is the symbol of France and the lotus plant is the symbol of Egypt. In all the designs for a 'Great coat of arms for Ukraine' (which, it must be said, has still not been finalized), you will always see a viburnum stem. And the anthem of the Ukrainian Rebel Army was also known as the 'Red viburnum'.

A special role in Ukrainian customs and traditions was played by the *rushnik*. The *rushnik* is a beautifully embroidered flaxen towel, which has a symbolic meaning. A *rushnik* with the relevant patterns and symbols sewn onto it was an essential prop in numerous ceremonies: the bride and groom would stand on a *rushnik* at weddings[59], and people would bring a *rushnik* to a woman giving birth, to wrap the new-born babe in it, or take it with them when meeting and accompanying guests whom they held dear; it would also be tied around the shoulder of *svati* (matchmakers), who were entrusted with going into the bride's house with the groom's wedding proposal (this tradition is still seen fairly frequently today).

---

59   This custom is alive and kicking today. It is believed that whichever of the bride and groom steps onto the *rushnik* first will be the head of the family. It can be a lot of fun to watch the bride and groom hurrying to get the toe of their shoe onto the *rushnik* in order to get the right to be head of the family.

Rushniki were also used to decorate icons. On many occasions I have seen *rushniki* being used to decorate a portrait of Taras Shevchenko, like an icon – such is the esteem in which he is held by Ukrainians.

Rushniki were also used to lower coffins into the ground.

Depending on their intended purpose, *rushniki* differed as regards the way they were manufactured and the way they were sewn. Different regions had their own characteristic colours and *rushnik* ornaments.

EMBROIDERY

Ukrainians love to decorate the world around them. When a Ukrainian built a house, its walls would as a rule be covered with white chalk, and then patterns, flowers and sometimes whole pictures would be drawn on the walls. This tradition of decorating the walls is alive and well today. Whenever I drive through a Ukrainian village, I'm amazed by the diversity of subjects depicted on the white walls of the buildings: you can see leaves, flowers, birds and patterns.

Decorating clothes has become something of a cult activity. The embroidery sewn onto the collar and sleeves of white shirts has reached virtuosic levels. Men's and ladies' shirts are all decorated with embroidery, as are garments worn on the upper body and headgear. The designs for ornaments, compositions and flower arrangements were passed down from one generation to the next, becoming traditions over time. Only qualified experts are able to explain the embroidery techniques used.

Given the vast amount of manual labour which goes into making these clothes, garments like this are quite expensive. Embroidered clothing can be bought at affordable prices at the 'night' market in Kolomyia, in the Ivano-Frankivsk region[60]. There, you can not only find a hand-embroidered shirt, but the embroidered item will have been made out of a home-spun fabric. Its authenticity is guaranteed. When you put on one of these shirts you will feel as though you have been transported to the sixteenth century, at least. Among the items seen as the height of fashion are the embroidered clothes for couples, i.e. shirts for a man and a woman which are embroidered with the same pattern. There are also some extraordinarily beautiful hand-crafted items and works of art. I'm sure every nation has things like this, in which it takes great pride. We are proud of our embroidered clothes.

In the various regions of Ukraine one can find different types and styles of embroidery, as well as different colours and techniques. It can assuredly be

---

60   This is by no means a secret, underground market. It's just that it opens in the wee small hours (at 4 am), and when the time what most people would describe as the 'early morning' arrives, all the goods have sold out and the market is closing.

said that the embroidered shirt has become a symbol of ethnic identification in Ukraine. When you put on an embroidered shirt, you are saying to the world: "I'm a Ukrainian!"

The patterns used in embroidery are decorative but have a symbolic meaning: there is the 'tree of life', symbolizing the unconquerable creative force, the 'grape', a symbol of wealth and a happy marriage, the 'periwinkle', a symbol of love, and the 'cock', which symbolizes the awakening of nature and the transition from life to death. Young women embroidering shirts today may not necessarily be aware of their symbolic meaning – they will simply say that "this was how my mother taught me to do it". Generally speaking, however, today's expert embroiderers tend to combine folk patterns and traditional patterns to their taste, and often use motifs taken from historical paintings.

Generally speaking, Ukrainian national dress is an eye-catching and original cultural phenomenon, just like the national dress of any other people. The national dress worn by Ukrainian women has always been particularly picturesque and original. It consisted of an extra-long embroidered blouse with a colourful belt tied around the waist, and a *zapaska* or *plakhta* – a garment worn around the waist, consisting of two patches of woollen fabric, partially sewn with a check pattern. In addition, women also wore a corset, i.e. a sleeveless garment, made of thin woollen material, velvet or silk, and a waistcoat with embroidered decoration along the hem. On the left bank of Dnieper this garment would have a pale grey thread sewn into it, on the sleeves, the collar, and the chest area and along the bottom of the shirt, whilst on the right bank, red and black trim would be used. Ribbons and *monista*[61] were worn as accessories with this garment, in order to give them a festive flavour.

In the early 20th century, *zapaski* and *plakhty* were gradually replaced by factory-made skirts and dresses, but even these had different characteristics depending on the region in which they were made. Ukrainian women used to wear low-heeled boots, fastened with laces or buttons, and in winter they would wear leather shoes embellished with a decorative piece, which tended to be red.

A special aspect of Ukrainian national dress for women was the garment worn on the head. This would indicate the woman's marital status: unmarried women would wear a garland decorated with various objects – pendants made of bronze or silver, coins, ribbons or flowers – whilst married women would wear an *ochipok*[62]. It was forbidden for married women to be bareheaded, since

---

61   A *monisto* is a long necklace made of beads, gemstones or coins.

62   An *ochipok* is a sort of cap made of fabric, with part of the back section cut out. Women would wear it over hair tied into two plaits, and the split at the back would be drawn tight with a lace. Since our women have always loved to dress up, and we love dressing them up, even this basic headdress (over

it was thought that this could result in a bad harvest, the death of cattle or other disasters.

National dress for men was less eye-catching but still fairly charactersful. The traditional costume for men consisted of a long shirt, wide bloomers[63] or narrow trousers, sleeveless garments comparable to present-day waistcoats, and belts with long tassels hanging from them.

Ukrainian men would wear flat shoes which were usually black. In West Ukraine, *postols* were widely worn – this was a soft shoe made of a whole piece of leather, with no sole sewn into them. So-called *lapty* – shoes woven together using strips of bark – were seldom worn. This kind of shoe was popular among the Karelians, the Mordovians, the Tatars, the Finns and the Chuvash. In the Russian worldview they became one of the most important symbols of traditional national life.

In the summer, Ukrainians would typically wear *bryls* – a straw hat with a wide rim. These are still worn in the summer months today, even in the city. In Huzulschina and in the Caparthians, men would wear black felt hats (known as *kresans*), decorated with a patterned buckle or multi-coloured laces, behind which a feather would be inserted. Winter hats were generally made of sheepskin or of cloth with a fur trim. Men's winter hats were pyramid-shaped with a rounded top[64] and a fur trim, or else made of sheepskin, with a base made of cloth. By contrast with Russia, fur hats with ear-flaps were not worn in Ukraine and are not commonly worn in the country today. The ear-flaps on such *ushanki* hats can be lifted up when the weather gets warmer and tied together with a bow either on the crown of the head or at the back of the head. The reason I mention this is that some Swiss friends of mine once asked me to find them a "genuine fur hat with ear-flaps", which to their minds was a symbol of this country. Such hats are a wonderful thing – they keep you warm and cosy and protect you from the cold, but they are not Ukrainian. In the

---

which women would wear something else when they went outside, such as a shawl) was made not only out of white canvas but also out of silk, gold-cloth or velvet. Even the most simplistic canvas *ochipki* would have some worsted woollen yarn sewn into them. Each part of the country came to have its own particular type of *ochipok*, sometimes featuring a very intricate design.

63   Interestingly, the trousers which were a traditional part of men's national dress in Ukraine were always very wide. I can understand why the Cossacks were so fond of these trousers. The Cossacks even used to sew large pieces of fabric in the middle of their trousers, so that as they walked along the middle of their trousers would almost touch the ground. Nikolai Gogol, the famous Russian writer of Ukrainian descent, who wrote a great deal about his native land, used to say of these Cossack trousers that they were "as wide as the Black Sea". Yet in these trousers the Cossacks would feel comfortable in the saddle when riding a horse with a broad back. Take any historical painting showing peasants making hay somewhere in the Poltava region and you will find peasants dressed in broad, white canvas trousers, bulging out like bubbles.

64   An indentation would be made with the palm of the hand on the top of these hats, as in a Borsalino hat, to make it look more dashing.

olden days something akin to this, known as a *malakhai*, used to be worn in northern regions of Ukraine, in Chernigovshchina, on the border with Russia.

In winter, men and women alike would wear leather coats made of tanned of sheepskin 'kozhukh'. A popular outer garment was an ankle-length coat which came in a variety of forms, made of woollen fabrics and cloth, either with sleeves or sleeveless (like a cloak): these were known as *zhupany* (a word which clearly has Polish origins), *svitky* (a Slavic word derived from the ancient word for canvas), or *yepanchi* (the name of this overcoat evokes the spirit of the Arab lands in the east, although it is more likely that the word was borrowed from the Turks).

These days, of course, European fashions are the order of the day. If you walk around any of our cities you'll see the same brands that you would find throughout Europe, and of course clothes made in China, Pakistan, Thailand or Turkey – just as is the case in your countries, in those countries themselves, and everywhere else. This is one of the manifestations of globalization, integration and unification, and there is no escaping this fact. Of course, in winter you will see all manner of jackets and coats made of synthetic materials and with synthetic linings.

Yet I perceive some reflection of our national traditions as regards winter clothing in the widespread attraction some Ukrainians feel towards so-called *dublyonki*, i.e. coats or jackets made of tanned sheepskin with fur on the inside – a kind of civilized form of the 'kozhukh' of days of yore. A *dublyonka* made of natural materials costs quite a lot of money, but is a must-have item in the wardrobe of those who can afford it.

On public holidays, however, many Ukrainians choose to wear an embroidered Ukrainian shirt under an outfit which would otherwise be European, and as a rule this look works a treat. As I wrote above, embroidered shirts are made to look very beautiful indeed in Ukraine. Picture the scene: a family is strolling along the sidewalk on a summer's day – a mother and father and their little kids – all wearing embroidered shirts, each one beautiful and designed exactly to the wearer's liking, and you are walking towards them, also dressed in an embroidered shirt. All of you feel as though you are among friends, get a sense of the familial nature of the Ukrainian soul, and you all greet one another happily: there's no two ways about it, this feeling of belonging is very pleasant.

LET'S TALK ABOUT FOOD

In relation to food, internationalization, globalization and standardization have, in my view, affected us far less than in the fields of fashion, cars and bad habits.

In the run-up to the Euro 2012 football championships I saw an online guide for German football fans getting ready to attend matches taking place in Ukraine. A substantial part of the guide was about Ukrainian cuisine. I found the content of this section amusing, because it was clear that the authors had a fairly superficial understanding of Ukrainian cuisine and the culinary tastes and habits of Ukrainians.

The guide stated, for example, that "*vareniky* are dumplings with a variety of fillings," "that practically all the dishes are fatty and contain meat", and that "Ukrainians' favourite vegetable is the gherkin". The guide expressed surprise that we do not have a set menu for breakfast: "In Ukraine people are equally likely to have sausage sandwiches or cherry strudel for breakfast."

One comment which caught my eye was the assertion that "at street stalls you can buy kabobs or sunflower seeds in their shells." These recommendations appear somewhat strange to us, and it occurred to me that I could just as easily make a faux pas like that if I tried to talk about German cuisine and about German people's daily diet. When we visit another country, most of us see the 'touristy' side of that country's cuisine, the side of it which is to some extent 'ceremonial'. We go and eat in cafes and restaurants, and our generous hosts strive to treat us to something more off the beaten track and a bit more interesting – something which will live long in their guest's memory.

Yet the day-to-day eating habits of various peoples may also seem a worthy subject of discussion, given that the menus and cooking techniques used reflect many aspects of life in that particular society. Among these are, for example, how much time it is considered normal to spend on cooking meals, which products are the most popular (and, importantly, which ones are easily accessible to the bulk of the population), and which members of the family take on most of the responsibility for feeding the others.

I can confidently state that Ukrainians always have a preference for home-cooked food. This preference extends to cover the time they spend at work, whether that be on the farm or in an office. Taking a pre-cooked, home-made meal to work is a very widespread habit. It may be that this tradition is one that has come down to us from the days when children used to take out a lunch cooked by their mother to their father as he worked in the fields, or when wives would give their husbands a so-called *tormozok* to take with them down the mine – i.e. a selection of foodstuffs to have for lunch. However that may be, nobody bats an eyelid when company employees take a plastic tub containing a pre-cooked meal out of their briefcase during the lunch break and heat up the contents in the microwave, before sitting down to enjoy it in a kitchen-diner set aside for this purpose. And these tubs don't just contain some slices of bread and a bit of smoked sausage. As a rule they tend to contain fairly complex dishes: chops with mashed potato, salads, stewed vegetables and hot meat.

The cafes that one finds near office blocks tend to serve appetising soups and home-cooked meat, salads and fruit compotes, rather than sandwiches or burgers. If they were to serve sandwiches they would soon run out of customers. That is the culinary tradition in our country.

I'm not suggesting for a minute that we don't have MacDonald's and the like here – of course we do, they're inescapable. And the fast-food outlets get plenty of customers.[65] We do not have any prejudice against fast-food outlets. Similar local chains are emerging here in Ukraine, such as *Puzata khata* and *Dva gusya*[66], and we also have local sandwich bars and alternative fast-food outlets serving jacket potatoes with various fillings. All this is here – and there's an abundance of it. One can also find small kiosks here, where before your very eyes the meat will be cooked on a vertical grill and you'll be given a kabob, or offered a doner – a Middle Eastern dish made of meat, vegetables and spices, wrapped up in some Pitta bread. Some people buy food from these kiosks. Frankly speaking, I'm not one of them. I have absolutely no confidence whatsoever either in the quality of the food served at these tiny, primitive kiosks, or in the levels of hygiene at such places.

---

65   I remember that a little girl I know from West Ukraine, after arriving in Kiev with her mother, asked me to take her to MacDonald's: she had dreamed of going there and heard loads about it, but in her home village there wasn't a MacDonald's, so she had had to wait until she got to Kiev. So off we went on a special trip to the nearest outlet, where we ordered hamburgers and coke. She later told her classmates back home how lucky she'd been, and where she had been taken. But for her this was a real adventure, something truly exotic. I've been to MacDonald's in Kiev, too – probably on a grand total of three occasions.

66   Our 'fast-food' restaurants, however, serve borshcht, salads, hot dishes with mushrooms and so on, rather than burgers and coca-cola.

Yet however many bars, cafes and restaurants we might have, it is not in these places that we have our breakfast, lunch or dinner in day-to-day life. To some extent, our habit of eating home-made food is the reason why the country's population has not had any problems with obesity, although there are of course exceptions to that rule.

And, it goes without saying, nobody here has "un-shelled sunflower seeds" for breakfast. It is not generally considered *de rigueur* to chew on sunflower seeds in a public place. If you spot someone munching on sunflower seeds in a public place, you can rest assured that the individual in question is an uncouth provincial with an outdated attitude. The eating sunflower seeds (or as it's known in our country, the 'nibbling' of sunflower seeds) is an old rural custom. One can imagine a group of guys and girls sitting on a bench somewhere in the countryside on the weekend, a hundred and fifty years ago, and laughing and joking with one another. And as they do so, one can picture them removing the shells from their sunflower seeds expertly with their teeth and spitting them out all over the place. It's more a pastime than a type of food. And what's more, the concept of hygiene was very different in those days from what it is today.

WHAT DO UKRAINIANS REALLY EAT, THEN?

Ukraine has long been famed for its cuisine. Some of the dishes served here are famed throughout the world. This can be attributed first and foremost to our exacting tastes and dietary habits, the diversity of the ingredients we use and the culinary techniques we favour.

Our women know how to cook home-made food and are proud of this knowledge. Our men sometimes praise the artistry of their wives and mothers, telling their friends: "You should try my Mom's preserved tomatoes (or pickled gherkins, or sauerkraut)." Many Ukrainian men are good cooks in their own right, incidentally. Cooking does not take up a great deal of time, and when a husband and wife do it together it can only enhance their love for one another and strengthen the family's ties.

I got out of bed a little earlier than normal this morning and washed a big piece of pork – 3 kg or so – then inserted a sharp knife into the meat, pushed the knife to one side and stuffed a mixture of salt and chopped pepper into the gap I had created, then added half a clove of garlic on top and pushed it into the meat. I did this ten times on one side of the meat and ten times on the other. This took me all of fifteen minutes. Then I went off to work on this book.

Then my wife got up, wiped the meat with the mixture of salt and pepper which was left over after I had stuffed the meat (this took 5 minutes) – and put the meat in the oven, in a casserole dish. I can already smell an enticing aroma coming from the kitchen now. This is the famous Ukrainian *buzhenina* (cold boiled pork) cooking. The stuffing you choose for this dish, and the herbs you choose to rub the meat in, depends entirely on your own personal taste. You can also try putting pieces of carrot in it. I have tried prunes, curry and chili. You can also use a bay leaf – either throw it into the casserole dish or stuff it inside the meat.

On this occasion we made it the simplest way we know how.

But no-one in this house will be going to MacDonald's today, that's for sure.

Let's take the well-known Ukrainian dish 'borshcht'. To tell you what borshcht is like would be absurd: after all, we don't generally try to explain to others what we feel when we look at a work of art, and tell them what's on the canvas. The same goes for borshcht: if you want to know how good it tastes, you have to cook it yourself. There are more than 30 ways to cook borshcht, and there are as many as 20 different ingredients which can be used to make it. I have appended a few recipes for everyday dishes and dishes for special occasions (including borshcht) to this book, and have a go at cooking and eating them it will definitely give you a more complete understanding of the ideas set out in this book.

Ukrainian cuisine contains tens of thousands of recipes for dishes which are easy to make and taste delicious. Many of them are notable for the successful combination of meat and vegetables they contain. Given that the guidebook for German tourists, which I mentioned earlier, talked about "*vareniky*, which are dumplings with a variety of fillings", I'll tell you a thing or two about *vareniky*.

The main difference between *vareniky* and *pelmeni* (the latter, incidentally, are a fantastic dish as well) is that the stuffing used in *pelmeni* is uncooked, minced meat. The only things used as a stuffing in *vareniky* are foods which have already been cooked or which do not need to be cooked. Some recipes for *vareniky* can be found at the end of this book, too.

In Ukrainian cuisine there are various methods of cooking food: it can be fried, stewed, boiled or baked. Among the most popular dishes are those cooked in special ceramic pots: roast meat, vareniky with sour cream, stewed cabbage or potatoes with meat and prunes.

And here's another important point: the dishes I have mentioned are not in any way unusual or solely intended for special occasions. On public holidays we cook a vast amount of food and a great variety of dishes – ham, pies or pastries stuffed with cabbage, meat or curd, *golubtsy*[67], jellied fish, various types of aspic, dozens of different salads, meat roulades, sweet pies, cakes and home-made tarts. And on top of that we also love making various types and kinds of home-made smoked sausage…

Each region in Ukraine has its own so-called 'crowning dishes', for which it is known. There is a dish called *galushki* which is made of dough. It is always described as being from Poltava, for the Poltava region is renowned for the art of cooking this dish. There is also a very tasty dish made of cornflour, sour milk and pork loin, which is known as *banosh*; and you won't find *banosh* without the adjective Transcarpathian immediately before it.

---

67 This is a mixture of chopped meat and rice, wrapped up in a lightly boiled cabbage leaf; the envelopes of cabbage are put into the pot and either stewed with tomato or boiled, and then heated up in a frying pan and served with garlic sauce.

There is a particularly strong emphasis on the different flavours in a dish in Ukrainian cooking, and for that reason a large number of herbs are used. Among the herbs used in Ukraine are cumin, onion, garlic, horseradish, mint, pepper, thyme, parsley and parsnip. A considerable number of dishes are flavoured with fresh dill and parsley.

Ukrainians' favourite drinks are kvass (wheat, beet, apple, birch, cranberry, guelder rose, raspberry or pear kvass); a drink called Uzvar, made of dried or fresh apples, pears, plums, cherries or beer.

We also like to make *home-made spirits*. I am not referring to that nasty, evil-smelling mixture of ethylated spirits, fuel oils and ethers known as *samogon*, which will be the death of your liver. Don't let anyone try to tell you that *samogon* is a traditional Ukrainian beverage.

Appended to this book you'll find some recipes for the home-made alcoholic drinks *spotykach* and *varenukha*. Try a small experiment and give your friends a pleasant surprise. In the olden days, home-made drinks involved the use of home-made vodka, whereas nowadays pure, factory-produced vodka is used, but the taste of it is softened and its strength reduced, and it gains additional aromas. It ends up tasting really good – but always remember to drink it in moderation.

Have a go at cooking a Ukrainian dish – your friends and family might just love it.

PORK "SALO"

My fellow countrymen will never forgive me if, whilst discussing Ukrainian cuisine, I were to fail to mention pork *salo* (lard).

In Ukraine, pork lard is part of our traditional cuisine. In the past, lard was an important part of the people's diet because of the high energy levels it contained (770-870 kcals per 100 g). A piece of lard, along with a slice of bread and an onion, was enough to give a peasant working hard in the fields the strength he needed, or equally a blacksmith or a fisherman. Nowadays, of course, people enjoy a far more diverse diet and do less physical work, so pork lard is an appetiser these days, rather than a main course.

Pork lard can be kept for a long time without being refrigerated – all you need to do is put some salt on it.

Picture the Ukrainian tradesmen (they were known as *chumaki*[68]), who set

---

68   The Chumaki were a class of merchants found only in Ukraine. In the first stage of their existence they were warrior-tradesmen. References to travelling merchants can be found in manuscripts chronicling events as far back as the 12th century. In the 14th century a special Chumak cart had already emerged, which was solidly built and had a large load-bearing capacity. In the 16th-19th centuries the Chumaks played an extremely important role in Ukraine's trade relations. On huge carts pulled by a special breed of Chumak bulls – massive beasts with long horns (this breed has almost been wiped out, and there only a few of the animals left, in zoos) – they would travel for many months from the Zporozhskaya secha to the Crimean khanate and back again. Before the advent of the railway, this was an extensive trade, which involved large numbers of people.
In addition to important trade with the Turks, Poles, Ukrainians, Novoserbs and Crimean Tatars, the Chumaks also had trade dealings (usually minor ones) inside the Zaporozhian Sicha as well, involving epanch, pigskin, arrows, onions, stirrups, sabres, fishing rods and so on. As well as the Secha, trade was also conducted at markets (in the villages in Kalmius, Bug, the Dnieper and so on). The trade carried out by the Chumak people was popular and held in esteem, since it was honest and fraught with dangers. The journeys made by the Chumak were very dangerous, and they were often attacked by bandits and Tatars. Due to the dangers associated with supplying goods, the Chumak rarely travelled alone. They often journeyed in large convoys. If they came under attack, the Chumak used to turn their wagons into a so-called *tabor* to protect themselves. Each convoy (the Chumak called it a *valka*) was led by a special *ataman*, who was elected from among the more senior and experienced Chumak: the ataman would indicate which route should be taken, appoint watchmen to keep watch on the cattle by night and by day, decide when to rest and when to move on, and resolve any arguments which broke out along the way. In addition to the ataman, each valka also had a *kuhar*, i.e. a cook, whose cart would contain food supplies, and also a cooking pot and a trivet. The Chumak usually carried about 50 poods (820 kg) with them, including as much as 60 to 65

off with their oxen for the Black Sea and the Azov Sea in search of salt and fish, which they then sold at the markets, as well as delivering other goods. Their journey would last from Easter (let's think of it beginning in April, therefore) until St Nikolai's Day (25th December). In these conditions, what sort of product could provide a guaranteed source of calories for these people? Salted pork lard was the only solution.

The first use of the word 'salo', accompanied by a description of the product, can be found in an Armenian manuscript dating from the 7th century, *A description of a Khazar feast*. In Ukrainian culture, something of a cult has developed around *salo*. For centuries Ukrainians were fond of eating salo, without even being aware of how good it was for them. Firstly, it contains arachidonyl acid (an Omega-6-unsaturated fatty acid), which helps with the synthesis of many hormones and the building of cell membranes, reduces cholesterol and helps the heart muscle, and it also provides many other irreplaceable amino acids and essential acids. Unlike other types of fat and meat, salo contains practically no cholesterol at all.

Modern science has also established that salo helps with the extraction of radionuclides. So it transpired that this much-loved foodstuff was even able to protect us from radiation after the notorious events in Chernobyl in 1986.

On top of this, if you apply some fresh salo to an aching tooth or a sore joint, the pain will subside. This remedy has been used for seven hundred years, and nobody has yet been able to explain why it is that salo reduces the pain felt in such cases.

Like a multi-coloured mosaic, Ukrainian cuisine incorporated recipes from all of the ethnically diverse peoples who have lived in this land of ours at one time or another. In a way which one would not find in any other country, all public festivals in Ukraine are accompanied by a slap-up banquet featuring all the gifts bestowed on us by our generous Ukrainian land.

---

poods (1000 kg) of salt. Several producers would set off together, under a mutual agreement. The total number of pairs of oxen in a convoy could be as many as 100.

PUBLIC HOLIDAYS AND FESTIVALS IN UKRAINE

It was my initial intention to compile a list of all the festivals in Ukraine, along with a brief description of the meaning of each one – and I found that I would need 150 pages. I reasoned that it would be best not to bother compiling the list. And yet one can learn a great deal about any people by looking at which days it has highlighted in the calendar as being of special significance.

Our people love public holidays and love celebrating them. In the Russian language the word for a festival or public holiday, *prazdnik*, is derived from the verb *prazdnovat*, which means to do nothing. In Ukrainian, the word *svyato* is completely analogous with the English word *holiday*, i.e. a holy day. In light of the tradition of drinking more copious quantities of strong spirits than normal during such periods of 'doing nothing', productivity in the workplace tends to be very low on working days which follow public holidays. When a public holiday falls on a Thursday, therefore, our government, aware of what is likely to happen, declares the Friday of that week to be a public holiday, so that we end up with four days off in a row, but then makes one of the following Saturdays in that month a working day, in order to make up for the shortfall in working days in the month.

The public holidays in any given year begin, of course, with 1st January, when we celebrate the New Year. The idea of celebrating the New Year was something that was thought up a long time ago by the Communists, as a way of distracting people from the idea of celebrating the birth of Christ on 25th December. And it could not be allowed for Saint Nikolai to come bearing gifts for the children on 19th December, so a neutral, non-religious character came along in his stead: Uncle Frost. Uncle Frost was a rosy-cheeked old man with a white beard, who wore a red fur coat and carried a staff and a sack. The sack would contain gifts which he had brought for the children, and he would also make their dreams come true. Before long he was joined by a girl called the Snow Maiden, who was supposed to be either his daughter or his granddaughter. The Snow Maiden is purely a fictional character – in fact more of a pantomime character. She was borrowed from an opera by the famous Russian composer Rimsky-Korsakov, in which the female protagonist – a girl made of snow – melted, the poor thing, when she decided to join in with a traditional spring-time pastime among young people: jumping over a fire.

We do not take our New Year celebrations lightly: people prepare their New Year banquet well ahead of time, and cook whatever they are capable of cooking; sometimes families come together to prepare the meal and celebrate together. On the menu will be various finely chopped salads, and dishes made of fish and meat. Those whose health allows them to do so stay up most of the night making merry – drinking, feasting, dancing and singing.

Special New Year programs are shown on the TV, including concerts and shows. In the corner of the room will be the *sine qua non* – a fir tree, decorated with colourful baubles, gleaming ribbons and lights. The festivities begin on 31st December, in the evening, and come to an end on the morning of 1st January – if anyone manages to last that long.

Some people spend the whole night at a restaurant, although most people choose to celebrate at home (because we'll have the chance to eat out at a restaurant when we have our New Year corporate party, in any case). Corporate parties are usually held between 25th December and 5th January, although they may also fall outside this period: it depends how lucky your company is when booking tables at one of the nice local eateries.

After that, Christmas is just around the corner. Orthodox Christians celebrate the birth of Christ on 7th January. For this holiday we go through the ritual of preparing a special dish called *kutia*, which is oatmeal made using whole grains of wheat (or, less often, barley or other crops, and latterly – using rice), with honey, dissolved honey or sugar poured over it, and with a topping of poppy-seed, raisins, nuts, milk or even jam. Kutia traditionally has a special Lenten 'milk' served with it in a separate jug: this milk is made of poppy-seed, walnuts or hazelnuts or a mixture of the two, or almonds.

For us, Christmas is one of the few holidays which we do not celebrate with guests, or as guests at other people's homes. It is a holiday which we celebrate *en famille*, a time when only our nearest and dearest are gathered around the table.

Next up, on 13th-14th January, is a holiday which is no longer celebrated anywhere else, only in Ukraine (and in Russia, of course – this holiday has a common origin for both our countries). This holiday is called *Old New year*. On coming to power in the Russian Empire in October 1917, the Communists decided to align the country's calendar with global standards. They declared 1st February 1918 to be 14th February, and thereby shifted the country onto the Gregorian calendar. The people raised no objections, of course, though in their heart of hearts they couldn't understand where those two weeks had disappeared to, and indeed the Orthodox church counts the days and religious holidays in accordance with the old, Julian calendar.

The upshot of this is that the 'new' New Year is of course a public holiday, and we enjoy celebrating it. But even little kids will be able to tell you that this New Year's Day is not 'the real one', and that the real one arrives on 13th January. If no snow is falling at the end of December, people say: "This isn't the real New Year, of course. New Year will arrive in two weeks' time." As you've probably guessed, we celebrate this 'old New Year' a little bit as well, if we still have any money left after the first celebration.

I have already mentioned, in the section about national traditions, that in days of yore various significant dates in the church calendar were attached to these days, and that folk customs included rituals such as girls making wishes to find out how likely it was that they would marry, carolling and *posevanie* ('sowing').[69]

19th January – the feast of Epiphany. Water is blessed in churches throughout the country, and this water is then believed to acquire special power and health-giving properties. The water blessed at Epiphany is used to heal wounds, and helps to ward off all manner of disasters. When you arrive home after attending the evening church service, you are supposed to sprinkle a little holy water in every corner of your home: this will ensure that your home is filled with order and tranquillity.

Today, we are seeing a return of the tradition of submersing oneself in a river or lake, through a hole in the ice, on Epiphany (which happens to fall during the coldest time of the year). A huge hole is made in the ice and people jump through it into the water, despite the temperature of the water being 4°C

---

69 Carolling is an ancient custom, dating back to the pre-Christian era. Young lads and little boys would dress up as mythical characters from fairy-tales, and go from house to house reciting special texts, usually ones which rhymed – and wish good tidings and joy on the people living in each house. Sometimes the 'mummers', as these amateur actors were known, would act out funny sketches. Special songs were written to accompany these rites, known as *shchedrovki* (acts of generosity). You have probably heard of one such Ukrainian *shchedrovka*: in English it is known as The Carol of the Bells. It is an interpretation of a folk song, by the talented 19th century Ukrainian composer Leontovich.

To show their gratitude, the home-owners would give their guests gifts of food and drink, so that the performers would have something to put on the table on public holidays.

Posevanie is another custom which dates back to pagan times. In those days, of course, the new year was celebrated at the start of spring, and it was therefore fitting to pour a handful of grain into the house (thereby 'sowing' it) and wish the occupants a good harvest.

Nowadays these traditions are only really observed in rural areas. Here, people still remember the words of the ceremonial songs, and take genuine pleasure in dropping in on their neighbours.

In the big cities, though, these traditions have been perverted: unscrupulous people send their little boys off to knock on doors in apartment buildings and ask for money, under the pretext of carolling. This is a standard example of begging, and is tied in with the exploitation of children and the abuse by parents of their rights.

and the air temperature being around - 15 °C. And no-one thinks anything of it. I have certainly never heard of anyone getting ill as a result of doing this. And don't go thinking that it's just young men that do this: you'll also see women of a certain age ducking under the icy water for several seconds. There is something of a trend among our politicians and other categories of 'celebrities' to submerse themselves at baptismal fonts – you can imagine how proud and winsome they look the next day, in the photos that fill the pages of the newspapers and glossies!

Bathing of this kind is preceded by luxuriant church services next to the hole in the ice, during which the water is blessed. It is believed that if you are baptized in a hole in the ice on Epiphany, you will enjoy good health for the rest of the year.

22nd January – Unification Day. This particular holiday is more political than the other public holidays. It was established by presidential decree in 1999. Yet it marks an event which, in every Ukrainian heart, will trigger feelings of both joy and sadness simultaneously.

Do you remember the 'Act of Unification' of 1919, which turned out to be more a declaration of intent than anything more lasting? During the Soviet era, it was forgotten. Yet the Ukrainian people's century-long dream of sovereignty for their state, which might unite all the different elements of the Ukrainian people, remained so powerful that on 22nd January 1990, when Soviet rule was still in existence, Ukrainians held one another by the hand and stood side by side, forming a human chain which went from Kiev to Lvov (a distance of 541 km), to celebrate Unification Day. According to official estimates, some 450,000 people took part in forming this human chain[70].

25th January – Student Day. There are a lot of students in Ukraine – some 2.2 million according to official statistics. 70-75% of school leavers decide to go into higher education. In the last twenty years, a huge number of universities and colleges have opened in this country. Yet these are all private academic institutions, without exception. This means that it costs quite a lot of money to study at one of them. As time has passed, it has become clear that not all of them are up to scratch – far from it. It comes as no surprise that our institutes of higher education do not feature in the rankings of the top universities in the world, released each year. There have been a few cases when private academic

---

[70] Unofficial estimates put the figure far higher. Creating huge human chains such as this is not an area in which we have a monopoly. On 29th November 2013, the day of the European Summit in Vilnius, 300,000 people held hands in a long line to demonstrate the Ukrainian people's desire to become a part of the European community, forming a chain which led right up to the border with Poland.

institutions have been forced to close, because the way they organized their courses for students did not satisfy even the most basic requirements.

The old, traditional state universities still enjoy far more respect and authority, although most students now have to pay to study at them, unlike in Soviet times.

During the first few years of independence, the private universities and colleges began offering courses in law and economics for huge numbers of students. Occasionally they offered combined courses in both subjects. I am firmly of the belief that combining these two subjects into a single degree is extremely difficult to do. Perhaps the object of this was to provide the country with a sufficient number of people who would be capable of making sense of the stormy world of the economic and legal order taking shape in the new state?

There was a disproportionately large number of people graduating as lawyers or economists. These days, high salaries are on offer for IT professionals, of which there is a shortage, whilst many lawyers and economists find themselves surplus to requirements.

Be that as it may, a holiday's a holiday – especially when it's dedicated to such a large cohort of young people. Concerts, plays, sketches, shows, processions – all this, and whatever else our fun-loving students dream up, takes place on this day. It is a very old holiday, dating back to the day when the plans for Moscow University were approved, under Empress Elizaveta Petrovna in 1755. The date on which the university was opened was specially tied to the day on which people remember the early Christian martyr, Tatiana of Rome, who was declared the patron saint of students. The holiday is therefore alternatively known as Tatiana Day.

Here in Ukraine, we decided to have another student day, just in case: International Student Day, on 17th November. It wouldn't be right for us to celebrate the founding of Moscow University here in Ukraine, after all. I have no doubt that our students celebrate both days.

Saint Valentine's Day on 14th February is a holiday that has not really caught on to any great extent here. Though young couples use it as another excuse for displaying their feelings for one another, no deep traditions have taken root here as they have in Europe.

The reason for this may lie in the fact that St Valentine's Day is followed by two serious holidays in quick succession. One of them is Men's Day on 23rd February, whilst the other is Women's Day, on 8th March.

The public holiday on **23rd February** was formerly known as Red Army Day. The Red Army was an institution with a special standing in Soviet society. Everyone was required to do military service. The only men who were exempted from it were those with physical or psychological conditions which made them utterly unfit for service. The official propaganda was at pains to put the idea into the public consciousness that service in the army was a prestigious duty, and that after completing his military service, a young lad would become a real man. Even men who did not serve as soldiers were sometimes conscripted in later life for what was known as 're-training' – short-term military courses lasting one to three months. Thus most men were connected to the army in some shape or form.

In the last few decades of the Soviet Union, the prestige of the army waned somewhat, and young men strove to avoid military service under various pretexts.

Nonetheless, in the public consciousness this day ended up becoming a public holiday, when all women congratulate all men and give them gifts. The Red Army has long since ceased to exist; the holiday has long since been known by a different name; some political figures are demanding that we stop celebrating it, describing it as an 'artificial' holiday from the Soviet era; compulsory military service has been abolished in Ukraine, and a different date chosen for celebrating Ukrainian Army Day…but no, the people stubbornly go on celebrating this day, and women still give gifts to the men in their lives on 23rd February.

The women don't have long to wait before they too are able to enjoy the next public holiday: **8th March**. This one is celebrated by the UN each year as *The International Day for the Struggle for Women's Rights and International Peace*. It began life as a day of solidarity for working women struggling for equal rights and emancipation.

No-one remembers this now, however, or at least no-one pays any attention to it any more. On this day, our women rule the roost: they are at the centre of our attention, and can do as they please. Men – even those with next to no talent on the creative front – try to recite lines of verse congratulating the women in their lives. And when it comes to presents, men with a conscience run the risk of going bankrupt on this day: they need to get something for their wife, their daughter, their mother, their sister and even their female colleagues at work. Giving flowers, at the very least, is obligatory – as inevitable as death and taxes. Florists hike up their prices significantly on the eve of the holiday, as you would expect.

Maslyanichnaya nedelya (Shrovetide week) usually falls in the middle of March. In the eyes of the Orthodox Church, this is the last week before *Veliky post* (Lent). On the horizon are seven weeks of strict dietary restrictions and frugal behaviour, so it is fitting to have fun and eat your fill at Maslenitsa. For the average person in Ukraine, this is nothing more than an opportunity to see off the winter and a good excuse for going out on the town and having plenty to eat and drink. Often there's still snow on the ground at this time. It's a joy to pour some mulled wine into a thermos flask with your friends, pick up a few tasty treats and head off into a big park or wood, to breathe in the chill air of winter for the last time that year.

In bygone centuries, of course, Shrovetide week was a very significant time, when each day of the week was associated with certain ceremonies. *Bliny* (small pancakes) would always be eaten[71]. Having said that, the requirement to eat *bliny* rather than anything else at Maslenitsa is more typical of Russia than Ukraine. Here, *bliny* were often replaced with *vareniky* containing *tvorog* (curd cheese).

In days of yore, people used to make a puppet representing 'Winter', and then set fire to it. Nowadays, of course, the only place where you'll see fire extravaganzas like this is at shows organized by professional entertainment agencies.

There is also an unofficial public holiday which we celebrate on **1st April**. It is called **Humour Day (April Fools' Day)**. On this day you're allowed to play jokes on your loved ones, friends and colleagues –they'll react in the spirit of the day and won't get angry with you. A large number of jokes, comedy

---

71   Below is a recipe you can use to make 12 *bliny*, incidentally. To make more, just increase the amount of each ingredient used, keeping the proportions the same. I've been known to bake fifty *bliny* at a time. They taste great with *Smetana* (sour cream), honey, a mushroom julienne or red caviar. There are loads of recipes for *bliny* – the one I'm giving you here is the simplest one of all. The best way to make them is in a non-stick frying pan.

What you'll need:
  Butter – for spreading on the *bliny*
  Milk – 200 ml
  Flour – 100g
  Sugar – 1 tbsp.
  Water – 75 ml
  Sunflower oil – 1 tbsp.
  A pinch of salt
  1 egg

Combine the flour and salt in a bowl and sift it through a fine sieve into a pan (if you're sure that the flour doesn't contain any unwanted bits and pieces like bits of fibre from the bag, or lumps, there's no need to use a sieve). Make an indentation in the middle, beat the uncooked egg into it and mix together, bringing the flour from the edges toward the centre. Mix the milk with the water and sugar. Whilst stirring constantly, slowly add the mixture obtained to the flour. Mix it until all the lumps have gone and the dough starts to have the consistency of thick Smetana. Add some vegetable oil and beat the dough with a whisk or a blender. Put a 16 cm frying pan on a high heat. Pick up a small knob of butter in a napkin and rub it all over the surface of the frying pan. You shouldn't spread any more butter than this in the pan. Pour roughly a third of a soup ladle of the mixture into the frying pan. Put the frying pan over the heat and make a quick circular motion with the pan, so that the mixture spreads all over its surface. After 30-35 seconds, flip the pancake over. Cook it for another 10-12 seconds. Once the pancake is cooked, put it on a plate and spread a little butter on it. Continue making pancakes until all the mixture has been used. Pile the pancakes on top of one another, spreading a small amount of butter over each pancake.

shows and funny stories can be found in the newspapers, on TV and on the Internet on this day.

At the heart of this public holiday, however, is the southern Ukrainian city of Odessa. Each year the locals organize a festival called *Yumorina*, and arrange a grandiose dramatized procession.

The people of Odessa are something of a special group of people. Founded right at the end of the 18th century, this southern port town became the crucible of the nation. Ukrainians, Russians, Jews, Moldovans, Greeks, Frenchmen and Germans – these are the elements which all contributed to the genotype of these people, who are famously known as *Odessity* in Ukrainian – 'Odessites'.

They are the descendants of sailors and fishermen, merchants and smugglers, stevedores, soldiers and artists.

They have their own distinctive way of speaking, intonation and pronunciation. Of course, they feel sad and put-upon at times just like everyone else, yet their ability to speak expressively and be witty, and their willingness to have a laugh and a joke at any time, have helped bring about the notion of the tireless resident of Odessa, who is tanned, fun-loving and well-to-do.

May is a special month as far as public holidays are concerned.

1st May is **Labour Day**. In the past, this was a Communist holiday for international solidarity among workers. Huge crowds of people would go out[72] into the streets and walk past the Communist leaders holding red banners, as the leaders stood on tribunes specially erected in the central towns and streets of the towns and villages. Columns of demonstrators, divided up by manufacturing plant, academic institution or research institute, would walk past for an hour and half, shout 'Ura!' ('Hurrah!'), then go off to celebrate at home, with their friends and family. The ways of Communism have long since become a thing of the past, and we no longer go out marching to demonstrate our loyalty to the ideals of Socialism. But the public holiday isn't going anywhere – we'll continue to celebrate it. 2nd May is a public holiday too, and on these days, if the weather's fine, the people in the city go on day-trips to the surrounding forests: they sit down around the fire with their friends, cook some meat on an open fire, go for a stroll and sing a few songs. In a word, the glorious month of May gets going in Ukraine, a month of new leaves, flowers, love and birdsong.[73]

---

[72] In truth, these huge crowds of people were 'brought out' into the streets by the Communist party organizers, since on this day there was a need to demonstrate the unity between the party and the people, and the universal satisfaction with the movement towards Communism. Yet there was nonetheless a sense of festivity in the air.

[73] In 2013, 2nd May fell on a Friday, and Easter was on 5th May, which was also a weekday. So in

Easter falls on a different date each year, depending on the lunar and solar calendar. In 2013 it was celebrated on 5th May, in 2014 it fell on 20th April and in 2015 it fell on 12th April.

It is a religious holiday, of course, but that does not stop it being a public holiday.

People who are not religious enjoy getting involved in the Easter merry-making, and many of them like to put boiled eggs, their shells decorated a bright brown colour, cakes with a sugar coating, and other products into a basket and go to the nearest church, where these foodstuffs are blessed by the local church priest from 3 am at night on 7th January.

Soon afterwards, on **9th May**, we celebrate **Victory Day**.

In Ukraine, the date on which the war with Germany ended in 1945 is marked on 9th May, rather than 8th May. It is not a day of grief, but a day when we celebrate victory.

During the Second World War, the risk that the Soviet Union would be wiped off the geopolitical map was very great, whilst Ukraine, as you will remember, was completely occupied by Hitler's troops. The victory that was won in this war was achieved through such a massive effort, and at such great cost, and the joy of victory so great, that our people pay their respects to those who fought in the war and honour the memory of those killed not through ceremonies of mourning, but by singing hymns to their glory.

Today, some political figures, whose goal is to distance themselves from the Soviet past, tell us that the war with Germany was a clash between Fascism and Communism for global supremacy, and that Ukrainians ought not to celebrate the end of the war as a day of victory for them.

It seems to me, though, that most families still have photographs of a grandfather in uniform, with medals across his chest, and that honouring the memory of those who died in the Second World War is something that is in our people's blood.

There are other war veterans in Ukraine too, of course – the ones who fought against the Soviet Army. These are the former soldiers of the Ukrainian Rebel Army. These men, too, have children, grandsons and great-grandsons, who think of them as heroes. And whilst those Ukrainians whose grandsons served in the Red Army consider the soldiers of the URA to have been enablers of the Fascists, there are other Ukrainians – the grandsons of URA soldiers – who think of the soldiers of the Red Army as an occupying force which seized control of Ukraine.

Time is a healer for historical wounds such as this, and it may be that a

---

May 2013 we had a whole week off work.

time will come when the Second World War will lose its material and human import, and become a subject for research by professors and historians.

There are several new political holidays in Ukraine: Constitution Day (28th June), National Flag Day (23rd August), Independence Day (24th August) and so on. These are not widely celebrated by Ukrainians, but they are nevertheless respected, all the more so given that the government has declared them to be non-working days.

And on top of that there are about a hundred and fifty so-called 'profession-related holidays': Customs Officer's Day, Fireman's Day, Meteorologist's Day, the Rescuer Day, Metalworkers's day, Bank Clerk's Day, Archive Worker's Day, Trade Day, Tax Officer's Day, Legal Expert Day, Architect's Day, Fisherman's Day, Veterinarian's Day, Pharmacist's Day, Notarius's Day, Miner's Day, Builder's Day, Bookkeepers Day…There are too many to mention. These holidays are celebrated by the people who work in these professions. Even if they happen to fall on a Saturday or Sunday, people will still gather round for a celebratory meal with their colleagues on the Friday – it's an obligatory ritual.

There are a whole host of military holidays: Armed Forces Day, Fleet Day, Air Force Day, Ground Forces Day, Airmobile Troops Day, Anti-Air Defence Day, Border Guards' Day, Interior Troops Day, Military Navigators' Day, Policemen's Day, National Guard Day, Road Traffic Police Day and plenty more besides.[74]

I'll draw this section on public holidays in Ukraine to a close by adding that in the lists of public holidays I found such wonderful phenomena as Astrologer's Day and Wedding Agencies' Day. Only the Good Lord knows who established those ones.

---

74   The problem is that although we have the holidays, Ukraine doesn't have an army. At least, not one that would be capable of defending its independence as a nation. We do not have the resources to maintain such an army. It was recently announced that we are going to see a shift to a professional, contractual army. It remains to be seen what comes of that. Will Ukrainians really want to serve in this army? The salaries on offer will be very low. Who would join such an army? Someone from a small village, with a poor level of education, who doesn't have any prospects of getting a better life for himself. And these days wars are fought with computers rather than pikes and spears.

THE ECONOMIC AND SOCIAL ENVIRONMENT IN MODERN-DAY UKRAINE

The history of the Ukrainian people is one that is capable of provoking bitter disagreements and engendering irreconcilable differences of opinion. Yet the question arises: what is there to argue about? It all happened, it has all been explained, and all the mysteries have been solved. All the heroes and villains are identifiable, and we know all their names. But alas, we go on fighting with every ounce of strength we have left to try and prove that the people who were declared to be heroes were in fact villains, and the ones thought of as villains were in fact heroes, a beacon of light for the nation who set a fine example for us to follow.

When we try to describe our customs and traditions, aspects of our culture and ethnic stereotypes, and even our favourite recipes, they are bound to become the cause of discussions – even if they are harmless ones – even though one would think it all ought to be perfectly clear: do we not celebrate the same holidays, and sing the same songs? Are they not founded on the same set of habits, morals and principles, which govern the behaviour between men and women, parents and children, and have done for centuries? Yet even in this case there are plenty of people who seek to interpret the purpose and meaning of an unwritten rule – and say to what extent it is compulsory – in different ways.

You can well imagine the kind of feelings which can be provoked by any attempt to describe Ukraine in terms of its contemporary political and economic components. Political figures, economic trends, legal regulations or social events are all interpreted by Ukrainians in completely different ways. Even within an individual family you are likely to find different readings of socio-political phenomena.

At the time of writing, opinion in Ukraine has once again been polarized, with the people in either camp sometimes holding mutually exclusive views as regards the path the country should take in the future. The discontent felt by the people with regard to the policies of the fourth President of Ukraine, Viktor Yanukovich, and his entourage ultimately led to him being removed from office. During the protest movement many lives were lost, cars and buildings were set on fire, and several hundred people were killed or wounded, or went missing without trace. Yet far from uniting Ukrainians, the revolution in fact put the country's territorial integrity at risk. Only time will tell how we are going to get out of this situation, and whether we will indeed be able to get out of it.

As a matter of principle, I am not going to give my verdict on any of the public figures in contemporary Ukrainian life. However hard I might try to be objective when describing a particular event in society, legislative act or economic phenomenon, there will always be an alternative point of view to be found somewhere, which will be diametrically opposed to mine, along with a different economic interest and a different kind of logic, which to its author will seem absolutely indisputable. Whatever I say about life in Ukraine today, my compatriots will undoubtedly start arguing and expressing their own personal point of view. This is also, incidentally, one of the distinctive traits of the Ukrainian people's national character: to have one's own personal point of view on absolutely everything.

My personal economic experience has been fairly diverse, and includes working for a state scientific and research institute, private companies, in trade and construction, for a bank and for an insurance agency. I have set up off-shore companies, and been the director of a tiny firm of my own, with a staff of two and a sub-division within a workforce numbering many thousands, at a big corporation. I have felt financial euphoria, and bitterness when my hopes turn to dust, and I've had my fair share of ups and downs – I've known all this and more. At present I am not setting up any new financial structures, nor do I have any well-defined political leanings; all in all, I hope I will be able to come up with a balanced analysis and paint an objective picture of contemporary economic life in Ukraine, and of the political life in the country, which stems from it.

The Ukrainian people's economic behaviour at present is determined, of course, by factors which emerged just over 20 years ago and which changed our lives drastically and radically. Let's refer to these, for the time being, as the demands of a free market economy.

On the other hand, of colossal significance is the fact that three quarters of the country's population were brought up in Soviet economic realities and in the midst of the Communist ideology. Anyone who has not lived here cannot really get a complete sense of the powerful imprint this left on people's mentality. I would not wish to draw a parallel between my country as it was in the Soviet era and the one described in George Orwell's dystopian novel *1984*. Yet one or two of the trends identified by Orwell were spot on, and one should not exaggerate the role played by the ideological charge with which the average Soviet person was force-fed, and which in many ways pre-determined his interpretation of his surroundings and his appraisal of it.

I feel the need to explain to my readers which factors shaped the mentality of the average Ukrainian in the Soviet era – otherwise the mind-set of the older generation, who make up a large part of the population, will be one that you find hard to understand. It is going to be a story about the past, the seeds of which are still giving rise to shoots in the hearts and minds of many Ukrainians, and having a very strong influence on the state of affairs today.

As I see it, the biggest weakness that our people have inherited from Soviet times is our complete inability to plan our economic future. The most serious financial operation of all is when we save up money so that we can make a fairly large purchase. Think about it: housing was generally given out for free (to those living in the cities, or course), or else people were given the promise of housing in the near future. At companies and firms, lists were kept of the employees who were entitled to be given their first apartment, or an extra-large apartment because they had a big family. The speed with which people moved up this waiting list would vary, and the housing provided was not particularly comfortable or spacious by modern standards, but it was free all the same.[75] And meanwhile the monthly payments for housing and communal services – electricity, gas, water, heating, the telephone and the radio – were fairly small. All the utilities expenses for one month taken together amounted to less than 10% of a family's income.

Medical services were free as well. You could always call a doctor from the local doctor's surgery to come and see you at home, and in serious cases an ambulance would come with a team of medics, and the patient would be taken away to a free hospital, and if necessary have an operation done on him or her. Women gave birth, old men had their spines straightened up – and no-one ever asked to see any money or insurance policies.[76] I certainly wouldn't

---

75   I hesitate to say it but perhaps the fact that this housing was free resulted in the vile habit among some people in the cities of writing offensive comments on the walls of apartment buildings, smashing the lightbulbs outside them, setting fire to the plastic buttons used to summon the lift, and throwing cigarette ends into the stairwells?

76   It's also true that many hospitals did not have any modern equipment, and that senior civil servants and party bosses were given special treatment, with access to the best medical experts. Yet the fact remains that even the most rank-and-file workers and peasants would never have dreamt of feeling the need to have money set aside in case they fell ill, and if a grateful patient wanted to thank his doctor, he would give him a box of chocolates, or a bottle of cognac, which was seen as a standard display of good manners.

want to exaggerate the quality of medical institutions in the Soviet era – far from it. There were some magnificent doctors in those days, of course, who were able to conduct unique operations in the capital's surgeries. The key word here, though, is 'unique' – i.e. rare operations, the sole examples of that type of operation that have been undertaken. I can remember the time when there was a dysentery epidemic, when, whilst I was still a child, I fell ill, and was taken to a free hospital, where all the beds were already occupied – it was an epidemic, after all. I was put in the corridor of this free hospital, in an old, flaky hospital cot with a metal frame. And there were plenty of others in the same position as me, in that corridor.

I remember what it was like years later, when my own child was very ill. The doctor treating him said that I had to go and find some powerful, effective medicines from somewhere, because the ones at the free hospital were having no effect at all.

There can be no denying that all of this took place. Yet the services that were accessible were genuinely accessible, and were provided for free. Under these circumstances, who would be likely ever to contemplate the need for medical insurance? There was nobody offering such insurance, in any case[77].

As for the possibility of obtaining a free education – wasn't that something to be held dear? Providing free education for pre-schoolers and schoolchildren – that goes without saying, it's what is generally done in the civilized world, and it's customary for Europe[78]. But the universities were free as well, and on top of that the students were given bursaries and grants; if they got good results in their studies, they would receive an even bigger bursary. When I was a student I married a girl who was also a student, and we both received bursaries, so I was not in a position where it was vitally important for me to seek out another source of income just to get by. As I've already said, communal services and so on were very cheap in those days.

In addition to the fact that so much was available for free, there were two ideological postulates which had an extremely serious impact on shaping the mentality of a substantial section of the modern population of Ukraine.

---

77   I suppose it has now become clear to you why it is that few Ukrainians give much thought these days to medical insurance, although the conditions under which medical services are provided have changed considerably, and nowadays it costs a lot of money to receive medical services – sometimes more than a person can afford. Our websites and newspapers are full of ads asking for charitable contributions to help provide treatment for children, women or young men.

78   There were certain peculiarities even in this regard, mind you. Believe it or not, teachers were obliged to spend time teaching the less able students after the school day had finished, and give up their free time to do so. The thinking behind this was that everyone had to do well in their studies – it was each person's duty to the country. Pupils who performed well were given a lot of encouragement, and sometimes received material rewards, albeit rarely. The child in question might be given a free trip to a good summer camp, for example.

What's more, these postulates were interpreted by us as dogma – as statements requiring no proof whatsoever.

The first dogma: the state will see to it that you are given work.

And this was indeed the case: every single person was guaranteed a job. The idea of not being in work was impossible, even for those who didn't want to work. People who were out of work were condemned by society, mocked in the media, and were sometimes punished by law for the crime of 'parasitism', i.e. a stubborn refusal to work, since this was seen as 'anti-social behaviour'. People had it drilled into them that 'If you won't work, you won't eat,' a slogan which signified that those who weren't doing any work would not be entitled to any social benefits at all.

Since there was always work to be had, there was always a working wage to be earned, and once you reached pensionable age you were guaranteed a pension – and take my word for it, the pensions given to veterans were sometimes equal to, or even higher than, the kind of salaries given to young men in employment. That said, an employee's salary often depended not on his personal capabilities, his contribution to the common goal or the results of the company's activities. In these circumstances, the best employees often felt as if they were being strangulated, and the worst ones prospered without deserving it. As some of my compatriots may remember, a system of bonuses was in place, but in effect this was a bonus that you received on a fairly regular basis, and which in a worst case scenario would be taken away as a result of 'bad' behaviour, such as being drunk in the workplace. Thus everyone could rest assured that they would have their salary paid to them twice a month, assuming the end of the world didn't come. It wouldn't be much, but it was guaranteed.

What if I wanted to increase my earnings? Let's imagine my entrepreneurial streak has come to the fore, and I've worked out a way to make money using an original idea and my own capabilities and labour? Not only was private entrepreneurship of this kind not encouraged: there were severe punishments for it. Private entrepreneurship was seen as a threat to the existing economic status quo, and such activity could result in criminal proceedings being launched[79].

The second dogma which was engrained in the minds of the Soviet person was that the period of flourishing was just a short time away. An extremely

---

79   A society in which the reigning ideology was one that did not encourage private initiative, in which people's quality of life did not depend much on how much they contributed to the 'common good', and in which the moral compass was set in such a way that inventiveness and entrepreneurship were condemned, if they resulted in private profit – a society such as this was destined to lose the economic competition with the other methods of organizing society, as indeed was the case with the Soviet system.

attractive utopia was invented, and given the name 'Communism'. Do you know how they defined this concept? "Communism is a classless social structure…in which…all the sources of social wealth flow all the way down, and there is the great principle of "from each – based upon their capabilities, and to each – based upon their needs". This meant that everyone would work as hard as they were able, and be able to consume as much as they wanted. And this paradise on Earth was just around the corner, and would be upon us in just a few years. I don't know to what extent fantasies of this kind worked as an incentive for the most able, the most talented and the most entrepreneurial, but there is no doubt that they did so for the masses. In the depths of people's minds was a certain expectation: the notion that soon all problems would take care of themselves – for the Communist Party and the Soviet state would see to it that they did.

And then suddenly: oops! All that changed. And I'm not talking about the collapse of the Soviet Union, or the fact that Ukraine obtained independence. The system of economic relations is changing radically, and in the new economic order – it's every man for himself! Can you imagine how that makes ordinary Ukrainians feel? The state in which you lived is no more. And not only has that state disappeared: it's taken the people's money with it, too.

As I mentioned earlier, the only action that people here used to take that was related to financial planning was saving up money for a big purchase. And a lot of people used to do so: to buy some furniture or a car, or to build a *dacha*. There was a lot of money held in the form of savings accounts. It is claimed that the total amount of savings was equal to the country's GDP. This money was held in accounts in the only state bank that existed, in Soviet roubles. And when the state ceased to be, so did the bank and the Soviet rouble, and therefore these savings ceased to exist as well.

What about the new state? The new state knew nothing about this money at all. It was scarce consolation to people that we began to see democratic reforms taking shape, freedom of speech, elections in which there were several rival candidates and the other benefits of the new political order. Under these new circumstances, the state quickly went from being a 'universal protector' to being everyone's enemy. The new Ukrainian establishment was clearly unable to cope with the new economic challenges it faced, and people were faced with a feature of the state machine known as the taxation system, something that was completely new to them. The tax agencies soon became corrupt, moreover, and began to be used by the group of oligarchs who had come to power against their economic rivals.

It was the Ukrainians themselves who took the decision, of course, when they said goodbye once and for all to the Soviet political and economic system in 1991. Yet none of them had any idea what a market economy was, how a democratic state ought to be structured, what the essence of the national ideology was to consist of, or what the objective for which the nation ought to be striving was. Economic and legal disorder resulted, the numerous gaps in the legislation were hastily filled in, based on the immediate needs of the present, as the group in power understood them to be. The people felt anger at the sense that their economic expectations had been frustrated, followed by disappointment and depression.

Political leaders in Europe sometimes criticize the Ukrainian authorities over the fact that the country's democratic institutions are not very well-developed. It feels as if they imagine that the only thing we're preoccupied by is making sure we have human rights here, as these are understood in Western Europe. Their comments about the rights of sexual minorities, political correctness and gender equality seem particularly absurd. I don't think that, after 20 years of development of the new social structure in Ukraine, the average Ukrainian would complain that democracy is not sufficiently developed in this country. The average Ukrainian will tell you that what he suffers from most is the lack of order, the corruption, and the abuse by those in authority of their position. The average Ukrainian wants the state to protect the fruits of his labour: as for the rest, he'll take care of earning it, creating it or building it himself. Moreover, that well-known democratic institution, free speech, has taken on such an extreme character here that a citizen's personal or business reputation can be destroyed via some untruthful or deliberately libellous statements made about them in the media – whilst the person who makes such statements goes unpunished.

It came as no surprise to me at all when a well-educated middle-aged man I know, who lives in Transcarpathia, in the far West of Ukraine (on the border with Hungary), expressed the view that our country doesn't need a parliament. This man, who has worked tirelessly for the last twenty years trying to increase his family's wealth, feels that the best solution of all for Ukraine would be to have a monarchy. I have heard this view expressed many times. That does not mean, I assure you, that Ukrainians are strongly attached to the idea of a monarchy. It is rather a defensive reaction to the economic and legal disorder from which the population has suffered in recent years. People are simply longing for a dependable and sustainable world order, in which everyone is able to work in peace, on their own patch of land, so to speak.

There is nothing surprising about this. In our country, the institutions of power have never been formed through universal democratic elections, in which everyone has an equal vote. Of course, under the Communist regime elections were nothing more than an imitation of the process, and before that, the territory known as Ukraine was ruled by the Russian monarchy for three hundred years. The Ukrainian people do not, therefore, have enough experience of influencing the decision-making done by the political groups in power in the country. The interaction between the ordinary Ukrainian and those in power has always been based on principles of non-interference: "our big masters decide things up there at the top, but we're just little people, so as long as it doesn't affect us, we don't get involved."[80]

Undoubtedly, the thing that had the greatest impact of all on forming the worldview of the modern Ukrainian was the absence, for decades, of the concept of 'private property'. When the concept of 'private property' is absent, it leads to the depersonalization of all property in general. The term 'personal property' once existed, but the difference between private property and personal property here has always been roughly equivalent to the difference between 'private property' and 'personal belongings', in English. And since everything around us is 'the people's' (this was how it was interpreted in the official doctrine – the means of production and manufacturing tools, the earth and the natural resources, the factories, the railways and so on – all of this belongs to the people), and since there is no doubt whatsoever that I am one of those people, then there can be no arguing with my right to put something that might come in useful in my pocket, at the firm where I work, and take it home with me. In the social mores of the day, it wasn't even seen as theft: people used the verb *vynesti* 'to take away', rather than *ukrast* 'to steal', and people who had committed countless acts of theft – petty ones, perhaps, but recurrent ones nonetheless – were known not as *vory* ('thieves') but *nesuny* ('takers').

In earlier periods during the existence of the Socialist state, under Stalin, 'takers' like this were punished severely. And yet theft of this kind still took place. But later on…

If my factory makes smoked sausage, then I'll always have a few packs of the stuff at home and so will my neighbours and relatives. I might decide to sell a bit of it to someone, at a cheaper price than they can get in the shops, or I might give some to someone as a gift. It doesn't matter: I got the smoked sausage for free, because I work at a smoked sausage factory, and I 'took it out' with me.

A worker at a car plant with the qualifications to do so might well take his own old banger to work, repair it, give it a new coat of nickel and fix the

---

80   It's only today, twenty years on, that Ukrainians have begun rising up against those in power, making demands of those in power and forcing those in power to do certain things. But this is the younger generation, who were brought up in an environment in which they had spiritual freedom, had access to information and became familiar with the conditions in which people live in other countries.

bumper – during normal business hours, of course, using the firm's resources and at its expense. If I did an office job and didn't manufacture anything, I'd still take something home – a pad of paper, a box of seals or a bottle of glue.

The state tried to fight back against this phenomenon: however small the stakes may have been on an individual basis, it was something that had a huge impact when everyone was at it.

The assortment of goods available in the shops wasn't very big, as a rule, and there weren't enough good-quality products on the shelves. The directors of retail companies were therefore among the most respected people in society. It wasn't possible just to go out to the shops and buy the most high-quality version of the product you needed: instead, you had to 'acquire' the product, in other words come to an agreement with the director (or head) of the shop, or with a salesperson or someone in the packing team, and pay them an extra 'commission' – only then would you be able to get your hands on the item. Only then, once they'd got what they wanted, would you be able to savour the feeling of having it in your possession. And what a pleasurable thing it was, to know that you had got your hands on something that no-one else had. People who were able to 'acquire' things in this way were greatly respected by their nearest and dearest. They really knew how to take care of business!

In America people will boldly assert: "I pay my taxes!" in an attempt to remind the administration of its duty to heed their personal opinion and rights. Here, by contrast, several generations of people have lived in a society in which the interests of the individual had to play second fiddle to the interests of society. As for what exactly the interests of society were, this was determined by the group of people who had seized power. And this group of people declared that the state was responsible for the fate of each and every individual, thereby absolving the individual of responsibility for itself. Many people professed that they felt grateful for this form of interaction: they didn't have to think about anything for themselves, for the people "up there at the top" knew better than them what ought to be done. And if any personal problems *did* arise, it was always easier to accuse "those at the top" of being responsible: "look what they're doing, they don't have any regard for the people at all."

This was the psychological preparation of ordinary Ukrainians prior to society's transition towards a market economy.

One of the most serious challenges facing the Ukrainian nation in 1991 was the work that had to be done in the field of state-building. The problem was that the national democratic forces in the country had no experience of creating and developing their own state. The entire history of the supporters of Ukrainian independence has been about resisting those in power: it has been a story of oppression, prison and exile. Ukrainian patriots were steeled in this battle, learned how to survive in it and passed on their ideas to later generations. But they were always soldiers fighting against something, eternal rebels, constantly in opposition. They never had an opportunity to learn about the positive work of creating a structure of state governance, administration, law-making and economic construction. For this reason, freed from the pressure of the totalitarian ideological machine, Ukrainian spiritual leaders focused their efforts primarily on the humanitarian front, in the field of the national language, and the country's symbols, monuments and place names.

The passion some people have in this country for giving cities and streets new names sometimes takes on epic proportions. I am firmly of the belief that geographical names and place names, and the names of cities and the streets in them, should be traditional, be well-founded from a historical point of view and remain unchanged for many centuries, unless the street in question is completely rebuilt. If the decision is taken to name a street in honour of some individual or other, then that person's achievements must be beyond doubt, indisputable and live long in the memory for many generations.

In our country, however, a strange custom has developed of changing the names of cities and streets for fleeting political reasons. This custom was something that was begun by the Communists after they seized power in the Russian Empire in 1917.

Dozens of cities were named not only after political figures who died long ago, but also after politicians who are alive and in office today. As for the names of Lenin and Stalin – two consecutive Communist leaders – there isn't a single city, town or village whose central square hasn't borne the name of Lenin, with the square next to it named after Stalin.

Over the course of several years, as battle raged among those at the very top of the Communist Party, various groups of leaders were revealed, one after the other, to be traitors and spies. Streets and indeed whole cities therefore had to be renamed in honour of different leaders.

Eventually, in 1953, Stalin died. Before long it was revealed that he was not a great leader, but a brutal dictator. His name no longer features among the names of streets and cities. And the same pattern was repeated endlessly: as each new group came to power, the epidemic of changing place names would spread once again.

Another funny habit that arose was to name streets after foreign political leaders, Communists and revolutionaries. Take Patrice Lumumba, for example: he was the Prime Minister of the Congo (modern-day Zaire) for two-and-a-half months in 1960, but today's young people have no idea who he was. Yet one of the streets in the centre of Kiev still bears his name.

Another example is the controversial Spanish republican politician, Julian Grimau, whose name is associated with brutal oppression of the opposition during the Spanish Civil War of 1936-1939. I wonder how many of the people currently living in Julian Grimau Street, in Dnepropetovsk, could tell you who he was?

When Ukraine obtained its political independence in 1991, our people had a sense of their 'separateness' as a nation. It was as if we suddenly remembered that we had a history of our own, and heroes of our own. And with a sense of enjoyment and a determination that were unparalleled, we began destroying all traces of our Soviet past in our place names. One can well understand why we rejected certain names which were entirely Communist in nature: Karl Marx Street, Lenin Street, Chekists' Street, October Revolution Street. Why, though, did we decide to rename streets which were named after famous writers or scientists? Was it that we wanted to get rid of anything and everything that was related to our Soviet past, and the symbols of Communism? In that case why is it that, to this day, there is a street in Kiev named after Uborevich, the Communist general and hangman, who brutally put down the peasant uprisings against Stalin's regime in Russia and Belarus?

In the city of Lutsk (in the centre of the Volyn Region), it was decided that 27 streets would be renamed. The names of Soviet guerrillas and Red Army generals, who had fought against the Germans during the Second World War, were to be removed. Why is it, then, that the city still has a street named after Kuibyshev, one of Stalin's closest associates? In the early 1930s he introduced a policy of forcibly joining up the peasants' smallholdings (known as 'collectivization'), which caused desperate, widespread resistance among the people and equally widespread and brutal oppression on the part of the Communist regime.

The hysteria with which we rename our streets is indicative of the wild nature of our political processes. For reasons purely to do with PR, politicians often focus their attention on issues related to the renaming of streets, to the rewriting of history, or to painting historical events in a slightly new light. Things are far more difficult when it comes to economic problems. It takes wit and wisdom, and willpower, to explain what needs to be built and how we are to go about building it; it is far easier to incite a crowd to tear something down, call it off, and give it a new name.

Yet even the new place names reflect the intense political passions of the present day. The murder of the journalist Gongadze, which was committed by a high-ranking bodyguard and his subordinates, caused a storm of discontent and led to two streets in Kiev being renamed in his honour. Yet many people, whilst sharing the dismay felt by the majority at such a brutal murder, are ambivalent about the person and activities of the journalist himself, and harbour doubts about whether his role in Ukrainian journalism was significant enough for him to be immortalized in a street name in an ancient city.

In the city of Lutsk, which I referred to above, the city's councillors elected to rename one of the city's streets in honour of Yulia Timoshenko, the leader of the political opposition, who at the time was behind bars after being given a prison sentence that was clearly motivated by the political interests of the group in power. The chairman of the city council had to remind the councillors – who were in the ecstasy of political opposition – that names were given to streets in order to immortalize the memory of a particular individual, i.e. after that individual's death. If they were to name the street after someone who was still alive, their actions might well be misinterpreted.

But whilst the patriots were busy renaming streets and tearing down statues of Soviet leaders, certain people took the helm of the economy, and for these people the colour of the flag was of next to no importance.

THE CAPTAINS OF UKRAINE'S MARKET ECONOMY

Where did they come from, the people who are currently running the Ukrainian economy? Where did these billionaires, bank owners, football club owners and philanthropists come from, in such a short space of time? It seems to me that four main methods can be identified, by means of which groups of people and individual businessmen were able to accumulate wealth and take ownership of major property.

Firstly, there was a group of people who had saved up significant financial resources, which they had probably converted into gold and gemstones. These people were representatives of that same cohort of store directors, goods storage site managers, warehouse managers, restaurant directors, and the really owners of 'underground' manufacturing firms (such firms did indeed exist, however hard the authorities tried to clamp down on them). They couldn't publicize their wealth: on the contrary, they had to keep it hidden from everyone. Their wives only wore the jewellery they owned in the presence of a close circle of friends, behind closed doors and with the curtains closed. Occasionally they were found, exposed, found guilty during trials held as a way of warning the others, and sent to prison. And yet this category survived, and formed one of the groups which, due to both their inherent entrepreneurial flair and the fact that they had some starting capital, were transformed into the effective owners of part of Ukraine's industrial and trade potential, created through the labour of many generations of people. This potential had lost its owner – the Soviet state – and acquired new owners during the transition to market relations.

Secondly, there was also another category of people, who enjoyed even greater influence and power in respect of property. These were the people appointed as directors of state concerns under the Soviet regime – at the very moment when that regime lost its grip on power in the state... The state had not disappeared, you might argue: it had a parliament, a ministerial cabinet, local authorities. This was indeed the case, but in Soviet Ukraine real power was not in the hands of the Supreme Soviet or the Council of Ministers – not for a moment. Real power was in the hands of the Communist Party. And this party – following the attempt by some of its most senior officials, in August 1991, to pull off a coup d'état, had been declared illegal.

Back then, the director of an industrial concern which might employee thousands of people, could become the outright owner of the firm, if he had enough entrepreneurial spirit. The legislation regulating private ownership of property was only just being formed, and it sometimes contained such unexpected standards that if you had the right amount of entrepreneurship, stubbornness and courage, and if you had the right contacts in the country's new establishment, you could really work wonders, and take possession of entire industrial complexes.

The accumulation of property in the hands of just a few was facilitated by an unusual mechanism, dreamt up by the leaders of the new state (although it should be pointed out that many of them held the levers of power in their hands during the Soviet era, too). All the property of the Soviet state on the territory of Ukraine was given a valuation (the criteria for this valuation, incidentally, remain shrouded in mystery, but a certain figure was put forward). The aggregate amount of property was divided up among the number of people living in the country. Each citizen of Ukraine was given a little piece of paper which stated that he or she was the owner of state property to the value of 1,155,000 Ukrainian *karbovantsy* – the equivalent of about 100 dollars at the time of going to press.

What was the *karbovanets*, you might be wondering? This was the currency of the new Ukrainian state, which was so badly made and so badly protected against counterfeits that in the countries bordering Ukraine people immediately started printing off this 'currency' using photocopiers. In exchange for this money printed using photocopiers, material assets (foodstuffs and industrial goods) were bought up and taken out of Ukraine in large quantities. Inflation in this period went through the roof. Before long the banknotes were available in denominations as high as 10 million.

Keep in mind that each person's share in all the nation's wealth had been put at just 1,155,000 *karbovantsy*. This sum had soon fallen in value from 100 dollars to about 1 dollar. What use was that to anyone? A window of opportunity was given, with a deadline by which each citizen had to choose which firm they wanted to take ownership of – otherwise their right to take ownership of it would simply expire and be cancelled. Ukrainians who worked at manufacturing plants might decide to become the 'owner' of the plant, with a one thousandth of a percent stake in it. There were some cases in which the workers at a firm pooled their share certificates, and formed a joint-stock company, based on the principle of collective ownership. Yet in these cases the stake owned by the firm's director and financial director was always considerably higher than the stake held by the rank-and-file employee. Thereafter the shares would be concentrated in just a few pairs of hands, and the formation of a group who were effectively the new owners.

What about people who worked as nursery school teachers, doctors or taxi drivers? These people simply had no idea what to do with their 'investment certificates'. Many citizens handed in their bonds to one of the investment funds, of which there was now a great abundance. The idea behind creating these funds consisted in uniting the right of many individual property-holders to part of the property of the state which had disappeared, with the aim of acquiring a firm of some sort. The promises made were the same ones made everywhere, since time immemorial: big returns, in a short space of time. Understandably, a large number of investment funds existed for just a brief period before suddenly disappearing along with your bonds, and from this muddled cocktail of incomplete laws and economic disorder, new owners of factories, newspapers and ferry companies emerged.

Sometimes it was even more straightforward than that. You would arrive at work to find that there were some cars parked outside the gates of your factory, and a group of stocky men would offer you a small sum of money in exchange for your bond – cash in hand, on the spot. The ordinary workers looked on their bond certificate as a useless piece of paper, the invention of those in power. Whereas if they got hold of some real money, they'd be able to go to the shops and buy something useful. The certificates were bought up like this in their thousands, at knock-down prices, and soon the firms had brand new, legitimate owners, who were able to present bond certificates in sufficient quantities to be able to obtain a controlling share.

I can't help but mention another category of *nouveaux riches* that emerged at that time in Ukraine: the people who belonged to criminal circles, the racketeers. The concept of a racket was something that people simply couldn't be aware of in Soviet times, since property was owned by the state and it was difficult to 'grease the palm' of a company director – he didn't own anything in person, other than his salary, and any attempt to demand something from him under threat of harming his business would be tantamount to pitting yourself against the state's entire law enforcement machine.[81] Under the new circumstances which had arisen, people had emerged who had to get involved

---

81   You will get a sense of how serious this is from the fact that for the theft of state property, the criminal code stipulated far greater punishments than for the theft of citizens' property. Criminals who caused damage to the state, valued at roughly the same as two economy-class cars, could be sentenced to the death penalty. The punishments for stealing private property were far less severe.

in low-level business just to ensure their existence: they had been separated from the pack, and were therefore defenceless.

Industry in the Soviet state was founded on the principles of cooperation in manufacturing. Just one or two large firms, or sometimes a few more than that, were manufacturing a particular type of product for an entire country with a population of 250 million people and an area of 22 million square kilometres (roughly the same size as North America). In the early 1990s, when, due to the disappearance of the economic ties which had existed in this huge country, and were now destroyed, the big firms were closed down, and people who worked at academic institutions were made redundant due to the lack of financing, all these people who had been left with nothing to do began to dabble in business, just to make ends meet. They set up stalls at markets in the towns and villages, to sell whatever they could – from cheap clothes imported from Turkey to tools and drills salvaged from companies that were going bust. They sold old clothes and shoes, books published 20 years previously, and hand-crafted items. People in rural areas sold foodstuffs at the markets: eggs, milk, curd, sour cream, vegetables, herbs and so on.

Slowly but surely people began to master the art of dealing in petty contraband goods, which were also sold at street markets.

What were the street markets like in those days? There were wooden tables and stalls, with covers over them to keep the rain off. And many tens and hundreds of individual traders who stood behind these tables all day long. The flow of hard currency that passed through their hands was quite considerable. And of course, before long people turned up who began to organize a racket, and demanded that these small traders pay them off. The racketeers quickly got a liking for this, got hold of weapons and went to the 'next level up', and began imposing a 'protection tax' from restaurants, private shops, garages, retail firms and so on. The moment anyone managed to set up a small but profitable business, the criminals might simply take him out of the picture through threats and violence.

On top of this there was also prostitution – illegal, of course, but very much a genuine and widespread phenomenon, which was soon under the control of the criminal gangs. There were also the gambling halls – legal and very much a part of life – containing thousands of 'one-armed bandits' which infected teens and the elderly, who put their last few coins into the wombs of these machines in the ephemeral hope of winning big. It doesn't take a lot of brains to work out that the gaming industry was not controlled by social welfare offices in local municipalities.

The lack of any genuine, effective assistance from the law enforcement agencies left small businesses with no choice but to turn a blind eye to the extortion by the criminals, and this meant that a flow of money was established which went right into the hands of the local mafia. This meant that the mafia now had capital which it could invest businesses which were above board. Criminal gangs began to emerge in the big cities, dividing them up into areas of influence. The initial capital made by certain individuals who enjoy considerable respect and influence today, and exert quite a strong influence on this country's policies, can be traced back to the wild nineties.

There were plenty of people who didn't quite make it through the wild nineties alive, incidentally. The market available to the racketeers was only so big, and the criminal groups began to clash over their areas of influence. What ensued was not exactly all-out street warfare between the gangsters, but a lot of people were shot dead in restaurants, apartment block entrances or in areas of wasteland. A huge number of expensive marble tombstones began to appear at the prestigious cemeteries in the city centre, beneath which lay the young men who were killed during this 'settling of scores' by the criminals. No-one is in a position to be able to confirm or deny the rumours that the intelligence services played a part in thinning the ranks of the criminal organizations. The official version of events, whenever there was yet another exchange of gunfire and two new corpses to add to the tally, was that it was the result of conflict between criminal gangs.

A time came when impudent young speculators, contraband dealers and racketeers began to feel as though they were the 'masters of the universe': they got their hands on the first imported Mercedes, and owned expensive restaurants; they made money hand over fist, and did not need to work particularly hard to do so; they hired expensive prostitutes and indulged in orgies in saunas. Burgundy club jackets came into fashion, and began to be seen as the traditional dress of a certain category of people who became known as 'new Russians'. This name had nothing to do with their nationality at all, incidentally. These were the people who handed out wildly generous tips at Egyptian resorts, and were rude and uncivilized towards the staff, thereby forming a particular view in people's minds about our 'eccentric nature'.

One particular theory about the origins of the money owned by another group of wealthy Ukrainians today is of interest. Some people are convinced that funds referred to as 'the party's money' were held in Swiss bank accounts. The story had it that these were funds which belonged to the central agencies of the Communist party and its youth wing, the Komsomol. After the CPSU was outlawed in 1991, this money ended up in the hands of the last people holding the reins: the ones who "knew the password", you might say.

Political commentators assured us, with stern expressions on their faces, that the Communist Party was not keeping any money overseas, and provided convincing evidence in support of this claim. Yet these experts were unable to explain how it was that there was now a group of young businessmen in Ukrainian society, who had formerly held significant positions in the party or the Komsomol; and these businessmen weren't just selling pies or serving coffee at kiosks – they were taking over banks which had just been set up, and so on and so forth. Some of them went bankrupt, and were cursed by the investors who had put their trust in them; but some of them stuck at it, made even more money than they had at the outset, and are now among the elite in Ukraine's financial and political establishment.

In other words, just as in the classic phrase ascribed variously to Rothschild, Rockefeller and Ford: "I'll answer for every cent, just don't ask me how I made my first million."

THE HETMANS OF MODERN-DAY UKRAINE

I think it will be of interest to have a look at who it is that the descendants of the Cossacks elect as their 'hetmans' – or to put it in today's parlance, as their presidents.

Our first president, Leonid Kravchuk, governed the country for 957 days (from 5th December 1991 to 19th July 1994). I consider it hardly surprising that he was elected President of an independent Ukraine. He had been involved in the governance of the country during the Soviet era as well. Moreover, Kravchuk was the chief ideologue of the Communist Party of Ukraine. When set against his ultra-conservative colleagues in the senior party leadership, however, he seemed like a progressive and democratic supporter of the nation's rebirth. Kravchuk secured 61.6% of the vote and his authority was beyond doubt. Seven days after he was elected, he signed an agreement on the termination of the USSR, along with the presidents of Russia and Belarus. At a ceremonial session of the Upper Rada of Ukraine on 22nd August 1992, in Kiev, the last president of the Ukrainian People's Republic in exile, Nikolai Plavyuk, gave him the state regalia of the UPR and declared that an independent Ukraine was the rightful heir to the republic. Kravchuk was an active supporter of the metropolitan Filaret[82] in the latter's efforts to create a Ukrainian Orthodox Church – a Kievan Patriarchate, which would no longer be subordinate to the Moscow Patriarchate.

Leonid Kravchuk is a well-educated man, and holds a degree in economics[83]. Nonetheless, it so happened that his presidency coincided with the start of Ukraine's transition to market-based relations, and the task of holding on to

---

82   Filaret had been excommunicated from the Russian Orthodox Church and been banned from it, which did not stop him taking charge of a four-million strong Orthodox religious community, consisting of 4821 parishes.

83   The degrees awarded in the Soviet era were recognition of the fact that someone had made a particular contribution to academic theory; degree candidates' dissertations had to pass a very serious review stage and a multi-stage check, and a huge amount of work and effort went into preparing them. I know this for a fact, because I went through the process of earning a degree myself.

the reins of Ukraine – which was hurtling ahead over the unchartered spaces of a hitherto unknown economic order, with all the ditches and potholes that entailed – was one with which neither he, nor his ministers were able to cope. The privatizations of the country's industry were accompanied by a considerable amount of corruption. Between 1992 and 1994 inflation soared to 1000%. Industrial workers, teachers and so on often had to wait many months to receive their salaries. The destruction of Ukraine's merchant navy on the Black Sea cast a pall over Kravchuk's presidency. An extremely profitable structure, which at the time of the collapse of the USSR was turning over $800 million dollars and making serious profits, suddenly became loss-making during the course of a short period of reforms, which were implemented under the pretext of corporatization; three hundred ships were sold off, the flows of money coming in were redirected to offshore banks, and the company filed for bankruptcy[84].

The appointment of the future President, Leonid Kuchma, as prime minister, and the handing over to him, with parliament's consent, of practically dictatorial powers, did not help to rescue the situation. Following numerous acts of protest, Kravchuk was forced to agree to an early election, in which he was beaten by his former prime minister.

Thus Leonid Kuchma came to power in July 1994.

Kuchma enjoyed the support of the so-called 'directorate', i.e. the leaders of the country's biggest industrial concerns. As someone who had once managed a missile manufacturing plant, the country's business elite saw him as one of their own. His campaign slogans – about industrial growth, and economics taking precedence over politics – struck a chord with people, and seemed wholly appropriate during the economic chaos which reigned supreme at the time. He introduced some fairly tough, authoritarian policies inside the country. In some cases this worked in Ukraine's favour, for example during the process of adopting the Constitution. As per usual in this country, the differences of opinion between the various political forces represented in the Supreme rada (the parliament) and the reluctance to seek compromises put at risk the ability to adopt the primary law in the country, without which Ukraine would be unable to think of itself as a fully-fledged state. As was his wont, Kuchma literally forced the deputies to reach an agreement, threatening to disband parliament, and eventually,

---

84 Parliament attempted to halt the 'corporatization' process, but the President used his edicts to reaffirm the authority of the Black Sea Shipping Company, which has come to be known here by the acronym Blasco. In 1998 the company's Director, who was found to have behaved unlawfully, was given a lengthy prison sentence, but after just two years he was released as part of an amnesty and went back to being a businessman.

during an all-night debate on 27th – 28th June, the deputies duly noted all of the President's critical remarks and voted to adopt all the articles under discussion. The document itself was far from perfect: experts point to a large number of mistakes and discrepancies in it, which have led to legal disputes. Nevertheless, 28th June – the day on which the Constitution of Ukraine was adopted – was declared a State holiday.

Leonid Kuchma's activities in the field of foreign policy were all about manoeuvring and a desire to develop relations with both Europe and Russia – the two economic and political centres which are struggling for domination in Ukraine. This was merely a continuation of the 'multi-directional' policy introduced by his predecessor, incidentally.

In spite of the scandals which shook his time in office, and the attempts made by the opposition to begin impeachment proceedings, some people look back on his presidency with nostalgia, as an example of political stability – by comparison with what came next. Kuchma managed fairly adroitly to shift the blame for any failings onto the government, getting through no fewer than 9 Prime Ministers during his time in office, including two future presidents. Nevertheless, during Leonid Kuchma's second term the fall in GDP was brought to a halt for the first time since 1992, and it began to grow once again. Inflation remained low and the exchange rate for the national currency was stable[85]. As you might expect, it was mostly the oligarchs that got rich – the quality of life of most ordinary people remained low, despite the undeniable upturn in the economy. Kuchma spent two terms in office – 3841 days in total – and, as you would expect, did not take part in the next election.

A terrible tragedy occurred during his presidency: during military exercises above the Black Sea, a Ukrainian anti-aircraft missile hit a Russian passenger plane which had begun its journey in Israel. Kuchma, somewhat at a loss as to how to respond, let slip the following remark: "We're not the first and we won't be the last, we mustn't make a tragedy out of this. Mistakes occur everywhere, and not just mistakes on this scale, but on a far

---

85   These successes are attributed in no small part to the Yushchenko-Timoshenko government, when the future president was in charge of the Cabinet and Yulia Timoshenko was Deputy Prime Minister. It was under their stewardship that the budget was balanced, order was restored to the fuel and energy complex, the debts owed on the payment of pensions and bursaries were cancelled, and the frequent power cuts which many towns used to suffer were brought to an end. These results played a considerable role in enhancing the popularity of Yushchenko and, to an even greater extent, Yulia Timoshenko. Yet at the same time there was resistance to them among representatives of big business, whose interests suffered due to the measures that were taken. Yushchenko was removed from office and a criminal investigation was opened against Timoshenko, and although she was required to spend 42 days in solitary confinement, the court found her not guilty, and she made a triumphant return to politics.

larger, global scale." A serious foreign policy row erupted. Ukraine paid out 5.6 million dollars in compensation to the victims' families, but never officially admitted responsibility for the incident.

Without question, the biggest blow dealt to Kuchma was the so-called 'cassette scandal'. The head of the technical security department in the presidential security detail, a man named Melnichenko, revealed that at his own personal initiative, he had recorded the conversations the President had in his office. The voices on the tape 'resembled' those of the president and the home affairs minister. The recordings suggested that Kuchma had allegedly instructed the minister of the interior, Kravchenko[86], to have the opposition journalist Georgy Gongadze[87] killed. The 'cassette scandal' resulted in the emergence of the protest movement 'Ukraine without Kuchma'.

When set against these events, the admonishments levelled at Kuchma for having facilitated the privatization of state property to suit the interests of his relatives and a close circle of friends are not taken very seriously, somehow. This is probably due to the fact that, if we take our national mentality into account, it would look strange if the president had acted in the interests of 'others' in a way that would damage the interests of 'his own kith and kin'.

In 2004 some historic events occurred in the political life of Ukraine, which demonstrated that the people will not tolerate it if their will is ignored, or if the expression of their will is manipulated.

As I have already mentioned several times, Ukrainians have striven for centuries to acquire the ability to build a national state of their own. At the present time, the greatest threat to Ukraine losing its independence stems, without a shadow of a doubt, from Russia. In Russia, the imperial ambition and ambition to be a great state, which, to put it bluntly, have become part of the worldview of even the poorest and most downtrodden Russian citizen, are being strengthened by the political views and objectives of the people currently ruling Russia. Therefore, when Prime Minister Yanukovich, in 2003, and his circle decided that the country should join the so-called Single Economic Area, a supranational entity incorporating the countries in the Customs Union – Russia, Belarus and Kazakhstan – both the political parties and huge segments of the population saw this as an attempt to reinstate the Soviet Union. This prompted millions of people to become politically active

---

86   Soon after Kuchma left office, Kravchenko was found dead at his dacha, on the eve of his birthday. The official finding that this was suicide is widely held not to stand up to criticism, since the former minister's death had been caused by two shots to the head.

87   Gongadze was the founder of the opposition online newspaper 'Ukrainian truth', which published stories that were strongly critical of Kuchma on several occasions. A high-ranking employee of the Ministry of Internal Affairs, who was suspected of murdering him, spent six years on the run before eventually being arrested, admitting his involvement and being sentenced to life behind bars.

to an unprecedented extent: to put it simply, they were afraid they might lose their Motherland.

Although there were a large number of candidates standing in the election (26), it was essentially a political battle between the Prime Minister, Viktor Yanukovich, and the leader of the bloc which triumphed in the parliamentary elections in 2002, 'Our Ukraine' – Viktor Yushchenko. The election was an extremely tense affair, taking place against the backdrop of unconfirmed reports that Viktor Yushchenko, one of the main candidates, had been deliberately poisoned. There were allegations of multiple breaches of the electoral laws, accusations of forging of votes and intimidation of voters, and of bias in the media.

According to the official verdict of the Central Electoral Commission, Viktor Yanukovich won the second round, with 49.46% of the votes. Yushchenko and his supporters, however – along with many foreign observers – declared that there had been large-scale falsifications during the election. There were a lot of people who witnessed voters being put under pressure by supporters of Viktor Yanukovich, as well as bundles of votes in his favour being thrown into the ballot boxes. This led to a serious political crisis and mass acts of civil unrest, which became known as the 'Orange revolution'[88].

---

[88] It was in November 2004 that our 'Maidan' form of national protest first emerged. In late 2004, tens of thousands of people from all over Ukraine gathered together on Independence Square in Kiev and declared: we'll stand here until honest elections are held. 'Maidan' was supported by mass protests in many regions. On certain significant days, up to half a million people would gather on the square. After the 'Orange Revolution' succeeded, reports came out to the effect that the acts of protest were funded by the USA, or by the now deceased Russian oligarch Berezovsky, and so on and so forth. I can well believe that funding was indeed received from these sources, but who received it? The political figures who took on the role of the leaders of the opposition? It may be that our friends from other countries judge things based on their own experience and on their own systems for organizing national protests. In this country, our 'revolutionary leaders' are, to be blunt, somewhat removed from the people. In order to support the activities of a protest like Maidan, which involved many thousands of people, you do indeed need funds. Voluntary help, in the form of the food and warm clothes that were taken to the Maidan protesters by sympathetic fellow-citizens, would not have been enough, on its own, for the activists to have been able to stay out there on the tarmac on those cold December nights. On the third day, however, Maidan gained the support of medium-sized business: the problem of securing material supplies, food and medical assistance was solved. The idea of business supporting popular protest movements is a pretty unusual phenomenon. At this time, though, there was an awareness in society of the threat that the socio-political group with whom Viktor Yanukovich was strongly associated might come to power. In the summer and autumn of 2004, cases of the forced transfer of ownership rights to specific companies from their owners to representatives of the politico-economic group in Donetsk were widely discussed in the world of small and medium-sized enterprises. The raids carried out by this 'Donetsk circle' on the business world gave rise to serious concerns, among large and, more importantly, active business circles, over whether or not their own businesses would be safe in the event of a victory for Yanukovich, and as a result there was a strong sense that he must not be allowed to win the presidency.
Ukraine's Minister of Internal Affairs was at pains to adopt a position of neutrality. The city's mayor, Alexander Omelchenko, opened up the doors to the mayor's office, and allowed medical assistance points to be set up there for the protesters.

OLEKSANDR SHYSHKO

Against the backdrop of the complex political situation, the Supreme Court of Ukraine declared the results of the 2nd round of the election null and void and ordered a re-run of the presidential elections in Ukraine. The re-run was won by Viktor Yushchenko (with 51.99% of the vote), who therefore took up office as the president of Ukraine.

Having swept to power on the back of a wave of enthusiasm from the public, Viktor Yushchenko initially benefited from a huge amount of trust from the people. Given that he had a majority in Parliament, he could have brought in radical reforms, and his political enemies would have been powerless to do anything about it. Yet, strangely, the new president revealed himself to be a weak administrator and a poor reformer. His decrees were often of a populist nature, and the decisions he made were impulsive and ill thought through[89]. Yushchenko soon began to have arguments with his peers from the days of the Orange Revolution, and ultimately he lost the support of Yulia Timoshenko[90], who was respected both by the politicians and the people. Timoshenko positioned herself as a protector of the state's interests and someone who was taking the fight to corrupt systems, when she spoke out against Yushchenko's idea of giving Ukraine's continental shelf to a private off-shore company, or when she got rid of the middle-men structures in the procurement system for energy sources.

I should point out that there was an unusual sense of unity in the country in this period, along with a sense of mutual respect and boosted morale. People began to treat complete strangers with benevolence, and smile at one another on crossing paths in the street or on public transport, in the office or outside their apartment block. This is no exaggeration. It was a fascinating time.

89   A great deal of puzzlement was caused, for example, by the presidential decree about the abolition of road traffic police. It is widely known that the Ukrainian road traffic police have a reputation for being extortionists and bribe-takers, who let those who break the rules of the road go free in return for a particular fee. The logical thing to do would be to hold checks, fire those caught with bribes, bring in new staff, and if need be give the police a pay-rise, so that it was harder to pay them off. But to wind up a whole police department? Who was going to make sure people abided by the rules of the road? After all, Ukrainians, to be blunt, are not among the most disciplined of drivers, and are capable of both speeding and drink-driving.

90   Yulia Timoshenko is one of the best-known stars in Ukraine's political landscape. With the support of the then Prime Minister Pavel Lazarenko, her company acquired a monopoly in the market for natural gas imported from Russia, and Timoshenko become one of the richest businesswomen in Ukraine. Following Lazarenko's resignation, her business was destroyed by the authorities, and she focused solely on politics, proving herself to be a good orator and a skilful political leader, and eventually becoming Ukraine's first ever female Prime Minister. Yet her background in business left her vulnerable to attacks from her political enemies, who are constantly looking into the operations of Timoshenko's former company to find new grounds for bringing criminal charges against her. There is no doubt that there may indeed be grounds for such charges. The so-called 'wild nineties' were a time of financial and legal disorder in Ukraine, when a lot of wealth was created that had dubious origins, etc. Timoshenko's actions whilst in office as Prime Minister saw her gaining approval, on the one hand, in the eyes of the nationalist and patriotic forces (for refusing to allow the country's key strategic companies to fall into private ownership, and for removing private middle-men in the field of the procurement of energy sources by Ukraine), and, on the other hand, caused puzzlement on all sides: by cutting out the middle-men in the supply of gas from Russia to Ukraine, Timoshenko ended up signing a deal under which the gas supplied to the country cost a lot more than it did when supplied through the middle-men...

TO GET UKRAINE

In foreign policy, Viktor Yushchenko was in favour of moving closer to the EU and the US, and advocated greater integration with Europe and the North Atlantic. On the issue of the installation of anti-missile defence systems in Eastern Europe, he was on the side of the US. Understandably, he made himself extremely unpopular in the eyes of the Russian government extremely quickly, in particular by calling on the nation to pay off the debt it owed to the Russian Federation for its gas consumption during the first years of independence, and in the transition to market relations as regards the stationing of the Russian Black Sea Fleet in the Crimea.

It must be conceded that Yushchenko was handicapped to a considerable extent during his time as president, because, at the apogee of the political crisis of 2004, President Kuchma, who was still in office and had retained his powers, only gave his consent to a re-run on condition that the president conceded many of his rights under the constitution to the prime minister.

Be that as it may, Yushchenko managed to position himself against both his political ally, Yulia Timoshenko, who had held the post of prime minister, and his adversary Viktor Yanukovich, who replaced her in this role. In 2010, Yushchenko decided to stand for the presidency independently, and consequently received just 5.45% of the vote – the worst result in world history for an incumbent president. Many believe that Yushchenko's behaviour facilitated Yulia Timoshenko's defeat in the presidential elections and the coming to power of Ukraine's next president, Viktor Yanukovich[91].

Viktor Yanukovich was elected president of Ukraine in 2010, securing 49% of the vote. This was the share of the vote that he was able to secure on a constant basis, because his supporters are concentrated in the densely populated industrial south-east of the country. There are particular socio-economic conditions which pertain in the east and south-east of Ukraine, and the political views of this group of people are defined by this fact. This is the area where heavy industry and mining are concentrated. Exhausting work in the mines and smelting plants was relatively well remunerated during the Soviet era, and workers were given various perks, and holidays at health spas and guesthouses owned by the companies for which they worked. The people in this region had a sense of pride instilled in them for the contribution they

---

91   An unsightly stain on Yushchenko's presidency was the case of the 'Hospital of the future'. In 2006 it was announced that a fund-raising marathon would take place to raise money for the construction of a modern hospital for children with oncological diseases. A group of businessmen came forward offering to contribute 2 million dollars in sponsorship. A huge number of ordinary people donated money out of the kindness of their hearts, from a couple of dollars to a couple of hundred, depending on their means. The project was carried out with the patronage of the president's wife. The hospital was never built. The money was nowhere to be seen at the bank. Not only are the explanations given by the directors of the 'Hospital of the future' fund about the missing cash flawed – they also make one want to open a criminal investigation.

were making to the country's economy through their hard, at times dangerous work. When the transition to a market economy occurred, miners and metal workers became much worse off. However, people began to blame this not on the new company owners, but on the collapse of the Soviet Union: "Life was better under the Communists!" A deep-rooted view took hold in these people that "The Donbass feeds Ukraine", whereas the Donetsk, Zaporozhye and Lugansk regions have long been subsidized, i.e. they receive more resources from the state's budget than they put into it.

A considerable proportion of the population of this region are ethnic Russians. In the big cities in the Donetsk Region, for example – Donetsk, Yenakiieve, Makiivka – there are more Russians than Ukrainians. Moreover, a sizeable number of the Ukrainians in this region consider Russian to be their native tongue – and 75% of the population of the Donbass speaks Russian. These factors – nostalgia for the USSR and the fact that Russian is so widely spoken – explain why the people in this region are inclined towards closer relations with the Russian Federation, and why they are somewhat cautious about the forces of nationalism and patriotism.

Moreover, the harsh living and working conditions lead to high levels of alcoholism and violent crime in these areas. Let me give you an example to illustrate this: in 2012, a total of 48,500 crimes were recorded in the Donetsk region, whilst 41,000 were recorded in Dnepropetrovsk region. In the regions in the extreme west of the country, the picture is completely different: 4200 crimes were recorded in the Ternopil region, 4800 in the Chernivtsi region and 4900 in the Ivano-Frankivsk region. The fact that the regions in the west of the country are less densely populated does not affect the comparative results as regards criminality: the East is ahead of the West on this count too, when calculated per head of the population. This means that many ordinary people in the east of the country are related to, friends with or know of someone who has been convicted of a crime in the past: for fighting, for example, or for vandalism or theft. To many people's minds, a criminal record does not amount to a black stain on a person's past history, which leaves that person excluded from society.

The tradition of working in the large teams – sometimes numbering many thousands – which formed the workforces at the plants and the coal companies, created in people, on the one hand, a sense of togetherness, of unity of opinion, a striving to abide by an idea that was shared by the majority, and on the other hand the habit of subordinating themselves to a leader, a boss, a director. These people are lacking that *khutoryanstvo* I referred to earlier, that striving towards independence, independent thought, which is considered a characteristic feature of the Ukrainian character. Bosses do not have too much trouble shaping the outlook of this kind of electorate, and aiming it in the direction required. The rank-and-file worker imagines that he doesn't really get the nitty-gritty of politics, that it's all a bit beyond him. And if his director has told him that he should vote for a particular candidate, because that candidate is offering the best programme, then that's exactly what he'll do – his seniors know best.

All these factors taken together led to a situation whereby voters in the south-east of Ukraine felt able to give their backing to a man such as Viktor Yanukovich. Europe may grumble about the fact that someone who had twice been brought before the criminal courts became president. For the average worker from Yenakiieve, though, Yanukovich was 'one of their own', someone with whom they felt familiar. He had had a difficult childhood – his mother died young. At 16 he took up a job as an ordinary worker at a factory. Yanukovich was a member of the Komsomol and a member of the Communist Party, and that meant he had genuinely been rehabilitated in respect of the crimes he had committed: say what you will, but people with convictions hanging over them weren't allowed to become members of the Communist Party. So as far as his past was concerned...These things happen, people make mistakes when they're young. Sometimes the mistakes they make lead to them being brought before the courts. On the flip-side, Yanukovich spent 20 years in managerial positions, and at one time (on the threshold of the 1990s), when a trend emerged for electing directors at general meetings of the workforce, rather than simply appointing them, he was twice elected to the position of director in a vote. He was governor of Donechina for five years. It was therefore no surprise that he had the backing of half the country's electorate.

After he was elected President, however, the worst fears about Viktor Yanukovich began seem justified. The people he appointed within the prosecutor's offices, the police and the courts unrolled a campaign of harassment against their political opponents, opening criminal investigations into them. Some were forced to flee the country as a result, and the leader of Yanukovich's political opponents, Yulia Timoshenko, was put in prison. The slogan 'everything for your friends, punishment under the law for your enemies' took on the most unbridled and perverse forms. The practice of redistributing profitable spheres of business to suit the interests of the 'right' people became commonplace. Not a single businessman who wasn't part of a narrow category of people classed as One of 'our lads', was able to feel secure. And whereas initially this was done to suit the interests of a group of oligarchs who had backed Yanukovich in his campaign for the presidency, the practice was later concentrated on the interests of a very small circle of people who were close to or had blood ties with the president – the so-called 'Family'.

OLEKSANDR SHYSHKO

A warning shot sounded for the president in 2012, when two new parties burst onto the parliamentary scene, one of which represented the nationalist wing of the political spectrum. The total share of the vote received by the party which backed the president fell, and in Kiev there were defeats for candidates who supported the government in every district. In late 2013, Yanukovich, a few days before a summit, and in a move which took most Ukrainians by surprise, refused to sign an agreement on an Association with the European Community and opted to go down a route of growing closer to Russia – and the response it promptly received was Maidan. Ukrainians don't want to fall under a Russian protectorate yet again.

Under pressure from the mass protests, the Cabinet, which consisted of loyal supporters of the President, was forced to resign, and Yanukovich fled to Russia. Due to the fact that senior officials in the Ministry of Internal Affairs made an attempt forcibly to break up the protest movement, which was initially a peaceful one, events took a tragic turn. Molotov cocktails and cobblestones were thrown, and there was death and bloodshed, with snipers on the rooftops, shooting in both directions, to provoke an escalation of the violence – and the Ukrainian people will not forgive their country's fourth president for these things.

The country had changed irrevocably. All new governments and all new presidents will need to take the 'Maidan' factor into account.

STATISTICS AND REAL LIFE

Somehow we have all grown used to saying that Ukraine is a poor country. Everyone tends to think of us as poor, and we have grown fond of complaining about life. In fact, though, Ukrainian entrepreneurialism, and our ability to adapt to any circumstances, create material values and earn money, have not been subjected to a proper, balanced assessment. Every day, the 'little man' in Ukraine, the small businessman, tradesman or farmer, is engaged in a constant struggle with his own state to try to keep hold of the wages in his pocket. There is a constant deficit in the state budget, and our civil servants are unable to find any solution other than to increase the tax burden. Consequently, the people try to apply all the wherewithal of their collective good sense in order not to pay these taxes. The people somehow sense that the holes in the national budget are caused by something other than excessive levels of consumption by ordinary citizens[92].

Take for example the centre of the country's coal industry – the Donetsk basin. 130 mines are owned by the state, and 30 are in private hands. Coal has been mined there since way back when, the mines are running dry, and the price of it is high. One tonne of coal, for example, might cost 600 UAH (60 Euros), or 800 UAH (80 Euros) or even 1000 UAH (100 Euro).

The state has established a kind of weighted purchase price – 750 UAH (75 Euros), to that the thermal power stations, which are the core consumers of this coal, all purchase coal under the same conditions. The difference between the set purchase price and the actual value is reimbursed to the

---

92   The annual losses from the national economy caused by the extremely wasteful consumption of energy sources amount to 14 billion Euros (Three times more energy is consumed per unit of production in Ukraine than in European countries, and twice as much as the global average). This sum would be enough to cover the annual costs on healthcare, defence and education twice over. The people, in their naivety, assume that the billionaire owners of industrial complexes and whole branches of industry ought to put their own resources into the modernizing of production processes. But since both the parliament and the government contain these self-same billionaires, or else are controlled by them, the solution that is always chosen is to expand the list of things that are subject to tax.

mines from the budget, using the taxes collected. The total amount that is paid back is growing year on year, and in the last 7 years it has grown four-fold.

These rebates from the state budget are unavoidable, and serve to keep our fuel and energy complex in working condition. In Ukraine, though, this mechanism works in its own particular way. The director of a mine will falsify his reports, hiking up the value to, let's say, 1200 UAH per tonne of coal. This means that he earns 450 UAH in reimbursements for every tonne.

What about the monitors on the side of the state? They come along and tell the director of the mine that some new equipment needs to be bought from a particular supplier, although this supplier's prices are 60% higher than elsewhere in the market. The thing is that the firm supplying the equipment is owned by the brother (or son, or friend, etc.) of the state monitor. This is an utterly corrupt system, of course, and although we were not the first to have invented it, we've certainly got it down to a fine art.

Not all sources of coal can be turned to profit through industrial methods: if the total volume of coal amounts to just 1000 tonnes, or even 20,000 tonnes, no-one is going to start bringing heavy machinery down here, or installing railway tracks. But if you bring a load of unemployed people along, and give them picks and wheelbarrows, then you can start mining coal. The value of this kind of coal is 50-100 UAH per tonne (5-10 Euros), because the working conditions are such that the workers don't even abide by the most basic of health and safety conditions, and no taxes whatsoever are paid to the state. This kind of coal can't be sold legally, of course. But you can always reach an agreement with the director of the mine, and add this illegal coal to the coal he produces through legal means. The mine will receive compensation from the budget for every tonne, and the director will have to share this with the dodgy supplier.

During the course of a year, 6 million tonnes of coal will be produced by the dodgy suppliers. The whole of the Donetsk coal basin has an output of 70 million tonnes of coal. The amount of compensation paid to coal mining companies in 2012 was 12 billion UAH (1.2 billion Euros). It's hard to fathom the sheer size of these numbers, unless you keep in mind that in the same year, the amount spent on healthcare was 6.3 billion UAH (half the amount spent on compensation) and the amount spent on culture was 2 billion UAH (just one sixth of the amount spent on compensation). So how much does one tonne of coal cost in real terms? Can you really use statistics to describe a situation like this?

I could paint a similar picture as regards our transport industry, too. And our construction industry. And the repairs to our roads, which are carried out every year, as if we lived in a region that was permanently suffering natural disasters. We see exactly the same thing in all these areas of life as well.

So how much does the Ukrainian economy actually produce, in reality – and what is the real size of its GDP?

The tax authorities estimate that the country's shadow economy is worth 350 billion UAH a year, and in their opinion this is a quarter of gross domestic product. Let's not get into an argument about it – other estimates have also been made. Suffice to say that the value of the profits coming into the budget in 2013 was defined as 363 billion UAH, and in 2014 – 395 billion UAH. Does this give you a sense of the sheer scale of our shadow economy?

If we take a look at those tax statistics again, they tell us that 170 billion UAH are paid as wages in 'envelopes' – this is money that is passed from hand to hand, isn't recorded anywhere and isn't subject to tax. What is forcing businessmen to pay this 'black salary', and forcing employees to agree to accept it? For the employee it doesn't make any economic sense at all: this kind of salary isn't taken account when calculating someone's pension, for example (i.e. their pension will be lower than it would be otherwise); and the employer could simply stop paying it in a crisis, and there would be nothing the employee could do and no-one to complain to.

The thing is that the tax burden on a company's wage bill, including all benefits and the income tax paid by employees, comes to 52% (i.e. for an employee to be able to take home 1000 UAH, the company must first deduct between 1070 and 1260 UAH in taxes and dues. So, as luck would have it, the interests of the employer and the employee coincide. When his salary is paid on a 'cash-in-hand' basis, the employee receives more money, and the businessman pays less tax.

And as for where the tax goes, I outlined this above when describing the peculiarities of the way in which our coal mining industry operates.

SLAYING THE DRAGON

Twenty-five years ago, a popular film was released in this country called 'Slaying the dragon', which was intended as a parable. The film's main message was this: it's not enough to expect some wandering knight to come over and slay the dragon that's terrorizing the citizens: instead, we need to make sure every citizen slays the dragon inside them. Corruption is something that reminds me of this dragon that has not yet been slayed[93].

Of course we don't like it that Ukraine is considered a completely corrupt country, and it's a claim I can't dispute. But having as I do a lot of experience of talking to foreign businessmen, I can confidently state that their attitude towards corruption in Ukraine contains an element of hope that they will find it easy to resolve various business and legal issues in the country. They suppose that since the civil servants are corrupt, all they will need to do is hand over a certain sum of money – and they'll be able to avoid obeying the law, or to receive preferential treatment that they don't really deserve. I want to warn you, in all honesty, that this is a sinful path, and one that hides a large number of dangers. They'll gladly take the money, of course, but there's no guarantee whatsoever that things will turn out for the best.

Given that corruption, as was noted in the First report on the campaign against this phenomenon to the EU, is present in all 28 countries of the European Union, and the total amount of economic damage it causes is

---

[93] It was neither us, nor you, that gave rise to this dragon – a dangerous beast, which bares its fangs when you try to wake it. At any rate, it is beyond question that the glorious Roman Emperor Julius Caesar was killed by a group of corrupt senators because of the attempts he was making to try and uproot the corruption that was widespread in the Roman Empire. The school of thought which maintains that the conspirators were supporters of the Republican model of governance and were trying to prevent Caesar usurping power, in my view, does not stand up to scrutiny, because by that time Caesar had already had absolute power in his hands for ages, and through this power he had bestowed many blessings on the ungrateful senators – but they wanted even more. Our historians tend to take the view that there were two Russian leaders who more or less managed to stamp out corruption: Tsar Ivan IV (Ivan the Terrible) (by ordering that those unmasked as bribetakers have their hands, feet and heads chopped off) and Josef Stalin, a name you will of course know (by creating an extremely wide network of informers, denouncers and secret agents, who made bribery an operation in which the chances of survival were extremely slim).

estimated to be 120 billion Euros, Ukraine has every right to become a valid member of the European community. The European Commissioner for internal affairs, Cecilia Malmstrem, has observed that the member states of the EU have done a great deal as part of the campaign against corruption, but the Report showed that they have not done enough. According to the results of a survey conducted by the European statistics agency 'Eurobarometer', 76% of Europeans feel that corruption is widespread in the EU, and 56% believe that the amount of corruption in their country has gone up in the last three years.

We are doing our bit to fight corruption too, but I fear we are not doing enough. 80% of those surveyed here don't trust the police or the courts, and believe that all matters dealt with by these state bodies are decided by money changing hands.

The NGO Transparency International conducts an annual survey called the 'Corruption perceptions index'. It is an assessment of how normal it is considered to give a bribe with the aim of resolving any kind of issue. In 2013, Ukraine was ranked 144 out of 177 states. I suspect that in this country, giving a bribe is seen very much as standard practice by the majority of the population[94].

Each new president declares a fresh crusade against this dragon. We have anti-corruption laws in place, and we even have special communications channels, both state ones and community ones, through which information about unlawful acts can be passed on. We can even point to some of the specific results this campaign has had. After all, the only examples of corruption that we know about are cases involving criminals who have been exposed and brought to book[95].

It's not just the small fry that we hear about, such as the doctor who demanded a bribe worth the equivalent of $60 from a worker who wanted a sick-note, so that he could take sick leave and still receive his wages. Some far bigger fish are sometimes caught too: the director of a scientific research

---

94 After taking money from a Ukrainian citizen, officials tend not to dare to 'forget' about keeping their promise. After all, I might approach them and start shouting: "You took my money – what about your end of the bargain?", and I'll tell everyone about it, both friends and people I don't know. And this is at the mildest end of the spectrum. But if you're a stranger, it's very easy to fool you. You won't try to appeal to the law enforcement agencies, because you have broken the law yourself – you have given someone a bribe. And if you try to use unlawful methods to try to influence the person who went back on their promise, that approach is bound to fail too. And this is why foreigners are seen by corrupt officials as cash cows, from whom money can be illegally extorted without punishment.

95 The new bridge across the Dnieper, in Kiev, cost two and a half times more expensive than the Viaduc de Millau in France (1 billion Euros as opposed to 400 million Euros), even though it took twice as long to build, is only half the size of the viaduct, and its supports are ten times lower. This isn't corruption: this is just the country growing a whole new generation of millionaires).

institute, for example, who asked for $11 million in exchange for agreeing to sign a lease agreement for real property belogning to the institute (which was state-owned, of course). A case that received a lot of attention in the press was the one involving a district judge in an appeals court, who was found to have over a million dollars in his office when it was searched. The judge categorically denied any involvement in corrupt activities, making up various improbable stories about where the money might have come from. Unfortunately for the judge, it turned out that the police had set up a secret surveillance camera in his office, which had recorded not only the handing over of bribes and the distributing of the cash among those involved, but also, completely by accident, some orgies in which the judge had indulged. He has now been sentenced to 10 years in prison, so he'll have plenty of time to come up with another explanation as to where all that money came from.

Not long ago, $870,000 was found in the offices of one of the managerial departments of the customs service in Odessa, with some of it stored in the director's office. For the customs services this is not such a huge amount, and this was probably the reason why the director was merely fired, rather than being punished more severely.

In July 2013, investigators from the General prosecutor's office arrested some individuals who had taken part in corruption by handing over a bribe worth the equivalent of $900,000. It turned out that the criminal was a member of the law enforcement agencies, and the bribe had been paid in exchange for his complicity in securing a large piece of land.

In August 2013, the rector of the National University of the State Tax Service was arrested and charged with having taken bribes. He had been a well-known and influential figure in the Party of the Regions, which was the party of power until recently, and he had also been a member of parliament, and so on and so forth. Those holding him were so careless that he was able to flee from under their noses and make his way to the United States, and he's still there today.

Those that have been implicated in criminal cases have also included directors of local state administrations, chairmen of autonomous agricultural bodies, detectives, and employees from the health inspection services: all of them want a piece of the 'pie' of corruption.

Yet this demonstrates that we are determined to fight back against corruption – if we weren't, how else would we have so many cases in which criminals have been caught out? There is no doubt that the role played by the mass media is huge. Journalists' determination to expose corrupt dealings of officials who are stealing money from the state budget is something that deserves a huge amount of respect. It was thanks to the mass media that it was possible to expose large-scale frauds such as the importing into the country of goods, free of customs duties, in the name of someone from a village in Western Ukraine. This man, who had been maimed in the Afghan war, was given a customized patent as a special concession, entitling him to import products for his own private purposes without having to pay any tax. Over the course of two years, 10,000 cars were imported into Ukraine at special discounted rates in his name, including half of all the *Maibakhs* in the country. The state lost out on $100 million in taxes.

In July 2012, the newspapers reported that the police in Slovakia had discovered a 700m-long tunnel which extended into Ukraine. The tunnel was a high-spec one, with plastic lining the walls and enhanced steel reinforcements, and a home-made train travelled through it.

On the day of its discovery alone, the police found 13,000 boxes of cigarettes inside the tunnel. The Slovaks were gobsmacked: they'd never seen anything like it, except in the movies about the border between the US and Mexico[96]. Drugs may have been transported through the Ukrainian tunnel, too (some white powder was found inside it, along with the cigarettes), and also illegal immigrants (when the building used to hide the entrance to the tunnel was searched, it was found to contain five passports belonging to Afghan citizens).

You can imagine how much influence the owner of this 'goldmine' must have, to have been able to build and use such a facility right under the noses of the border guards! There was someone on the Slovak side receiving the goods too, incidentally, and this explains why the search for the tunnel was initiated not by the Slovaks, but by the Germans, who were troubled by the constant flow of contraband cigarettes into their territory.

All the incidents of corruption in Ukraine that I have told you about share one thing in common: they are the cases which we already know about. Freedom of speech and freedom of information, which we have now won, are playing a decisive role in the fight against corruption. The things that society is finding out about now can no longer go unpunished. If our citizens feel that the turpitude seen in the behaviour of the people entrusted with governing the country exceeds a particular 'permissible' threshold, Ukrainians will leave their *khutor* and come out onto the streets. And then the officials who have had their snouts in the trough will either flee the country or end up in the courts. Until our democratic structures have 'matured' as they need to, until the traditions of a state governed by

---

96 The Guinness Book of Records really should send over some representatives so that they can verify this record. Contraband cigarettes aren't just taken out of Ukraine, incidentally. According to data from the law enforcement agencies, 7 billion cigarettes are exported from Russia, Moldova and Belarus each year. Only about 0.3% of this total is seized at the border.

the rule of law have gained a stronger foothold, the people will be forced to try to control their 'elected representatives' themselves.

We still have a lot of work to do in this particular area. For example, we need to get to the bottom of why a state agency entered into an agreement to manufacture "tent pegs for marking out the borders between plots of land" worth 450 million Euros. According to reports in the media, the company which won the tender to manufacture the 'tent pegs' was set up in 2010 with a share capital of a thousand UAH (90 Euros), and is owned by a company from Cyprus (why was I not surprised to hear that). The most interesting part is that installing markers on the borders of land plots isn't even something that's compulsory: you just do it if that's what you want to do. But anyone looking to sell their plots was going to be forced to buy some new 'tent pegs', otherwise the deal wouldn't go through. In this regard, many will recall a recent occasion when motorists were forced to purchase fluorescent stickers for their bumpers, or else their cars would fail their MOT. This strange new law was repealed before long, but someone somewhere managed to make a few million dollars whilst it was still in force.

We also need to get to the bottom of the supplies of so-called 'humanitarian aid' to Ukraine. The value of the humanitarian aid sent into Ukraine in 2012 is estimated to be worth almost $57 million dollars. According to experts, a substantial part of this is contraband. Not long ago the Minister for Social Policy, tired of the constant pressure from his own colleagues, announced in parliament that it was being proposed that 148 cars be imported into the country in the guise of humanitarian aid. These included 53 expensive cars (24 Volkswagens, 11 Mercedes, 6 Audis, 5 Toyotas and a Lexus). For reference: in February and March 2013 the Ministry of Social Policy received 450 requests to have shipments of goods classified as 'humanitarian aid'. I can picture the scene: all those poor, downtrodden Ukrainians, who have been waiting for humanitarian aid for so long, joyfully get behind the wheel of a new *Lexus*.

There is also an investigation taking place in relation to a certain charitable foundation in the Volyn region, which passed on goods imported as charitable aid to retail firms, so that they could sell them for profit, and did not shy away from doing so right there in its offices.

These days, people react strongly and in no uncertain terms to impudent attempts to break the law, or to avoid punishment for crimes they have committed by making use of corrupt connections[97]. Things have reached a very

---

[97] One case that received a huge amount of coverage was an incident in the city of Nikolaev, when three young men raped and beat up an 18-year-old girl and threw her into a fire. The police tried to afford the culprits special protection, because one of them was the son of "people of wealth and influence". Anger flared up throughout the whole country, and people took to the streets to

poor state of affairs, of course, when people in the law enforcement agencies, and representatives of the executive, are themselves guilty of committing crimes. It is a poor state of affairs when law and order is not enforced, when too many privileges are enjoyed by those in power, and when the law is applied on the basis of the social and material position of the person caught up in the judicial system.

We are tired of all this. Events in recent years have shown that the Ukrainian people has no intention of resigning itself to this and forgiving the criminals. However patient the Ukrainians might be as a people, and whatever might be said about the *khutorite* mentality, when it's each man for himself, those who try to test the Ukrainian people's patience for too long are making a grave mistake. At times like this, Ukrainians remember "that we, brothers, are of the Cossack bloodline". The events that took place at the start of 2014 showed what happens when we remember this.

---

protest, demanding that the criminals be given the most severe sentence of all, and collecting money to pay the victim's healthcare costs. In spite of the treatment measures taken, the girl died in agony. The perpetrators were given lengthy prison sentences, and the ringleader was given a life sentence. In another case, in the town of Vradievka, in the Nikolaev Region, police units tried to hide the fact that a police captain and a senior lieutenant had been involved in the rape and attempted murder of a local shopkeeper. Local residents stormed the district police headquarters and broke down the doors. Mass acts of civil unrest, which were supported throughout the country, led to the criminals eventually being given severe sentences.

It goes without saying that there is nothing good about the fact that measures like these have to be taken to ensure law and order, in a European country in the 21st century. On the other hand, though, it demonstrates once again that the Ukrainian people can't just be turned into a submissive crowd. Two hundred years ago, an envoy from the Kingdom of Sardinia at the Russian imperial court, Joseph de Maistre, wrote a line which was to capture the popular imagination: "Every country has the government it deserves." As the events of recent months have shown, Ukrainians have no intention of putting up with either a bad president or a corrupt government.

A FEW CONCLUSIONS THAT CAN BE DRAWN AT THIS STAGE

So what have been the results thus far of Ukraine's existence as an independent state, the largest state in terms of its territory in the entire history of our people? Has life got better for us? Has our country got richer? What parameters can we use to draw conclusions about people's wealth?

I just don't know.

The task I set myself was to help foreigners gain a better understanding of Ukraine. I can honestly say, now, that I sometimes find it hard to understand it myself.

GDP has still not reached the level it was at in 1990, and is currently at about 70% of that level. There is a very simple reason for this: after the collapse of the USSR, gigantic firms which had in the past served the needs of the domestic market for the whole of the Soviet Union, shipyards, munitions factories and so forth either reduced their levels of production or ceased operations altogether. The degree of sophistication of our technological processes and equipment which we inherited from Soviet Ukraine was not high enough for us to be able to enter the global market at that stage. A drastic and destructive process of de-industrialization took place. For this reason we are currently suppliers of raw materials at this stage, and I suspect that the rapid development of nanotechnologies will need to be put on hold, although in the fields of IT technologies, metallurgy, chemistry and agriculture Ukrainians have become strong competitors.

There are some things that we now have in greater quantities. The openness of the Ukrainian economy has led to progress being made in one of our traditional and most important sectors: agriculture. As of 1st January 2012, there were 40,965 farm holdings in Ukraine. The output produced by farmers accounts for almost 20% of GDP. And this share is growing with each passing year. In recent years, global capitalism has managed to transform the decaying collective farms from the Soviet era into successful agricultural enterprises, and introduce modern technologies and effective agricultural machinery. Ukraine produces a lot more grain than it used to: in 1991 the amount of grain produced was almost 39 million tonnes, while in 2011 it was 57 million tonnes. Bread has become one of our core exports. 140 countries purchase our agricultural products.

We have fewer cows, pigs and sheep these days (4.4 million in total in 2012, as against 24.6 million in 1991), but it remains a mystery to me why it is that in Soviet times there was a constant shortage of meat, and the meat available in the shops was sub-standard, whereas today the shelves in the supermarkets and at the markets are heaving with meat and meat-related products.

Exports are on the increase (they have grown by a factor of 4.5 since 2001, to 82 billion dollars), but imports are growing too (they have grown by a factor of 5, to 91 billion dollars), and for this reason we have seen a trough in the trade balance.

One of the things we export is arms. According to the official statistics, we are the world's 4th biggest arms exporter (1.3 billion dollars in 2012). Our arms are even bought by the USA and Germany, although the weapons in question are of course rare and out-dated fire-arms. In addition to the old arms reserves which remain from the Soviet era, which are surplus to requirements for Ukraine's relatively small army, we also sell some new weaponry, created and manufactured at Ukrainian arms factories, including some fairly modern tanks and some amphibious hovercraft.

Our economy has a high energy dependence on supplies of organic fuel, which contribute 65%.[98] The technologies applied consume a lot of energy and are outdated, and as a result we waste 3 times more energy than the countries in Europe.

Light industry is developing in a unique way. In recent years it has been showing steady growth. At the same time, while of clothes have been imported into Ukraine from Asia and Europe, and Ukrainian factories have sewn clothes for the whole world. There isn't a single European clothing brand that doesn't have its clothes made for it in Ukraine. Our sewing factories make things out of foreign materials to order for brands like Zara and Hugo Boss. The world-famous brand Lener Cordier manufactures 1 million items at Ukrainian plants, and imports these goods to the West.

We don't publish as many books as we used to – but only because of the growing popularity of e-books. In recent years I have hardly bought any traditional books, but my e-book is full of hundreds of Ukrainian works and

---

98   Since this fuel is supplied predominantly from Russia, our northern neighbour turns this factor to its political advantage to the full, putting maximum pressure on both foreign and domestic policy in Ukraine.

foreign literature. The Ukrainian people are still avid readers, just as they always have been.

The number of newspapers and magazines that are published has increased. The print-run of major newspapers stood at around 51 million in 2011, as compared with 27 million in 1991. There were 2886 magazines and other periodicals and recurrent publications in 2011, with a combined print-run of 316 million, whereas in 1991 there were only 194, with a print-run of 95 million.

And what about the people, how has their standard of living changed? If I try to define the standard of living of some kind of 'average' Ukrainian, I'm going to get stuck.

According to statistical data, the average monthly salary of workers in Ukraine (expressed in dollars) ranges from 300 dollars in the countryside to 500 dollars in the capital. The average salary throughout the country in 2013 was 400 dollars a month. The working population of Ukraine currently stands at 14 million. There are 13 million pensioners. The remainder of the population are kids, teenagers, students and the unemployed (unemployment is at 8% - according to the official statistics, at any rate). Thus, if the statistics are to be believed, Ukraine's workforce as a whole earns a total of 67.2 billion dollars in wages.

So in that case let's ask the statisticians to try and explain how it is that Ukrainians managed to acquire the 7 million cars that are registered in the country? Every year, between 200,000 and 240,000 new vehicles are bought. A single car costs around 30,000 dollars on average. This means that Ukrainians spend 6.6 billion dollars on cars each year. A litre of petrol costs a dollar fifty. Driving to work and back for a month will set you back 450 dollars at least. Experts maintain that according to data regarding sales and primary registration of vehicles, the number of new cars in January 2014 was 11,840. Thus Ukrainians spent more than 300 million dollars on new cars in January 2014. What's more, by comparison with January 2013, the proportion of 'budget' cars had gone down, whilst the proportion of 'premium' and 'luxury' cars had more than doubled.

One square meter of housing, on the primary market, costs between 800 and 1000 dollars. Each year, 10 million square meters of new housing is put up. This housing may not necessarily all be sold straight away, but after all I'm not taking into account the statistics for sales on the secondary market, i.e. residencies built previously, which are being transferred to new owners. So it is fair to say that Ukrainians spend at least 8.5 billion dollars on housing a year.

Alcohol consumption in this country stands at 15.5 litres of pure alcohol per person per year. This means that the amount spent on beer, wine, rum, liqueurs, vodka and cognac is at least 382.5 million dollars a year. It's difficult to give a more accurate figure, as the prices vary so greatly - some alcoholic drinks cost up to twenty times as much as others.

There are 16.5 million smokers in Ukraine. A packet of cigarettes costs about 1.2 dollars, on average. This means that Ukrainians spend 7.2 billion dollars on cigarettes every year.

The total turnover from all retail trade in the course of a year is 100 billion dollars.

The total amount of savings held by the population in the banks is in excess of 80 billion dollars. Net purchases of convertible currency (i.e. the amount by which purchases exceeded sales) amounted to 782 million dollars in November 2013, and 940 million dollars in December: people had stocked up on foreign currency in case the hryvnia collapsed. There is no doubt whatsoever that a lot of money is spent on buying foreign currency from the 'bins', i.e. things that are not essential for people's everyday needs.

The Ukrainian people pay the equivalent of 226 million dollars a year to insurers under accumulating life insurance policies. This type of insurance is not all that common for the time being, with roughly 1.6 million people insured each year, but this figure is growing.

The number of Ukrainians who went on holidays to other countries in 2012 stood at 2.76 million. A holiday in Turkey (the most popular tourist destination for Ukrainians, and also the cheapest) costs at least 500 dollars a week. We can conclude, therefore, that Ukrainians spent 1.4 billion dollars[99] on trips to foreign holiday destinations in the course of a year. The number of people who went on holiday to destinations inside the country in the same year was 807,000 people. There are 45,000 restaurants, bars and cafes in the country, 48% of which are owned by legal entities and 52% by individuals. Needless to say, these are not struggling to attract clients, nor are they going bankrupt.

In Ukraine's capital, 1000 people have officially declared themselves to be millionaires. Their aggregate annual income was more than 1.2 billion dollars a year (how much they each declared, specifically, is something only the tax authorities can tell us). The official figures tell us there are 2500 millionaires in the country. I am emphasizing the words 'officially' and 'declared', because

---

99 The actual figure is higher, of course, because there are plenty of holidays that are more expensive, and last longer, and Turkey accounts for just one third of the total flow of tourists, while Ukrainian holidaymakers spent fairly large amounts at seaside resorts on day-trips, eating out at restaurants and souvenirs. I don't think it would be wildly inaccurate to multiply this figure by a factor of 2.5. The total number of Ukrainians going on holiday to foreign destinations was 23.4 million people. From a statistical point of view that would be half the country, but in actual fact the reason for this is that people living in the border regions cross the border many times a year to visit their relatives, look for work, do a bit of business or do a bit of smuggling of contraband goods.

there are of course a couple of other words that apply – 'unofficially' and 'undeclared'.

The cost of a cinema ticket ranges from 2 to 10 dollars. Let's take a mean cost of 5 dollars. There are 2.2 million cinemas in the country, which attract 15 million cinema-goers in the course of a year, which means that at least 75 million dollars is spent on cinema trips alone. Our 570 museums are visited by some 22 million people a year. 7 million people go and see a play at one of our 130 theatres each year.

A population which is struggling to eke out an existence (according to the official data, 26.5% of Ukrainians are living below the poverty line), simply cannot afford to spend so much on cars, new apartments, entertainment and spirits, whilst also having tens of billions of dollars in savings. What do the statistics tell us about the average salary in the country in the light of this?

Communal services have to be paid for, too (on average these cost 15% of an employee's wages), as do white goods and electronic goods (6.4 billion dollars a year), clothes, textbooks for the kids, books, gym and sports club memberships, bowling trips and tickets to the football. It goes without saying that there is a massive amount of inequality between our citizens in terms of their material wealth. There are poor people, there are those that are poverty-stricken, and there are billionaires. But something else is obvious, too: the country has a "shadow economy"[100]. This is not about contraband goods or the exploitation of illegal immigrants. We are talking about the normal production of goods and services, which are not taken into account by the tax authorities.

I'm not going to start speculating about where the oligarchs keep their money. Let's try to have a look at how the "little men" in Ukraine try to provide themselves with a decent quality of life.

Let me give you a few examples.

I bought 100 kg of potatoes from one of my neighbours, who had grown them on a little plot of land next to his dacha. How are this transaction and this produce to be recorded by the tax man?

For many years now, a woman who lives near me has sold home-made pickled vegetables next to our apartment block. There's another woman who has sold home-baked pies with various fillings, near the entrance to the metro, for many years. A friend of mine manages a small garage. Services

---

100 I have already explained the reasons why it came into being: the state does not provide the normal relationship between the salaries people have earned and the amount they actually take home, due to the excessive tax burden on the people. Moreover, major property owners do not carry their fair share of the tax burden, because they engage in tax evasion by setting up their companies in "tax havens" and off-shore countries.

are paid for in cash, and most of his staff don't have employment contracts and also receive their wages cash-in-hand. The spare parts used to repair vehicles are bought at the market, which isn't subject to any controls or records whatsoever, either. Who is likely to start recording the price of spare parts taken from cars which have been written off? Who can actually record the volume of services provided by a hairdresser or a manicurist at someone's house? How are we to record the contribution made to the economy by a friend of my son, who collects old computers and repairs them in his apartment? The man in the flat above mine repairs shoes (and very good at it he is, too – better than any of the officially licensed cobblers – so we always recommend his services to our friends).

It's entirely possible that somewhere, in some ever-so-obedient, ever-so-law-abiding country, private entrepreneurs like these would be asked questions such as: "Why don't you declare your income?" Over here, a situation like that would cause two fatalities: the tax inspector would die of fright if he was ordered to ask questions like that of the local citizens, and the average local citizen would be so stunned that someone was asking him these questions that he would drop down dead too. This state of affairs has not arisen because Ukrainians are born scoundrels and tax avoiders. It's just that we know full well that taxes represent payment for the upkeep of the state, which is supposed to provide a system of law and order, guarantee people's security and manage the process of development in the country. And if the state does none of these things, then the man in the street becomes a member of the 'front for resistance to the tax authorities' – an agency which isn't registered anywhere, but is very real.

In the 2008 presidential elections in the USA, an ordinary citizen named Joe Wurzelbacher – a plumber by trade – shot to fame when his six-minute conversation with the presidential candidate Barack Obama was broadcast on the US TV channels. Obama's rival, Senator McCain, deemed it necessary to contact Joe and tell him how he would have answered the question. So what was Joe's question? He had asked about the reforms to the tax system proposed by Obama. Both Obama and McCain knew that Joe the Plumber was their employer. He paid their salaries, because he paid his taxes, and for this simple reason he was entitled to know what they were spent on.

This is the kind of approach we like. We too want to know what the taxes taken from us are spent on. What we know thus far is that 80 million dollars a year were spent on meeting President Yanukovich's needs. We have been told that Ukraine's new government intends to cut the amount spent on the state administration by 20 billion UAH (roughly 2.5 billion dollars) without damaging the way this system functions in any way: there would simply be a reduction in the number of personal Mercedes given to civil servants, and some of the more excessive exemptions enjoyed by them would be abolished. There are good grounds for believing that the resources available to the economy and the amounts which can be added to the budget are fairly sizeable. As a bare minimum, we need to clip the wings of the 'dragon' of corruption I referred to in the previous section of the book.

I would therefore ask you to try and understand us Ukrainians: we can only be law-abiding people who pay their taxes if and when the people ruling the country behave similarly. For the time being, the struggle for a better quality of life incorporates the struggle against the tax authorities.

There are 2700 licensed markets in the country, 400 of which are food markets[101]. To analyse the turnover at these markets, the prices, the profits and the salaries earned by the stall-owners would be an impossible task, and no-one is even attempting to do so. There is only one figure that I can quote: each year, 3 million tonnes of produce – a quarter of all the foodstuffs in the country – is sold at these food markets. And I would like to emphasize the fact that these are the markets which are "officially licensed". Many thousands of small, unlicensed markets crop of from time to time in the villages and towns, or beside crossroads. During the fruit and vegetable harvest, the entire highway is lined with containers filled with the fruits of people's orchards and gardens, with their owners sitting next to them: you can pull up alongside them and buy a bucket of fresh strawberries, apples or apricots, or a basket of mushrooms picked a short time ago in the woods[102].

Don't go thinking that sales of foodstuffs grown in people's own private farmsteads or orchards are just a small, exotic part of the overall picture. These growers are the core suppliers of everyday foods of mass consumption to the domestic food market. They produce 82% of all our milk, 52% of our meat, 78% of our wool, 97% of our honey, 98% of our potatoes, 86% of our vegetables, and 85% of our fruit and berries. Moreover, these farmsteads perform some important roles in society: they give people the ability to grow their own food, enable people to be self-employed, and give them a source of income and a financial platform.

---

101   The city markets today consist of huge pavilions with long stalls, divided into sections, with hundreds of stall-owners standing behind the counters. For our purposes it's irrelevant whether or not these stall-owners are the people who produce the goods. These days, practically all sales are controlled by middlemen, who buy goods from the farmers wholesale.

102   Ukrainians love buying food at the markets. You won't find food that's past its best here, as often happens at the supermarkets. At the market everything's open, you can see what you're buying, and you can do a bit of haggling over the price (and if you buy a large quantity of something, you're sure to get a discount); stall-owners at the markets, desirous of securing your custom in the future, will occasionally throw in an extra handful of goods for free – "with compliments from the boss", so to speak.

Thus, if you were to form an opinion based on the data in the official statistics, we are poor, and therefore either stupid or lazy. But in truth, Ukrainians are intelligent and hard-working – it's just that when faced with the destructive tax legislation, we have no wish to give up the fruits of our labour to all and sundry.

THE THINGS WE DISLIKE

Certain aspects of life in this country make an unfavourable impression on visitors. To be frank, there is a great deal that we ourselves are unhappy with, and we do not accept that it is our due and we must accept it, nor do we intend simply to resign ourselves to it.

We don't like the awful state of our roads. The technologies used to lay the road surfaces are simply not good enough to meet modern standards, and became out of date long ago. Moreover, they are constantly disintegrating, because the funds and materials set aside for road repairs are often pocketed by corrupt officials. After being "repaired" in the summertime, most of our roads are falling apart by the following spring and turning into an obstacle course for cars. Naturally, huge amounts of money are once again set aside for repairs, only for the same thing to happen. And if you think about it, if the roads were to be repaired in a high-quality manner, so that they didn't need to be repaired for several years, then no funds would be set aside for this purpose from the state budget, isn't that so?

We don't like the fact that there is an epidemic of tuberculosis in Ukraine. According to the official figures, there are 700,000 people suffering from tuberculosis in the country, but experts claim the real figure is twice that.

We don't like the quality or condition of housing in Ukraine. Just 7.4% of the residential housing currently in use in Ukraine was built after 1991. The rest of our residential buildings are much older, and 41.5% of them were commissioned before 1960. A quarter of the housing supply consists of apartment blocks built using simplified technologies between the 1950s and the 1970s. Assembled using concrete panels which were fastened to one another using so-called 'ears' made of metal, these buildings are slowly but surely falling to bits. They were cheap, and provided affordable housing for great for large numbers of people. But after five years they are no longer fit for purpose.

We don't like the fact that skyscrapers with 30-40 floors have been put up in the historic centres of our biggest cities (the ones with a population of a million or more). These buildings are over 120 metres tall. The maximum height of an external fire-escape is 45 metres. What are we to do if a fire breaks out? And the buildings are built so close together that when you glance out of the window, you can see what's going on in the building opposite, down to the smallest detail. Our cities are losing the beautiful, traditional look they used to have.

We don't like the fact that 33% of our utilities networks – the water pipes, the sewers and the central heating – are in a state of disrepair. Sewage networks built before 1917 are still in use today. They are badly damaged, overloaded and in need of immediate re-laying and replacement. Repair vans parked in the road above the latest burst water pipe or sewage pipe are now a common sight. The water supply to residential buildings and offices is often switched off, because yet another hole in the pipes needs to be patched up.

We don't like the fact that there are so many beggars on our city streets. People who have been unlucky in life for various reasons (they fell ill, lost their job, and lost their home after running up debts), and now have to provide for themselves somehow. On the streets of our big cities there are huge numbers of homeless people, who usually gather together in groups next to our railway stations. They have long, unkempt beards, they've been burnt by the sun, they're dirty and dressed in rags, and they're in a poor state of health. Many people point out that this never used to happen under Communism.

Beggars stand in the underpasses, next to shops and in busy areas, with one arm stretched out. Among them there are a large number of young people, of both sexes. They hold little boards containing a handwritten note explaining how they came to be in this position.

The fact that you often see the same handwriting being used for these notes, and that they are often written in the same style, leads you to believe that they are produced centrally somewhere. Indeed, it is an established fact that begging is in the hands of well-organized mafia gangs, whose members drop off these paupers at their "posts" in the morning, and then come round in the evening to collect the "takings", leaving the beggar with just a small cut – enough to buy some cheap food and poor-quality spirits.

Our people are, on the whole, benevolent and capable of feeling sympathy, and often drop not only coins, but also banknotes into the boxes left out on the ground. The total amount of money that a single beggar can collect in one day is more than the daily wage that workers can make through honest toil. What's more, companies – whether privately owned or state-owned – may well delay payment of an employee's salary for several months – and how people survive at such times is a mystery to me. Often entire workforces have to be asked to go on unpaid leave.

We don't like the fact that the new times have brought with them phenomena which were previously unheard of, such as unemployment, bankruptcy, racketeering, mafia 'hits' and pyramid schemes.

We don't like the colossal amount of stratification within society. Luxury homes that look like palaces, owned by the *nouveaux riches*, are being put up one after another. Brands like Mercedes, BMW and Lexus no longer raise any eyebrows – Bentleys and Lamborghinis are now all the rage (although, given the state of our roads, where are people supposed to take them?). And yet there are many people who face great problems and difficulties in their lives. The pensions paid to people who have worked hard for forty years are so small that they can't get by on them. The chasm between the rich and the poor in Ukraine is more akin to what you might find in an African country, rather than a European one. Needless to say, this is a huge source of anger for large numbers of people in the country.

It is only natural that political forces describing themselves as Communists or socialists make use of this anger and cultivate nostalgia for our Communist past. And some people start to think to themselves: wouldn't it be worth exchanging the freedom to express our own opinion for a great sense of security, for a world in which people weren't at risk of being kicked out of their apartment due to debt, and for a guaranteed salary and pensions which are the same for all? Wouldn't it be worth exchanging our ability to travel to foreign countries (if you've got the money and the Embassy agree to give you a visa, which is far from guaranteed these days) for the option to send our children to a free summer camp? They'd be able to enjoy hot meals with the other children in the canteen, wander around a forest full of pine trees and watch some movies for kids at the cinema, all under the supervision of specially trained teachers. These days, the children of the average 'little man' in Ukraine get their education on the streets and from the Internet, and I wouldn't dare to say which of these sources of 'education' is the more dangerous. In brief, shouldn't we bring back the economic system set up by the Communists?

We don't like the constant increases in the cost of goods and services. In the Soviet Union, one of the strongest propaganda tools was the regular announcement of cuts in the prices of various groups of products. This was intended to provide evidence of the efficiency of the Soviet economy.

If there were increases in prices in certain cases, this was accompanied by a mass propaganda campaign, explaining that the increase was a necessary but temporary measure. For example, the 450% increase in the price of coffee was explained away with reference to the failed harvest in Brazil. There were several increases in the price of so-called "luxury items" – jewellery, crystals and rugs. The vast majority of the population were not affected by this. In the

USSR there was in fact a surplus of money among the people, who were not provided with the goods they wanted. Cars were seen as luxury items, and cost about 40 times the average worker's monthly wage. There would nevertheless be queues of people wishing to buy a car at the car plants, and occasionally one of the perks enjoyed by the top-performing employees was the right to buy a car, using money from a special fund set aside for a specific factory.

There were no increases in the price of foodstuffs, however, rent payments were low, and electricity, water, gas and heating were very cheap. A litre of petrol cost less than a litre of mineral water. The cost of bread, milk, vegetables, meat, beer and a ride on public transport remained unchanged for decades.

I can remember a time in the mid-eighties when, under the pretext of the battle against excessive consumption of spirits by the people, the price of vodka went up. Quite simply, some new, more expensive brands appeared on the shelves, and the old, cheap ones disappeared[103]. This situation could not last long, however: it led to a mood of discontent and the rebirth of an underground industry in the production of alcohol. Cheaper spirits therefore made a return to the shelves. Officially, however, it was as if there had never been a rise in prices: it was just that the cheap brands disappeared, and then came back again.

These days, you can quite easily walk into a shop and find that you have to pay quite a bit more than you paid yesterday for the same products. Those with a bit of sense when it comes to money realise that the rise in prices is to a large extent down to the increase in indirect taxes, i.e. once again what we see is an attempt to shift the problems of a badly run budget onto the ordinary citizen.

---

103   It must be said that in our country, experiments involving restrictions on the consumption of spirits always end in failure. We have a century-old tradition, handed down from generation to generation, of making home-made spirits. As soon as the increase in prices for factory-made alcohol makes it profitable to distil spirits using any raw materials containing starch in your kitchen at home, this spirit immediately starts to be manufactured. And if you're too lazy to do it yourself, you can always find someone who'll be willing to sell you some. The state has gone to considerable lengths to try to root out such behaviour, introducing a fierce propaganda campaign and bringing in tougher punishments under civil and criminal law. The public consciousness has always had a soft spot for artisanal distillation, however, and people were always more likely to sympathize with those who make home-made vodka than to judge them. Before long, therefore, the state had to give in and allow cheap brands of spirits to be produced once again.

A FEW THINGS THAT WE LIKE

The fall of the iron curtain opened up a new world to Ukraine. Whereas prior to that Ukrainians picked up their ideas about what life was like in foreign countries from the TV programme 'The movie travellers' club', now they had themselves turned into travellers. For Soviet citizens, a holiday in Bulgaria had been the trip of a lifetime. Now, though, people were able to see the world – the USA and Israel, Turkey and the Caribbean, Germany and the UAE – and they realised that the concept of 'quality of life' was a far cry from what the leaders of the Communist Party had told them it was. Thousands of Ukrainians set off on holiday to Western Europe every weekend. With each passing year, the number of countries in the world which have not yet become holiday destinations for Ukrainians falls. The list of our favourite holiday destinations includes all kinds of exotic places: Mauritius, Bali, Vietnam, Sri Lanka. This is something that we like, of course.

One of the most important phenomena and benefits of worldwide civilization, to which the ordinary Ukrainian has been able to secure access, is of course the Internet. I think that if our country was still run by the Communists today, the Internet would only be available to state and academic institutions, by special permission and subject to strict controls. In a country in which the only correct opinions were those that were in line with the official ideology, the Internet would be a very dangerous tool for dissidents. In the past, even our radio sets had a very limited range of short-wave frequencies, and couldn't pick up the frequencies on which Russian-language radio stations in the West, such as *Golos Ameriki* (Voice of America), *Nemetskaya volna* (the German wave) and the BBC. Restricting access to the Internet, which today seems to us to be the very embodiment of the freedom to spread information, would be very easy to do. There would be no Internet providers offering to connect you up to the worldwide web. But times have changed, the Internet is accessible again, and one can only be amazed at how rapidly the number of gamers, hackers, spammers and Internet addicts in this country has shot up. More than 14 million Ukrainians use the Internet on their mobile phone.

Just as in any normal country, people here make friends over the Internet, organize flash-mobs, buy products, and hack into people's bank accounts. And, of course, they sometimes express their opinion on all manner of subjects, sometimes in very uncivilized terms, unfortunately, using vulgar and offensive language.

We like the fact that we can go and watch films in 3D at the cinema. We like the fact that we can buy Samsung TVs with plasma or liquid-crystal screens for about the cost of one month's wages, because we remember a time when a colour TV made locally, with a beam tube, cost three months' wages.

We like the big supermarkets, full of produce, and we like the fact that we can choose between twenty different types of bread, rather than two, and fifty different types of smoked sausage, rather than one. It may well be that to European readers, this particular 'like' of ours will seem amusing, but you've been living under your own particular economic system for two hundred years, whereas ours has only been going for twenty. We are still in the habit of comparing life with how it used to be.

It is very important that the attractive sides of the new world, for the average Ukrainian, prove to be more significant than the inherent downsides to this new world.

IN PLACE OF AN EPILOGUE

I have described my country as I see it from the inside. My views are, of course, subjective ones. You are free to form your own opinion.

We aren't complaining, and we aren't asking for people to like us. But it is very important to us that people understand us. We are a very peaceful people, we don't have any reason to start conflicts with our neighbours or any territorial claims, and we don't wish to bring up ancient grievances. What we want is to be given the opportunity to build, at long last, our own country, which we have tried so many times to create, and lost so many times.

The problems we have don't pose a threat to anyone: they are our own problems, and our leaders, though they may not always be successful, are ours, too. We sometimes change our government because we feel that we deserve a better alternative – albeit using methods which Europe has long since grown out of the habit of using.

We need a little time to organize our lives better, draw up some plans for the future and work out where we are going; some time to get who we are. To get Ukraine.

SOME TRADITIONAL UKRAINIAN RECIPES WHICH YOU SHOULD TRY IN ORDER TO GET A FULLER UNDERSTANDING OF THE IDEAS SET OUT IN THIS BOOK

UKRAINIAN **BORSHCHT**

Below is a recipe for Ukrainian borshcht, which the professional chef Sergei Dzhurenko published on his website. It is a very good recipe and was written in a humorous way, which is why I chose it.

So here's the recipe for red Ukrainian borshcht.

The quantities below are enough for 6-8 portions, depending on how hungry you are. And if you have any left over, you can leave it in the fridge for a couple of days – it will only get tastier. It takes two and a half hours in total to make the borshcht in a pan. It's fun to make things like this with a friend or partner, at the weekend: one of you can peel the veg while the other one washes the meat…It really helps to encourage mutual understanding and peace in the family home.

Our chef writes: "To boil Ukrainian borshcht, you need three things: inspiration, inspiration and a little more inspiration. You can find everything else at your local bazaar or shop."

This is what you need to buy at your local shop or market:
1. Some meat – either pork or beef (or both together): up to 1 kg
2. A carrot
3. 3-4 potatoes
4. A glass of beans

A sprig of parsley with its stalk (if the parsley has had its 'green tail' chopped off, you'll have to buy a bit of parsley stalk separately) 1 piece

1 large red beetroot
1 sweet pepper, red
2-3 cloves of garlic
1 onion, finely chopped
½ a head of cabbage. In Ukraine, a head of cabbage usually weighs one-and-a-half kilograms, so make the necessary adjustments
Salt, black pepper, herbs to taste
2-3 spoonfuls of tomato paste. You can also use ketchup of course, but tomato paste is a very filling, bitter, thick condiment, whereas ketchup is more runny, and it's hard to tell how much you need.

Here's a direct quote from Dzhurenko:

"You've got to buy some meat. How can you possibly call it borshcht if you haven't put meat in it? The best option is to go for a variety of meats. A little bit of pork, ideally the ribs, and a little bit of beef – again, it's best to go for the ribs. A little bit of chicken: strangely, the best bits to go for are the neck, the head and the wings. In rural areas, people tend to add a little bit of old yellow *salo*, and always keep a box of this type of *salo* in their store-cupboard. And a bit of chicken bone for the pot, that's essential.

Pour some cold water into a pan. The pan should be more than half, but less than two thirds full.

Heat the pan on the hob. Bring it to the boil.

Meanwhile we need to wash the meat. We slice into fairly large pieces, weighing 40-50 g each. We leave the bone whole. We separate the ribs and cut them into slices 5-6 cm long. The pieces of chicken are going to go into the pot whole.

We put all the meat in the boiling water. It's essential to get rid of the foam.

Then we add 2-3 bay leaves and a whole sprig of parsley, and add a little salt and pepper. You can also add a mixture of spices to add flavour, but don't 'over-*borshcht*' your *borshcht*.

Boil the flavoursome meaty broth for at least an hour. The meat should become tender and start coming off the bone.

When the broth is ready, we take the sprig of parsley and the bay leaf out of it. We add the beans, which we have put in water in advance (ideally the night before).

We wait until it starts to boil, turn down the heat and boil it for 15-20 minutes. The beats should be slightly undercooked.

We add the chopped carrot, onion and pepper to the broth. It's up to you how big or small the pieces are. Next we add the crushed garlic cloves.

We leave the broth to boil for 10-15 minutes.

After this we peel the beetroot. Many people like to sauté it in oil or *salo* first. That was how my grandmother used to do it. At one time, however, it was quite hard to get your hands on beetroot that was the right colour: it was usually too dusty and therefore turned a little bit white. Nowadays, beetroot is a deep, dark violet colour, good enough to paint your wallpaper with it. I throw in the beetroot raw. And what a wonderful hue it lends to the broth…fantastic!

Feel free to grate the beetroot using a coarse grater, or alternatively to chop it into thin strips. The latter tend to look nicer. Add the beetroot to the boiling borshcht. Give it a good stir and admire its fabulous colour!

We then cook it for a further 10 minutes and immediately add some large pieces of diced potato. In theory, there's nothing wrong with putting the potatoes in whole and crushing them when they're already in the borshcht.

Once the potato has boiled – this usually takes 15 minutes or a little longer – we add the tomato paste. This is strictly a matter of taste! For every 6 litres, I add 3 heaped tablespoons. Then I give it a little try. The borshcht should have a slight bitterness to it – a bitterness that's barely noticeable.

The tomato paste should be left to boil for 5-10 minutes.

We then add some finely chopped white cabbage! Add enough to ensure the borshcht isn't runny. The cabbage in borshcht is like the alcohol in vodka: irreplaceable!

Many chefs like to add pickled cabbage to their borshcht. I suppose there's nothing wrong with that. It's not something I would do though.

I like it when the cabbage is a little bit hard. I boil it for no more than 5 minutes.

It's essential to add salt and pepper to the borshcht, to taste. You should also add some finely chopped sprigs of parsley and dill.

Turn the heat off straight away and leave it to stand until the following morning. Seriously! The tastiest borshcht of all is borshcht that is eaten the day after it's cooked. And it's essential to add some *Smetana* (sour cream), but it mustn't be the thickest type: ideally it should be home-made or 10-15% fat *Smetana*.

It's simply irresistible!

And after that it's just like in the fairy-tales: a plate of flame-red borshcht! Smetana!!! Chopped onion! Garlic! Fresh bread, or, if you really want a treat – dumplings with garlic! A bit of spring onion and some green garlic and it's sheer indulgence. Plus a shot of freezing cold vodka!!!!

And there you have it! Call an ambulance, I've gone crazy – I'm off to eat my borshcht!"

So there's a little recipe for you, from a professional. Give it a go, you'll get a flavour of the Ukrainian spirit!

UKRAINIAN VARENIKY

Below is a recipe for *vareniky* with potatoes and mushrooms, from the amateur chef Vladimir Mikhalko (the author of the recipe recommends mushrooms which we call *lisichki* (Pfifferlingen – wild mushrooms), but you can also use other types.

For the *vareniky* dough

- A glass of water, 200-250 g (in Ukraine, the tradition is to raise the dough not in water or milk, but in a bonny-clabber or a dairy whey)

- Flour, 250-300 grams
- Salt, 1 teaspoon
- Sunflower oil, 1 tablespoon
- A filling for the dumplings made of potatoes and mushrooms
- Several large potatoes
- Mushrooms
- Chopped onion
- Salt, to taste

Method:

First of all, peel the potatoes, chop them up and put them in a pan to boil. The water should just cover the potatoes. Don't forget to add some salt to the water.

While the potatoes are boiling, prepare the filling. Boil the mushrooms in some salted water. You should wait until the water starts to boil, then pour the water out. Pour in some more water, then add some more salt and leave it to boil for 5-10 minutes.

Pour the mushrooms into a sieve and put them to one side to cool. Finely dice the onion and fry it in a frying-pan in some sunflower oil until they are half-cooked.

Once the mushrooms have cooled, chop them up and add them to the frying-pan with the onion. Add a little salt and fry the contents with the onion, until the onion starts to turn gold.

Then make some mashed potato using the potatoes, which will be cooked through by now. To do this, pour all the water out of the pan. Put a nice big bit of butter in with the potatoes and add a tiny bit of milk – you don't want the mash to be two runny. Now mix the potatoes together, making sure there are no lumps.

Now mix the mashed potatoes with the fried mushrooms and onion. Taste it to see whether you need more salt, and add a little bit of freshly milled black pepper.

While the filling cools, it's time to make the dough for the *vareniky*.

Pour a glass of water into the mixing bowl for the dough, add the flour, and add the salt and sunflower oil. (You can tell immediately that this recipe was written by a man. Female cooks in Ukrainian always mix their dough the other way round. They pour out a heap of flour onto a clean wooden or plastic surface, then make a hole in the heap and gradually add the liquid (water, milk, sour milk, whey or eggs – different people have different recipes. You mix the dough a little more each time you add more liquid, until all the flour has been 'caught', and the dough is the right consistency, and not too stiff.) Mix well with a spoon. Pour some flour onto the work surface and lay the dough out on it. Now roll out the dough, sprinkling flour over it, until it becomes springy.

Roll out the dough into thin pancakes and cut circles out of it using a large teaspoon. In the centre of each circle of dough we place the filling. Stretch out the dough slightly and fold the sides over, so that the filling is wrapped inside it. Give the ends of the *varenik* a good pinch, so that they don't come unstuck in the water. Once the *vareniky* are ready, put them on a board, tray or large plate sprinkled with flour.

Now boil the *vareniky* in boiling, salted water until the dough is cooked. Before serving, put the *vareniky* on a large plate and add a large knob of butter on top, so that the *vareniky* don't stick together and to make them taste even better.
Dip the *vareniky* in Smetana and put them in your mouth immediately!

Bon appétit!

You can also enjoy *vareniky* as a dessert, by using strawberries or cherries for the filling. Here's a recipe for *vareniky* with cherries, for example.

Ingredients:

- 2 eggs
- 4 tbsp of milk (approx. 65 ml)
- ½ tsp salt
- 1 cup of flour (the ratio required is 1 part flour to 4 parts liquid)
- 300 g of cherries
- Sugar – to taste
- 1 tbsp potato starch

Beat the egg in a small bowl, add the milk (or water), add the salt, pour in the flour and make some dough, held loosely together. Roll the dough into a ball, sprinkle a little flour over it and leave it to stand for 20 minutes (this will allow it to get softer and improve its consistency).

Prepare the filling:

mix the cherries with the sugar and starch (the starch will stop the filling escaping from the *vareniky*). Cut out a small piece of dough and roll it into a sausage, then slice this sausage into little pieces.

Roll out each piece and put the filling inside. The dough should be nice and thin.

Give the ends of the *vareniky* a good pinch (stick the ends of the *vareniky* together very carefully, so that they don't fall apart in the boiling water) and boil them in some salted water for 5-7 minutes.

Once the *vareniky* are ready, take them out using a slotted spoon, transfer them to a pot and sprinkle sugar over them so that they don't stick to one another.

A FEW RECIPES FOR UKRAINIAN DISHES SERVED ON PUBLIC HOLIDAYS

FISH IN ASPIC

Ingredients: 0.5 kg filet of trout, skin off (we still see trout as something a little exotic; other kinds of fish, sourced locally, are used more often – but they still taste just as good), 1 carrot, 1 onion, 1 sprig of parsley, 3 apples, 1 lime (or lemon), 50 g of gelatine, 300 ml of dry white wine, 300 ml of clear apple juice, 2 bay leaves, mustard, a clove, freshly milled black pepper, salt.

Cut the filet into slices and boil them in a litre of salted water, adding the carrot and onion whole and the sprig of parsley. Once the water comes to the boil, take out the fish and strain the broth. Bring to the boil. Mix in the gelatine. Take a fish-shaped mould, fill it 1/3 full with the liquid and put it in the fridge. Once it has cooled, add the fish, carrot, and some slices of apple with the skin peeled off and the seeds removed over the aspic, to form the scales. Make an eye using a little circle of red chilli pepper, and make the head and tail using the zest of the lime. Pour the remainder of the gelatine broth on top and allow it cool in the fridge. Before serving, put the base of the mould in some hot water for a few seconds, then cover the mould with a plate and quickly turn it upside down.

RECIPES FOR **KHOLODETS** (ASPIC)

Kholodets (aspic) is traditionally served at Christmas and Easter. It is not difficult to make, but it takes quite a long time (6-7 hours). The key thing is to choose the right meat. The meat must be fresh and smell good. Pig's trotters, which are an essential ingredient of *kholodets*, can only be used if they are clean and have a smooth surface. In Europe, where the quality-control for the food in the shops is of a high standard, this advice is less relevant. But in this country a lot of food is bought at the markets, where the foods sold come from small farms, so for our cooks, knowing how to choose high-quality meat is an important skill.

The meat and the jelly are equally important in *kholodets*. For the meat to taste good, it should be boiled on a slow heat – it should be 'boiled on needles', as we like to say – so that air bubbles form on the surface of the broth no more frequently than once a minute. This method of cooking enhances the broth too, incidentally.

Good cooks don't add any gelatine to help the jelly to cool. Two types of meat components are added: the bones (pork, beef or both) and the skin (this is what is used to make the jelly) – and the meat itself (lean veal, or the breast or legs of poultry).

It's important that the ratio of meat to water should be high, 1:1 or 1:1.2. Never add water to the broth in which you are boiling the meat – if you do, the jelly won't form. Immediately work out how much broth you need (it should be boiled until it has been reduced by at least a quarter).

It is entirely up to you whether to add herbs to the *kholodets* or not. Garlic is usually added to the hot, boiled *kholodets* and left in it for 15-20 minutes, then taken out. The herb most often used for *kholodets* is a bay leaf. You can also add peppercorns (black, white, green, pink or a mixture), cloves, allspice or thyme. As well as chopped onion, you can also add use the green part of a leek (saving the white part for other dishes), carrots, parsley or coriander stems (no leaves!), celery stalks, and parsley and parsnip roots.

Some people like the broth in their *kholodets* to be transparent, whilst others prefer it to be a honey-gold colour. To make it transparent, give the bones used in the *kholodets* a good wash in some very cold water, constantly removing the foam from the broth. To add more colour, add an onion, with the peel still on (make sure you give it a good wash first, of course) or a carrot (whole), or fry the flesh of the meat at the start in a dry pan, until it browns (5 minutes).

Here's a little recipe for one of the other types of *kholodets*:

AMBER KHOLODETS

Ingredients: 2 pig's trotters, 2 chicken breasts, 1 turkey leg, 2 chicken legs, 1 large onion, 1 carrot, 3 bay leaves, freshly milled black pepper, salt.

Wash the pig's trotters and scrape them with a knife. If the legs have got blood on them, leave them to soak for an hour, or preferably longer, in some cold water. Wash the rest of the meat thoroughly as well. Peel the carrot and wash the onion without removing the peel. Put the meat and vegetables in a 5 litre pan, add some water, bring it to the boil and, turning the heat down as low as it will go, so that air bubbles appear at the surface not more often than once a minute, boil for 5-6 hours.

After the first hour, take out the chicken breasts, and after another thirty minutes take out the chicken leg, then leave the other ingredients to boil until the time is up. Lastly, add salt and pepper to the broth to taste, bring it to the boil, and then turn off the heat. Take the rest of the meat and the vegetables out of the broth using a slotted spoon. Add some crushed garlic (3 large cloves). Allow the broth to cool until it reaches room temperature, then strain it through a fine sieve. Chop the meat up into very thin slices and put them in some moulds prepared in advance for the *kholodets*. Pour the broth over them and leave to chill in a cool place (on the balcony, for example), then put it in the fridge for several hours. Serve with mustard, horseradish sauce or vinegar.

For the meat component, you can use beef tongue instead of the poultry legs and chicken breast. In order to get rid of the foam on the meat, take it out of the boiling broth and pour some ice-cold water over it.

Here's a lighter recipe for *kholodets*, ideal if you're on a diet…

CHICKEN KHOLODETS

1 turkey leg, 1 young chicken weighing 1.5 – 2 kg, 1 chicken breast, 1 sprig of parsley, 1 large onion, 2 bay leaves, salt, pepper; for decoration: eggs, carrots.

Wash the meat in cold water and place it in a large pan. Add the parsley, onion and a bay leaf, bring to the boil, then turn the heat down as low as it will go and leave it to cook, removing the foam from time to time. After 1 hour, take out the chicken breast; after another hour, take out the chicken, and then leave the turkey to cook for another 2 hours. Add salt and pepper to taste. Take out the meat, and allow the broth to cool. Prepare some moulds for the *kholodets*. Boil the eggs (there should be half as many eggs as there are moulds) and the carrots.

Slice the boiled eggs in half and cut the carrots into pretty shapes (little stars, crescent moons, flowers). Pull the meat apart with your fingers or cut it into slices. Put half an egg at the bottom of each mould, with the sliced side facing downwards, add the carrots and the meat, pour the broth on top, allow it to cool until it reaches room temperature, then allow it to form a jelly in the fridge.

When you serve the *kholodets*, divide it into portions – slices, cubes or segments.

Try serving *kholodets* in the old, Slavic way: with a salad made of parsley, dill, spring onion, lettuce, radish and fresh vegetables, with a dollop of Smetana and a drop of vinegar. The contrasting flavours and textures will really give the *kholodets* something extra!

HOME-MADE DRINKS

This is how the simplest type of *kvass* is made:

- 8 litres of water
- 60 grams of fresh, 'live' yeast
- 1 cup of sugar
- 1 loaf of rye bread weighing 500-700 grams
- Ginger

Cut the bread into slices and put them in the oven on the highest setting until they turn brown – the darker you make them, the darker the kvass will be – but don't overcook the bread, or the kvass will taste too bitter.

Boil some water in a large pan, take it off the heat, add some sugar and the toasted bread, and leave it to cool, until the water becomes just slightly warm. Once it has cooled, take out a little of this water in a cup and dissolve the yeast in the cup, then pour the solution back into the pan. At this point you should stir the contents of the pan with a spoon, so that the yeast is evenly distributed.

The pan should ideally be covered with a piece of fabric or cheesecloth (so that none of the flies attracted by the smell of the fermentation process fall into it). You should start this process in the evening, because the kvass will take one and a half days to ferment, and most of the fermentation process will be complete by the next morning.

Once this period has elapsed, strain the kvass into a different pan through a cheesecloth – at this point you can add some more sugar to taste, but don't but too much in, or else the kvass will end up being too strong. Pour the strained, sweetened kvass into 3 litre bottles (you'll be able to fill two of these, because some of the liquid will stay inside the bread), and put a pinch of ginger into each bottle (this will add extra fizz to the kvass, giving it a sharper flavour). Cover the bottles with saucers – not lids – and leave the kvass to stand for another day in the fridge, or overnight.

At the end of this period, there will be a residue at the bottom of the bottles, and you should carefully pour the kvass through a sieve into new bottles, trying not to disturb the residue; then put the ginger back into the kvass.

The kvass should be stored in the fridge. As a drink that quenches your thirst, kvass is streets ahead of any factory-made beverages you'd care to name.

HOME-MADE SPIRITS

Here's a recipe for a drink known as *spotykach* (this name derives from the verb *spotykatsya*, meaning 'to stumble' – you'll need a designated driver if you're planning to have some!).

Ingredients:
300 grams of fresh cherries (without their stones),
15 prunes,
300 grams of sugar,
1 bottle of vodka (0.5 litres).

Method:

Pour the sugar over the cherries and leave them overnight. Then heat the cherries until all the sugar has dissolved. Add the prunes to the pan, then take it off the heat and leave it to cool. Transfer the cherries to a bottle, pour in some water and leave for two weeks in a covered dish. Then strain the *spotykach* so that you get rid of the bits of cherry, pour into bottles and store them away somewhere.

This is a dessert drink, and should be drunk in small shot-glasses after dinner.

Here is a recipe for a drink called *varenukha* (the name comes from the verb *varit*, 'to boil', but it would be more accurate to describe it as stewed).

What you'll need:
2.5 litres of vodka
¾ cup of flour
2.5 cm peeled root ginger
1/2 tsp ground cinnamon, cloves, allspice
100 g dried cherries
1 tsp butter
100 g dried apples

60 g dried pears
60 g prunes
2 bay leaves
600 g honey

1. Thoroughly wash all the fruits, and put them in a large, non-metallic bowl, pour in the vodka and allow it to stand for 5-6 hours.

2. Mix the flour with a small amount of water and sunflower oil, combine it to form a thick dough, with the consistency of plasticine.

3. Pour the vodka and the crushed fruits into a large enamel (or ceramic) pan, and add some honey, spices and a bay leaf.

4. Heat up the oven to 100°C. Cover the pan with a lid and seal the edges securely using the dough you prepared earlier. Press down on it a little and then put it in the oven for 10-12 hours.

5. Strain the drink through a sieve, covered with 2 layers of moist cheesecloth. Pour it into bottles and store them in a dark, cool place. *Varenukha* can be served either hot or cold.

Dear Reader,

Thank you for purchasing this book.

We at Glagoslav Publications are glad to welcome you, and hope that you find our books to be a source of knowledge and inspiration.

We want to show the beauty and depth of the Slavic region to everyone looking to expand their horizon and learn something new about different cultures, different people, and we believe that with this book we have managed to do just that.

Now that you've got to know us, we want to get to know you. We value communication with our readers and want to hear from you!

We offer several options:

- Join our Book Club on Goodreads, Library Thing and Shelfari, and receive special offers and information about our giveaways;

- Share your opinion about our books on Amazon, Barnes & Noble, Waterstones and other bookstores;

- Join us on Facebook and Twitter for updates on our publications and news about our authors;

- Visit our site www.glagoslav.com to check out our Catalogue and subscribe to our Newsletter.

Glagoslav Publications is getting ready to release a new collection and planning some interesting surprises — stay with us to find out!

Glagoslav Publications
Office 36, 88-90 Hatton Garden
EC1N 8PN London, UK
Tel: + 44 (0) 20 32 86 99 82
Email: contact@glagoslav.com

Glagoslav Publications Catalogue

- *The Time of Women* by Elena Chizhova
- *Sin* by Zakhar Prilepin
- *Hardly Ever Otherwise* by Maria Matios
- *The Lost Button* by Irene Rozdobudko
- *Khatyn* by Ales Adamovich
- *Christened with Crosses* by Eduard Kochergin
- *The Vital Needs of the Dead* by Igor Sakhnovsky
- *METRO 2033* (Dutch Edition) by Dmitry Glukhovsky
- *METRO 2034* (Dutch Edition) by Dmitry Glukhovsky
- *A Poet and Bin Laden* by Hamid Ismailov
- *Asystole* by Oleg Pavlov
- *Kobzar* by Taras Shevchenko
- *White Shanghai* by Elvira Baryakina
- *The Stone Bridge* by Alexander Terekhov
- *King Stakh's Wild Hunt* by Uladzimir Karatkevich
- *Depeche Mode* by Serhii Zhadan
- *Saraband Sarah's Band* by Larysa Denysenko
- *Herstories*, An Anthology of New Ukrainian Women Prose Writers
- *Watching The Russians* (Dutch Edition) by Maria Konyukova
- *The Hawks of Peace* by Dmitry Rogozin
- *The Grand Slam and Other Stories* (Dutch Edition) by Leonid Andreev
- *The Battle of the Sexes Russian Style* by Nadezhda Ptushkina
- *A Book Without Photographs* by Sergey Shargunov
- *Sankya* by Zakhar Prilepin
- *Wolf Messing - The True Story of Russia's Greatest Psychic* by Tatiana Lungin
- *Good Stalin* by Victor Erofeyev
- *Solar Plexus* by Rustam Ibragimbekov
- *Don't Call me a Victim!* by Dina Yafasova
- *A History of Belarus* by Lubov Bazan
- *Children's Fashion of the Russian Empire* by Alexander Vasiliev
- *Empire of Corruption - The Russian National Pastime* by Vladimir Soloviev
- *Heroes of the 90s - People and Money. The Modern History of Russian Capitalism*
- *Tsarina Alexandra's Diary* (Dutch)
- *Everyday Saints and Other Stories* (Dutch) by Archimandrite Tikhon

More coming soon…

www.ingramcontent.com/pod-product-compliance
Lightning Source LLC
Chambersburg PA
CBHW020904080526
44589CB00011B/433